"There She Is, Miss America"

"There She Is, Miss America"

The Politics of Sex, Beauty, and Race in America's Most Famous Pageant

Edited by

Elwood Watson and Darcy Martin

Cax

First published 2004 by
PALGRAVE MACMILLAN™
175 Fifth Avenue, New York, N.Y. 10010 and
Houndmills, Basingstoke, Hampshire, England RG21 6XS.
Companies and representatives throughout the world.

PALGRAVE MACMILLAN is the global academic imprint of the Palgrave
Macmillan division of St. Martin's Press, LLC and of Palgrave Macmillan Ltd.
Macmillan® is a registered trademark in the United States, United Kingdom
and other countries. Palgrave is a registered trademark in the European Union
and other countries.

ISBN 1–4039–6301–0 hardcover
ISBN 1–4039–6302–9 papberback

Library of Congress Cataloging-in-Publication Data
"There she is, Miss America" : the politics of sex, beauty, and race in America's
most famous pageant / edited by Elwood Watson & Darcy Martin
    p.   cm.
  Includes bibliographical references and index.
  ISBN 1–4039–6301–0—ISBN 1–4039–6302–9 (pbk.)
   1. Beauty contests—United States—History.   2. Miss America Pageant—
History.   3. Feminine beauty (Aesthetics)—United States.   4. Racism in
popular culture.   I. Watson, Elwood.   II. Martin, Darcy.

HQ1220.U5T48   2004
791.6'2—dc22

                               2004040002

A catalogue record for this book is available from the British Library.

Design by Letra Libre, Inc.

First edition: August 2004
10 9 8 7 6 5 4 3 2 1

Printed in the United States of America.

Contents

Acknowledgments

This book emerged from years of curiosity as well as the dearth of scholarly writing about the Miss America Pageant. A number of people and institutions contributed to this undertaking in various ways. It is here where we take the opportunity to thank them.

To Brendan O'Malley, editor of History and American Studies at Palgrave Macmillan, our deepest thanks for his invaluable assistance and patience in dealing with us as we went through the laborious process of preparing and editing this manuscript for publication. A huge thank you goes to Ms. Deborah Gershenowitz and Dr. Michael Flamini who had enough faith and insight to believe in this project and diligently fought for it. We also owe an enormous debt of gratitude to the fine scholars who contributed to this anthology.

Individually, Elwood Watson would like to thank the following: I am deeply grateful to my Siblings—Bruce, Marsha, Eric, Susan, Steven, and Stephanie who provided encouragement and love during this time period. Special colleagues and friends at East Tennessee State University and elsewhere provided strong words of support and encouragement to me as I endured through this process—Dr. Colin Baxter, Thomas Young, Mary Alexander and Tamara Baxter, Scott Lanzendorf, Dr. Brian Mc.Knight, Dr. Russell Wigginton. Dr. Howard Johnson, Dr. Wunyabari Maloba, Dr. Dorothy Drinkard-Hawkshawe, Dr. Juliet Walker, Dr. David Payson, Dr. Jennifer Harris, Michael Bowen, and Dr. Robert Thompson. Special thanks to my co-author Darcy Martin.

Darcy Martin expresses her heartfelt gratitude to the following: First and foremost, I cannot thank my professor, Dr. Stevan Jackson, enough for his inspiration. Little did we know that a graduate class project would become a book! I appreciate the collaborative experience of working with my professor and colleague, Dr. Elwood Watson. Special thanks to the strong and beautiful women of the East Tennessee State University Women's Studies Steering Committee who have encouraged and nurtured me, especially Dr. Amber Kinser, Dr. Marie Tedesco, Pat Buck, and Harriet Masters. I am fortunate to be surrounded by some extraordinary women—my three daughters, Lori Adams,

Sherri Wallis, and Julie Bell; my lovely granddaughter Jessica Adams; my delightful sister Jymie Anderson and her daughter, my niece Jennifer Anderson; my colleague Cynthia Lybrand; and my dearest friend of nearly 40 years and wise counsel, Liz Sefton. The fabric of my life is woven from their love and friendship. There are men who are special to me including my brother, John Powers; my brother-in-law Ken Anderson; my sons-in law, Jim, Preston, and Jeff; my favorite (and only) grandson, Christopher Adams; and my good friend. Bob Sefton, who once said, "You ought to write a book." This project would not have been possible without the love and support of my soulmate, Richard Martin. For 43 years he has been the constant in my life, my best friend and ultimate critic—I love you.

Our appreciation goes to the Journal of Popular Culture and past editor Ray Browne who published our first article on the pageant, and special thanks to the Miss America Pageant for making this anthology possible.

"There She Is, Miss America"

Introduction

Elwood Watson and Darcy Martin

"There she is, Miss America,
There she is, your ideal."

*T*he Miss America Pageant has provoked a wide range of responses throughout its history. *Time* critic Richard Corliss wrote, "It's gaudy, it's fake, it's real, it's live! We hate it. We love it!"[1] Former Miss America Chief Executive Officer (CEO) Leonard Horn referred to the pageant as a competition that "promotes healthy competition and breeds character among young women."[2] Robin Morgan, feminist scholar and former editor of *Ms.* magazine, responded that it was "the classic entity where racism, sexism, and homophobia are merged into one."[3] Corliss's comment captures the kitschy, glitzy, carnival-like atmosphere that he experienced while covering the pageant, while Horn's invokes the years of training, hard work, and competition that most of the contestants endure before having a chance to wear America's most coveted crown. Morgan's critique attacked what she sees as the perennial blond-haired, blue-eyed, heterosexual, Barbie doll-like archetype that the pageant has rewarded for most of its history. These few remarks constitute a small sample of the broad spectrum of sentiments proffered by observers of the pageant. Such varied reactions no doubt indicate that the pageant touches a nerve in the American psyche.

Perhaps the Miss America Pageant's ability to generate strong feelings has contributed to its endurance; few American popular culture institutions have lasted as long. The Miss America Pageant has survived financial hardships, scurrilous allegations in its formative years, the Great Depression, World War II, the modern feminist movement, the sexual revolution, the Vanessa Williams scandal, and more recent controversies: the 2002 Miss North Carolina pageant scandal[4] and Miss America 2003 Erika Harold's controversial platform advocating sexual abstinence.[5]

This anthology grew out of the response to an article we published in the *Journal of Popular Culture* in which we looked at the history of the pageant and sought to understand its long-standing popular appeal.[6] In our view, the microcosm of the Miss America Pageant provides invaluable insight into broader changes and trends in American culture for most of the twentieth century and into the present one. For better or for worse, the pageant reflects commonly held values, beliefs, and attitudes that Americans share about women. As psychologist Jill Neimark observes, "The Miss America contest has always knit together in its middle-class queen the deep schisms in American society. Whether her contestants flaunt pierced belly buttons or Ph.D.s in veterinary medicine, wear pants or ball gowns, Miss America is a mirror of America, even now."[7]

Even though the pageant has enjoyed a prominent place in American culture throughout its long history, few serious studies of it exist. Historically, scholars have overlooked or dismissed popular culture icons like the Miss America Pageant as areas worthy of research. Many feminist scholars find beauty pageants and beauty culture in general a problematic topic. Some would dismiss writing about an institution that so clearly oppresses and commodifies women as a waste of time. Pageants unquestionably objectify the female body, drawing attention to contestants' breasts, the smallness of their waists, the length of their legs, and appearance of their hair. It can be argued that they deny a participant's humanity on a fundamental level, basing her worth solely on her physical appearance.

Other feminist critics, however, argue that pageantry and beauty culture deserve scrutiny so that their negative influences can be understood and combated, while another segment sees a more complicated picture: Pageantry and beauty culture offer some women a certain level of empowerment and agency. Historian Kathy Peiss's 1997 study of the evolution of the American cosmetics industry, *Hope in a Jar*, embodies this ambiguity, contributing to the ongoing debate whether the use of cosmetics imprisons women or fosters healthy self-expression.[8] This volume embraces the position of cultural critic and contributor Sarah Banet-Weiser, who argues in her 1999 book, *The Most Beautiful Girl in the World: Beauty Pageants and National Identity*, that pageants' emphasis on public spectacle and display, their emulation of monarchy and medieval pageantry, and their relentless articulations of a dominant norm of femininity make them a ripe subject for academic inquiry.[9]

Part I: History

The chapters in the first section of the book look at the pageant through a historical lens, examining the first decades of the pageant. What follows is a brief synopsis of the pageant's history that places each piece in its chronological context. On September 7, 1921, the first Miss America Pageant took place (although not yet given that name), as part of a weeklong festival then titled "A National Beauty Pageant/Fall Frolic," in Atlantic City, New Jersey, with eight contestants sponsored by national newspapers. The pageant itself was initially called "Atlantic City's Inter-City beauty contest." The special event was born out of several local hoteliers' desire to prolong the summer resort season. Margaret Gorman, a fifteen-year-old schoolgirl from Washington, D.C., became the first recipient of the crown.[10] Her victory inspired the admiration of many Americans who saw in Gorman all the basic virtues of American womanhood. President of the American Federation Labor Samuel Gompers publicly hailed the judges' choice. Gompers reportedly told the *New York Times* that Gorman "represented the type of woman that America needs, strong, red-blooded, able to shoulder the responsibilities of homemaking and motherhood. It is in her type that the hope of the country rests."[11] The period immediately after World War I presented challenges to the very fiber of American society; the Bolshevik revolution in Russia called the future of capitalism into question, while new archetypes like the suffragette and the flapper destabilized traditional roles for women. The choice of Gorman harkened back to a more comforting era, and the pageant itself enshrined the notion that women ought to pursue beauty, not sexual pleasure or political power.

Despite this nostalgia for an earlier time, pageant promoters took advantage of the new mass media, borrowing promotional ideas from film studios that had launched the bathing beauty as a successful cinema character.[12] As the 1920s progressed, the pageant began to achieve nationwide fame. In the years that followed, the roster of candidates increased from eight young ladies to more than seventy entrants representing thirty-six states and Canada. In 1923, for the first and only time in pageant history, a contestant won back-to-back Miss America titles when Ohio's Mary Katherine Campbell, who had defeated reigning champion Margaret Gorman the previous year, returned to capture her title. Campbell's winning streak abruptly ended in 1924, when she narrowly lost the Miss America crown to Philadelphia's Ruth Malcomson.[13]

Its popularity with the public notwithstanding, the beauty tournament's success was interrupted by a series of embarrassing incidents that focused an unflattering media spotlight on the event. First, officials forgot to include a no-marriage clause in the original set of rules; thus, several married contestants participated in the pageant. Their presence was deemed as highly inappropriate at this time. (Although divorced women may compete, the unmarried rule remains in effect.) Contestants representing cities or states in which they did not live was a frequent problem. The pageant's reputation was furthered tarnished when several women's clubs labeled the competition as "indecent" and a number of New York newspapers ran inflammatory articles about the supposedly loose morals of the young women who participated in the pageant. In some cases, newspapers retracted their stories.[14] Norma Smallwood, Miss America 1926, in a daring move, refused to crown her successor and left Atlantic City for Hollywood when she became aware of the fact that she would not be financially compensated for crowning the next winner. By the late 1920s, the detrimental aftermath of such publicity, compounded by early effects of the Great Depression, eroded critical financial support from the resort's business community, and the fall frolic and National Beauty Tournament were discontinued in 1928.[15]

In Chapter 1, contributor Kimberly Hamlin examines the pageant's early years and how they reflected contested proper roles for young women. Hamlin notes the marked contrast between the image of young womanhood espoused by male promoters of the pageant and the "new woman" persona projected by the feminist suffragettes, and argues that the pageant's early popularity "was an outgrowth of deep-seated and widespread cultural unease over the changes in gender roles resulting from the passage of the Nineteenth Amendment and women's increasing presence in American public life." Further, she contends, the early pageant years reflected the striving to determine women's "proper place," an unresolved battle that continues to the present day. It is quite telling that the pageant was first held the year after women gained the right to vote.

Although America found itself dominated by terrible social crises in the 1930s, due in large measure to the Great Depression, an attempt was made in September 1933 to revive the pageant. That year another fifteen-year-old, Marion Bergeron of Connecticut, won the crown. (To date, Bergeron is the only New England contestant ever to win the pageant.) The determined efforts of pageant director Armand T. Nichols could not sustain the pageant's revival and, however, charges of fraud, married contestants, falsified residences, and other factors culminated in the pageant failing to take place in 1934.[16]

It returned in 1935 with Henrietta Leaver, Miss Pittsburgh, capturing the crown. Immediately after the ceremony, Leaver became the subject of controversy when it was learned that she had posed for a naked statue. Newspaper accounts of Leaver posing in the nude made national headlines, although Leaver vehemently denied such charges, insisting that her grandmother was present with her at the time of her photographs. Nonetheless, press coverage was merciless. Thus, the image of young women with questionable morals still lingered over the pageant. At this defining moment pageant officials realized that changes had to be made.

In the summer of that year, pageant officials turned to a twenty-nine-year-old southern woman with years of experience in public relations named Lenora Slaughter to help salvage and promote an image that would be necessary in order for the pageant to gain the credibility it needed if it were to have any long-term success. Slaughter served as director of the pageant until her retirement in 1967. During her long tenure, Slaughter was credited with restoring and maintaining dignity and morals to the pageant. It was under Slaughter's reign that contestants were kept at a safe distance from unscrupulous men, including some male chaperons. Contestants also had to sign a clause that assured pageant officials that they had not committed any acts of "moral turpitude." This document of rules stated in effect that in order to be a pageant contestant, a woman could have never been married, been pregnant, borne a child, been arrested, and so on. Slaughter later inserted another, more controversial rule (although probably not for the time period) into pageant bylaws. This clause stated that contestants had to be in "good health and of the white race."[17]

The fact that a new, no-nonsense woman was at the helm of the organization, unfortunately, did not eliminate the recurrence of a number of embarrassing situations. Bette Cooper, Miss America 1937, horrified pageant officials by abandoning her post. The reason given for her disappearance was Cooper's desire to stay in school. Pageant officials eventually selected Alice Emerick, Miss Texas, as the winner. In 1938, Miss California, Claire James, declared herself Miss America, rather than the judges' choice that year, Miss Ohio, Marilyn Meske. Judges refused to award James the crown because she violated pageant rules by wearing mascara. For a number of years afterward, James went around the country referring to herself as a former Miss America.[18] It was also in 1938 that a talent component was added to the pageant, another brainchild of Lenora Slaughter.

Miss America survived the critical decade of the 1930s to emerge into the 1940s with a new confidence to keep the pageant's momentum growing. During this decade several changes were introduced to ensure the pageant's rise in popularity. The name "Miss America Pageant" was adopted as the official title of the contest. Also, the Convention Hall in Atlantic City became the new home of the pageant. In addition, restrictions were imposed governing the composition and conduct of judging panels, and a pageant sorority, Mu Alpha Sigma, was organized. Then, after the first runner-up to Miss America 1940 returned to Atlantic City the next year and effortlessly walked off with the crown, a rule was invoked prohibiting contestants from competing in the national contest more than once.[19] The first academic scholarships were also awarded during this decade.

As America's involvement in World War II escalated, the military commandeered much of Atlantic City. The glamorous Boardwalk hotels were transformed into barracks housing thousands of soldiers, and Convention Hall became an Army Air Force training site. During one month in 1942, even the glittering lights of the Boardwalk were dimmed when its was suspected that Nazi submarines lurked offshore. Despite the pageant's newfound temporary housing in the Warner Theater, the military conditions made it nearly impossible to conduct the production effectively, and much thought was given to discontinuing it until the conclusion of the war. Eventually city leaders decided that the pageant should be continued because it provided a positive moment in an otherwise dark time. The pageant also decided to focus its efforts on persuading college students to enter the pageant, and in 1943 Jean Bartel became the first student to win the Miss America Pageant.

The debate over whether Miss America is representative of the modern American woman began during the 1940s at the onset of World War II. The portrayal of Miss America as a strong, independent, contemporary woman who embodies her current era runs head on into an image that she is an anachronistic, retrograde, docile, and antiquated relic whose time has long passed. With war following on the heels of the Great Depression, traditional domestic roles were thrown into disarray. By 1943, government and industry began to actively recruit women for a rapidly shrinking workforce. The previous negative stigma attached to employment for married women diminished, and the propaganda of the time period advocated that women enter the factories as part of their patriotic duty in order to keep the economy stabilized while their husbands were off fighting overseas.

As American history scholar Elaine Tyler-May notes, these "women rushed eagerly to take challenging and well-paying defense jobs, recruiters did their best to claim that the work would not diminish their femininity."[20] "Rosie the Riveter," a young woman in overalls working to build ships and planes, became a national symbol. Pictures of attractive "Rosies" graced magazine covers and posters. In chapter 2, contributor Mary Anne Schofield looks at what happened to the pageant during the war years and how the emerging image of the working woman and Miss America fared during this period. As Schofield notes, the pageant gained approval to continue during the war from the War Finance Department because it "was considered a major opportunity to sell war bonds." She argues, "Miss America of the war years is the antithesis of the [strong, formidable] Rosie the Riveter," and examines "the popularity of the pageant during the years [as it] speaks to the predominant woman question of the period."

Upon the conclusion of World War II in 1945, the pageant returned to Convention Hall, where it continued to gain in popularity. In September 1945, the scholarship fund was established and Bess Myerson, Miss New York City, became the first recipient of a Miss America Scholarship. For many years, much to the consternation and dismay of the Miss America Organization (MAO) officials, the issue of racism had plagued the pageant. For most of the pageant's life, a contestant's whiteness was a given. In chapter 3, contributor Sarah Banet-Weiser uses the selection of Myerson, the only Jewish woman to wear the crown, and jumps forward to examine the case of Heather Whitestone, who, in September 1994, became the first and only Miss America with a major disability. Banet-Weiser uses these two cases to explore the "material, ideological, and cultural politics of whiteness" within the pageant arena, arguing that by 1995, "the reality of identity politics . . . [was] not the celebration of difference, but rather the flattening out and diffusion of racial identity in ways that 'accept' difference while not posing a threat to the dynamic power of whiteness." Both Myerson and Whitestone offered the appearance of "difference" (and thus the pageant's tolerance of it) while at the same time maintaining the pageant's standard of whiteness. Some would later argue that the first African American Miss America, Vanessa Williams, also would maintain this standard with her light-skinned complexion.

By the end of the 1940s, support for the pageant was at an all-time high, and its scholarship fund grew rapidly. The pageant increasingly cultivated the wholesome girl-next-door image of its contestants. And in an effort to bring dignity to the image of Miss America, 1948 marked the first year that the winner was crowned wearing an evening gown instead of a bathing suit. This change caused an uproar among the press corps, many of whom stormed out of Atlantic City. The press eventually returned and BeBe Shoppe of Minnesota was crowned Miss America that year.

The 1950s ushered in revolutionary changes to the pageant. The first involved Miss America's title, which was officially postdated to allow most of the queen's reign to take place during her actual title year. In September 1950, Yolanda Betbeze was crowned Miss America 1951, resulting in no selection of a Miss America 1950. The arrival of television in the early 1950s wrought unprecedented change on American society, providing a persuasive means of transmitting ideas, values, and cultural norms.

The first telecast of the Miss America Pageant in September 1954 helped to solidify further the event's hold on the public imagination. An audience of 27 million Americans was able to witness the pageant on live television. Equally important was the introduction of corporate sponsorships.[21] The pageant quickly became an annual family viewing event, particularly among the female members of American households. The schedule of events was modified to accommodate the telecast, and more performance and choreography were added. Pageant historian A. R. Riverol writes, "Television had, has and will leave its mark on the basic structure of the pageant as experienced live and in person in Convention Hall."[22]

Lee Meriwether, Miss California, was crowned Miss America 1955, the first Miss America crowned in front of a live television audience. That year the pageant also introduced a master of ceremonies, Bert Parks, who was an instant hit with both viewers and contestants. It was Parks who inaugurated one of the most famous features of the pageant: the singing of "There She Is: Miss America," written by composer Bernie Wayne. The song was an immediate hit with viewers, and except for three years (1982, 1983, 1984), it remains the official song of the pageant. In 1958, the pageant switched from ABC to the more powerful CBS network, and ratings continued to increase.[23] The 1950s proved to be an enormously successful decade for the pageant. Full state representation had been achieved, the scholarship program had reached $250,000 in funds, and audience viewership had tripled. In many different ways, popularity of the Miss America Pageant peaked in the 1950s.

Television altered the nation's political landscape, as demonstrated by the House Un-American Activities Committee hearings, the consequent downfall of Senator Joseph McCarthy, and the presidential campaign of John F. Kennedy. Television permeated every aspect of American culture, affecting many cultural institutions that pre-dated it, including the Miss America Pageant. Yet even during the tumultuous 1960s, Miss America still ranked either as the first or second most popular broadcast eight out of ten years.[24]

In the 1960s, for some the pageant became emblematic of the 1950s postwar naive optimism and conservatism that was rapidly being undermined by social turbulence. Perhaps the pageant's most emblematic moment of the 1960s came in 1968 when 200 angry feminists demonstrated in front of Atlantic City's Convention Hall while the pageant was in progress. That a group of radical feminists would choose the pageant as a site of protest indicates the cultural power it wielded even during that turbulent moment in American history, and perhaps throughout its over eighty years of existence. The group, known as the Women's Liberation Front, marched on the Boardwalk, where it was alleged that they burned bras, refused to speak with male reporters, chanted anti-pageant slogans, crowned a live sheep, and tossed bras, girdles, makeup, and hair curlers into a "freedom trash can."[25] Despite the protestors' threats to disrupt the telecast, the disturbance was not audible to television viewers; the broadcast continued without incident.[26]

The pageant's swimsuit competition was no doubt a significant part of what some feminists found (and still find) offensive about the contest. Since the pageant's inception, it has remained the most popular and perhaps the most highly contested fixture of the contest. The introduction of other elements at various times during the pageant's history—for example, talent, evening gown, interview, personal platforms—and the quiz has not detracted from the appeal of beautiful young women parading on stage in their swimsuits. Miss America 1951 Yolande Betbeze's refusal to pose in a bathing suit during her reign was responsible for the manufacturers of Catalina swimwear withdrawing their support of the pageant (forming their own pageants, Miss Universe and Miss USA in 1952). Church leaders often spoke out against beauty contests, and, in 1959, the Catholic Church renewed its ban on them, threatening contestants with expulsion from church-run schools or participation in the sacraments.[27]

By the mid-1990s, growing numbers of American women (including some pageant contestants themselves) were becoming increasingly disturbed about a contest that unabashedly promoted the fact that it distributed more than $60 million in academic scholarships to young women throughout the nation but continued to allow bathing suits to be an important part of the competition.[28] Thirty years earlier, their mothers and grandmothers echoed similar sentiments. During the September 1995 pageant, viewers were allowed to phone in to pageant headquarters and vote whether the pageant should either preserve or abolish the swimsuit competition. Opponents argued that having young women parading around in swimsuits and high heels was insulting and outmoded. Proponents argued that discontinuing the swimsuit competition would result in the demise of the Miss America Pageant. In the end, voters decided by a margin of 80 percent to 20 percent to maintain the swimsuit competition.[29] Prior to the viewers' vote, a poll taken of the fifty contestants revealed that forty-two of them said "they did not have a problem with waltzing around in public in swimwear." One of the small minority of no votes referred to the swimsuit competition as a "veiled strip show."[30]

In 1997, for the first time in fifty years, pageant contestants were allowed to wear two-piece swimsuits. Then CEO Horn assured the public that the change was to promote individuality "and is not, we repeat, not a ploy to boost ratings."[31] The swimsuit controversy continues unabated, with this segment's name being changed in 2001 to "Lifestyle and Fitness."[32] What may have begun as "a gesture of defiance against the lingering clouds of Victorian prudishness," as writer Candace Savage notes, has perhaps become a mark of submission to the patriarchal ideals of femininity.[33] In her book *Beauty Bound*, Rita Freedman wryly observes, "The freedom to wear a mini-bikini or a skin-tight tank suit feels liberating only to someone with a skin-tight body."[34] It is doubtful, considering its long history, that the swimsuit controversy will dissipate any time soon.

Part II: Gender, Race, and Identity

The Miss America Pageant, with its claims to represent an American feminine ideal, has always raised interesting questions of gender, race, and identity. The chapters in the second part of this book explore these questions as they pertain to the more contemporary history of the pageant. Since America's earliest origins, race has been an enigmatic societal issue. From sports, to politics, to education, to media, the subject of race and racial identity has remained a perennial factor, whether directly or indirectly, in the lives of all Americans. The great black scholar and intellectual W.E.B. DuBois echoed a prophetic message when he predicted, "the problem of the twentieth Century would be the problem of the color line."[35] Ideals of beauty and femininity have long been intertwined with race in American society. All too often, images and representations of black beauty have been denigrated, obscured, or ignored by the dominant white culture, as evidenced by stereotypical portrayals of all black women as "Mammies," "Sapphires," or "Jezebels."[36]

For most of the twentieth century, particularly after the 1920s, one of the major themes that dominated the history of American women was the growth of what Betty Friedan labeled "the feminine mystique."[37] This twentieth-century version of nineteenth century Victorianism saw the cult of domesticity and the institution of motherhood as integral for American women (meaning white middle- and upper-middle-class able-bodied women), to have fulfilling lives as well as to provide them with a sexual aura that was desired by powerful men.[38] By the 1950s, the ideology of the feminine mystique had firmly etched itself into the fabric of a segment of American culture. This was a mind-set that advocated home economics and mother's clubs and resoundingly rejected the institutions of organized feminism that had coalesced during the Progressive Era.[39] In most of the popular literature between 1920 and 1960, the predominant images of black women were ones of domestic figures like Aunt Jemima.[40] For the most part, there were no black counterparts to white sex symbols such as Marilyn Monroe and Ann-Margret; such figures were largely absent from the pages of magazines and newspapers. Lena Horne, Dorothy Dandridge, and Eartha Kitt were rare exceptions.

A few examples of black cultural symbols assuming a place of preeminence in the wider society. For example, during a brief period in the late 1970s, a number of white women, so impressed by the cornrows that actress Bo Derek wore in the movie *10*, began to adopt this form of hairstyle for themselves. A segment of the media was enamored with Bo Derek's cornrows. This fact was not lost on a number of black women who expressed resentment because Derek received so much attention and more, unfairly so, credit for inventing a hairstyle that black women had been wearing for centuries. Such complaints made the media reexamine its prior assumptions.[41] Historically, female archetypes in popular culture such as the girl next door, the movie star, the tough-minded professional woman, supermodels, and the revered cover girl have all been seen as white.

By the 1990s, the racial and ethnic diversity of American society had at last begun to be reflected in popular culture, challenging its historical standard of whiteness.[42] The Miss America Pageant placed itself squarely in the center of the national discussion on issues such as identity. The pageant, as Sarah Banet-Weiser notes in her book, *The Most Beautiful Girl*, "accommodates diversity, performs and exercises toleration, and effaces any obvious signs of particular ethnicities or races."[43] During much of the 1990s, nationwide debates surrounding issues of diversity and identity politics were acted out on the beauty pageant stages, couched in terms of traditional liberal rhetoric of individual achievement.[44]

One of the various strategies involved in managing diversity is through the representation of difference.[45] Banet-Weiser describes Miss America as " . . . the face who is simultaneously the face of America, the face of womanhood, and the face of diversity," and argues that "the presence of Black and brown female bodies on the stage does not dismantle the privilege of whiteness that frames the pageant." To the contrary, such a false image of pluralism works to include whiteness as a powerful force in the game of diversity.[46]

Contemporary society is replete with cultural images based on race, ethnicity, gender, and class. When these factors are combined, a plethora of diverse cultural images emerge. For example, the cultural image of African American women is different from that of European American women, Native American women, and Asian American women. While cultural images of most racial and ethnic groups have changed over time, the cultural images of African American women have changed only minimally.[47] Despite the fact that the white cosmetic world and consumer markets largely ignored them, many black women were deeply immersed in the psychology of the "beauty myth."[48]

In the 1960s and 1970s, while many white feminists were complaining about the sexist nature associated with the Miss America Pageant and many black authors were examining the retrograde psychological, social, and emotional impact that societal beauty standards imposed on black women, a number of black civil rights groups charged the pageant with racism and complained of the dearth of minority contestants as participants. As the civil rights movement gained momentum in the mid- to late 1960s, it began to pressure the pageant to publicly voice its commitment to increasing minority participation. In 1970, Cheryl Brown, Miss Iowa, became the first black woman to compete in the national contest.[49] In the September 1976 pageant, Miss Delaware, Deborah Lipford, became the first black woman to place in the top ten. Although these were important milestones, the issue of race would continue to haunt the pageant throughout much of the decade.

The continuing stigma of racial bias associated with the pageant began to diminish as the 1980s started off on an inspiring note. In the September 1980 pageant, for the first time, two black contestants, Doris Hayes, Miss Washington, and Lencola Sullivan, Miss Arkansas, placed in the top ten. Sullivan shattered another racial barrier, becoming the first black to finish in the top five; she was fourth runner-up.[50] Three years later, the scenario repeated itself. However, the sixty-second Miss America Pageant would be one that would forever alter the history of the annual event. September 18, 1983, was indeed a day that changed the Miss America Pageant. Two black finalists, Suzette Charles and Vanessa Williams, not only made the top five, but emerged as first runner-up and Miss America 1984. Their victories made headlines around the world. Prominent black publications such as *Ebony* magazine ran cover stories on Vanessa Williams.[51]

The fact that a black woman finally wore America's most coveted crown for young women was the subject of considerable debate. A number of African American women expected this precedent-setting event to have a positive effect on every medium that was used as a vehicle to transmit images.[52] Congresswoman Shirley Chisholm remarked, "Thank God that I lived long enough to see this nation select a beautiful young woman of color as Miss America."[53] Many black women believed that since a black woman had been accepted as America's symbol of womanhood, black women would gain greater access to mainstream society.

Despite praise in some quarters, Williams's victory was not without controversy. There were some who believed that her selection was due to the fact that Miss America was an antiquated and outmoded pageant that needed to inject a new enthusiasm among the American public. Within certain segments of the black community, some questioned whether Williams's green eyes and golden brown hair made her "sufficiently" black enough. Not long after her crowning, the Congress of Racial Equality (CORE) issued a statement declaring Williams as not "in essence black."[54] Williams was also the recipient of death threats among white racists who resented the fact that a young black woman finally wore America's most coveted crown. Thus, for many, the selection of Williams was not based on her qualifications but, rather, racial politics.[55]

Throughout most of her reign, the mainstream media portrayed positive images of the new Miss America. She enjoyed tremendous popularity among all races and was undoubtedly one of the most popular Miss Americas ever, and the media covered Williams' activities on an almost daily basis. Near the end of her reign, during the summer of 1984, a rumor surfaced that nude photographs had been taken of Williams prior to her participation in the pageant. By July 21, the news had made the major media outlets. That same day, pageant officials issued a statement in which they gave Williams seventy-two hours to relinquish the crown. Three days later, on July 24, 1984, in an emotional press conference, she did. First runner-up Suzette Charles fulfilled the remaining seven weeks of Williams's reign and became the second black woman to wear the Miss America crown.[56]

The same controversy that marred her reign was prevalent in Williams's post-reign as Miss America. There were those, particularly black Americans, who felt that much of the same mainstream (white) media that had earlier treated Williams with such adulation were now reverting to the same malicious reporting and sordid tactics that they had previously used in describing black women. One tabloid paper went so far as to run the headline, "Vanessa the Undressa." In radical black circles (some who initially had ambivalent feelings toward Williams), there were those who argued that Vanessa Williams was the victim of a "racist conspiracy" designed to dismantle all positive achievements by black

Americans. Surprising to some (primarily whites), much of the black media's handling of the problems that led to Vanessa Williams, the first black woman crowned Miss America, abdicating her title was considerably different from that of the mainstream media. For example, Susan Taylor, then editor-in-chief of the largest black women's magazine in the nation, *Essence,* offered understanding and support that was, at the time, representative of most black female publications and black publications in general.[57]

In the year that followed, subtle and overt comparisons were made between Vanessa Williams and Sharlene Wells, Miss America 1985. Wells, a twenty-year-old white Mormon from Utah, was touted throughout her reign as a paragon of virtue with high moral standards. Some critics argued that such remarks were designed to reinforce the stereotypical image of angelic purity associated with white womanhood and denounce the reductive image of wanton sexuality associated with black females.[58]

As the 1980s progressed, the issue of race continued to resurface from time to time. In 1987, Toni Seawright, a twenty-three-year-old black college student from Moss Point, Mississippi, became the first black woman crowned Miss Mississippi. Although other black women from southern states had participated in the Miss America Pageant, the fact that Mississippi, a state that had a notorious legacy of violence against and mistreatment of blacks, selected a black woman to represent the state made for national attention. In the weeks prior to the pageant, Seawright made the talk-show circuit as curiosity about her increased. She was fourth runner-up in the 1987 Miss America Pageant.[59]

In September 1989, Debbye Lynn Turner, Miss Missouri, became the third black woman to wear the Miss America crown. Interestingly, the first runner-up that year was an Asian American, Virginia Cha. Two minority contestants of different ethnicities in the top spots that year was another pageant first. The following year, September 1990, Marjorie Judith Vincent, Miss America 1991, became the fourth black woman to win the Miss America title. Two consecutive black winners was another historic milestone.[60] The last four minority women to win the pageant were Kimberly Aiken, Miss America 1994, the pageant's fifth black winner; Angela Perez Baraquio, Miss America 2001, who made history by becoming the first Asian American woman to win the crown; multiracial Erika Harold, Miss America 2003, and Ericka Dunlap, Miss America 2004, the pageant's seventh black winner.

Unlike early minority pageant winners, these women's racial identity generated minimal response from the media. By the time of Turner's victory in 1989, each of their victories spawned little controversy. One reason for the lack of controversy may have been (particularly in the victories of Aiken, Baraquio, and Harold) that by the early 1990s, multiculturalism and political correctness had become permanent factors in American life. Cultural pluralism had become a major issue in American society, and issues such as race and gender were approached with increasing sensitivity.[61]

As minority women began to win the pageant, the question of what is beauty became even more prevalent. Vanessa Williams's light-skinned features, Suzette Charles's biracial background, Debbye Turner's darker, yet Anglo-looking, features, and Marjorie Vincent's classic black features were the subject of commentary. Some journalists argued that Marjorie Vincent's crowning was really the first time that a black woman with traditional features won the crown. As journalist Valerie Helmbreck noted: " . . . Yes, having a Black Miss America was a breakthrough and Vanessa Williams was the first to achieve it. However, until Vincent, there hadn't been a Black woman with dark skin and classically Negroid features to wear the crown. . . . Vincent with her luscious lips, broad nose and full cheeks didn't fit what had become the conventional mold. She was talented, smart, poised, Black, and very ethnic looking. And Bert Parks said she was our ideal and bid her to 'go out and greet your subjects.'"[62]

Awarding the crown to Williams, in many ways, intentionally or not, validated the prevailing white standard of beauty rather than championing a larger standard that accepted black beauty on its own merits. In chapter 4 contributor Valerie Kinloch asserts that the Miss America Pageant personifies the racist politics of identity through symbolic meaning making. She further argues that the pageant has historically promoted and accounted for the beauty of white female bodies by disregarding and failing to acknowledge how certain "multiple meanings, images, and representations" are represented within the black female body. Kinloch examines Williams's abbreviated reign through the lens of the work of prominent black scholars such as Cornel West, bell hooks, Patricia Hill Collins, and Toni Morrison, among others.

This desire of many black women to conform to Eurocentric standards of beauty had its roots in the world of the rising black middle class of the 1920s. Many blacks of the middle and upper classes were extremely light-skinned. A number of these women became preoccupied with passing. As seen in the literary work of Nella Larsen, some manipulated their light-skinned privilege to gain acceptance in the larger white world.[63] At times, these women were willing to exoticize themselves in promoting black female popular culture figures of the 1920s, at times producing a nonthreatening, domesticated version of African American femininity. These women attempted to define their racial, class, and gendered status through consumer performance. Despite the fact that Larsen's work was fiction, her characters bore many parallels to the reality that was facing the small number of well-educated, affluent black women of the 1920s. The term "mulatto" was one that described biracial or fair-complexioned African American females who possessed features that were considered European. Thin lips, long straight hair, slender nose, slim figure, and fair complexion are the physical characteristics that make up this image, conforming more to the American standard of beauty than any of the other images. The mulatto is a black woman who is so close to being white that she attracts a white male who would marry her, thus becoming her Prince Charming and she his Cinderella. We saw this image in movies like *Pinky* (1939) and *Imitation of Life* (1959). The unfortunate reality (both in film and fiction) is that there is no black fairy tale with a happy ending. The biracial/mulatto black woman cannot enter into a happy marriage with her suitor because she possesses one drop of black blood and is, thus, black.[64] Many of the aforementioned cultural images that symbolize African American womanhood have been modified over time, and, although cultural changes have taken place, these traditional cultural images are still evident.

Later in the twentieth century, other writers began to view black women and their quest for beauty in a different light. The works of Toni Morrison, in particular, have all addressed the issue of black women and the body. From *The Bluest Eye*[65] to *Jazz*,[66] Morrison offers up a view of the body identified not by its completion, but rather its lack of wholeness.[67] In all of her works, Morrison has dramatized the perils of color obsessions. Through her literature, she has shown the disparity that often exists between women's desired bodies and the body that they have. Other black women, such as legal scholar Dorothy Roberts, argue that the black body has often been maligned, devalued, and disrespected from slavery to the present.[68]

Fair skinned, young, flowing lustrous—typically blond—hair, sensuous but demure, carefully groomed and elegantly gowned, the myth of what constitutes the highest echelon of female beauty and femininity endures through our images of Miss America and Cinderella. As Cinderella endures as an icon of beauty and femininity for young girls throughout the world, so, too, does Miss America construct femininity and beauty for American womanhood. In chapter 5, contributor Iset Anuakan looks at fairy tales, and princess literature in particular, and their relationship to the Miss America Pageant and the ways that both inform and maintain our cultural biases against minority characteristics of beauty, or what Anuakan describes as the "dark feminine." Anuakan argues that the pageant fosters a fading ideal of beauty that systematically restricts a variety of women from participating due to cultural, racial, and physical differences.

In chapter 6, a study of pageants conducted in the southern tri-state region known as Wiregrass Country (portions of Georgia, Florida, and Alabama), contributor Jerrilyn McGregory explores how small southern communities and beauty pageants interact to create an environment that reinforces, perhaps unintentionally, the romantic image of the "southern belle": feminine, delicate, vulnerable, and, most important, white—what McGregory refers to as the "old cult of true womanhood."

Further, she notes, participation by black women in pageants has not created a truly multicultural event. McGregory contends that, although the new Miss America Pageant is promoting an image of female independence, progress, and inclusion in the broadest sense, this image, in reality, is a mirage. Rather, she argues, the pageant possesses a "Stepford wives"–like quality that demands that all participants—and particularly minority women—look as demure and European as possible.

For those who believe that the pageant has finally moved beyond "the race issue," consider the comments of two contestants in recent pageants: "In the Miss America Pageant there's always one or two black finalists now, and you never saw that before. I don't think that's a coincidence, I really don't."[69] "[T]his Miss America hopefully will not be a ploy for P.C. correctness in that the girls are judged on the content of their character rather than the color of their skin."[70] Race undoubtedly remains a contentious aspect of the pageant, as it does of American society at large.

Part III: Personal Reflections

In all of the criticism and scandal surrounding the Miss America Pageant, the hard work and sacrifice of the contestants often is overlooked or forgotten. In an undeniably biased 1997 editorial in support of the pageant, former Miss America CEO Horn argues, "I wish once and for all that the American public's attention could be shifted to the exceptional young women who participate. . . . How about some headlines for them?"[71] Pageant participants have trained for many years in areas such as music, dance, physical fitness, and modeling. In recent decades, most are college graduates, many with advanced degrees. They have worked to cultivate their appearance and develop the poise and presence necessary for success in the many levels of the Miss America program.

One of the major appeals of the pageant is the sense that the contestants represent old-fashioned, small-town America and its values. The Miss America organization website enthusiastically promotes to potential applicants this small-town focus, extolling "The road to the Miss America competition begins in a town near you." Each year, for more than 12,000 young women, this proves true. In Part III, contributors Donelle Ruwe, Mark Eaton, and Gerald Early reflect on their personal experiences with the pageant from vastly different perspectives, spanning more than twenty years of the pageant's history. One a contestant, another a teacher of contestants, and the third an interested bystander, their chapters reflect their perceptions and personal conflicts in their understanding of the many nuances that constitute the pageant.

Although "feminists are often accused of being anti-beauty," psychologist Rita Freedman contends, "there is a difference . . . between protesting the damaging effects of a beauty myth and opposing the value of beauty itself."[72] In chapter 7, contributor Donelle Ruwe agrees. As a former beauty pageant contestant and now an English professor, Ruwe explores her "surprisingly positive, perhaps even feminist" experiences within the Miss America Pageant system. In addition to providing important perspectives on local and regional pageants and their relationships with their communities, Ruwe discusses two of the essential characteristics of the pageant: the surprisingly sisterlike unity of the participants and the enjoyable "kitschy" quality of the pageant itself. Recognizing that Miss America is an "imaginary construct," Ruwe uses her personal experiences within the pageant system to explore "an admittedly problematic construction of gender." More important perhaps, Ruwe explains how she was able "to participate in a process while simultaneously critiquing that process."

Oklahoma City University is a school with a national reputation for recruiting young pageant winners and grooming them for the Miss America Pageant.[73] During his tenure at the university, contributor Mark Eaton was introduced to pageant culture, and in chapter 8 he writes about two pageant contestants who were among his students. With relative ease and great relish, some feminists, among others, often denigrate much of mass culture, whether it is NASCAR, beauty pageants, Hollywood films, "reality" television, or the like. To fail to engage mass culture on any level is to deny important aspects of many people's everyday lives. As avowed feminist Eaton became better acquainted with his students, his early disdain for the pageant evolved into a deeper understanding of what motivates young women to dedicate long hours and hard work to pageant competition. In light of his interaction with these women, Eaton acknowledges that "a much more pliable feminism for practical living" is needed, a feminism that does not outright reject these women's motivations or experiences.

In chapter 9, distinguished cultural critic Gerald Early writes about Vanessa Williams, arguing that she was reminiscent of famous, beautiful black women of earlier years such as Lena Horne and Dorothy Dandridge. Although his essay was written twenty years ago, it remains relevant, because as we will see in his chapter and others included in this anthology, the issue of race remains a conundrum in our society. Combining personal experience and acute insight, Early tackles the complexities of racism to peel away the many layers of racial biases and ambiguities. He explores the hollowness of Williams's victory, noting cultural acceptance of black women who are successful and embraced by the larger society and the rejection of angry black women who have been shunned by society. Early described Miss America as a multifaceted, complex American fantasy of femininity.[74] In so doing, he faced the same challenges we all face in our attempts to develop a context for understanding the Miss America Pageant.

As editors of this anthology, we, too, come from vastly different experiences and backgrounds. One of us is a product of Generation X, a young male African American history professor, who came of age in the 1980s, and the other is a white female women's studies scholar who grew up in the 1950s. Our mutual long-held fascination with the Miss America Pageant resulted in this collaboration.

It cannot be denied that, for many Americans, the pageant is seen as either culturally irrelevant or as an anachronism and a throwback to the supposed wholesomeness of the 1950s and early 1960s—a time when uniform suburban homes, white picket fences, three kids, a doting June Cleaveresque wife, and a strong, confident, responsible husband went to work everyday wearing one of the two gray flannel suits he owned.[75] This imagined society with white, middle-class, largely Protestant, heterosexual, able-bodied people considered the norm made others seem either invisible or unimportant. With the advent of the twenty-first century, this is still the mind-set that many individuals associate with the pageant.

Whatever its connotations, the Miss America Pageant endures as a fascinating and revealing icon in American culture. In discussing the so-called bra-burning 1968 feminist protest of the pageant, Rita Freedman accurately described some of the confused emotions the pageant elicits in women who denounce the pageant, but also often count themselves among those who faithfully watch it year after year. She pointed out, "Even the most 'liberated' among them responded at a deep emotional level to the sanctification of female beauty . . ."[76]

The question remains: Does the pageant reflect the attitudes and beliefs of the majority of Americans, or do most find it boring and tiresome, as did the first Miss America, Margaret Gorman Cahill, in her later life?[77] If television ratings reflect societal beliefs, then the consistent decline in recent ratings support the contention that the pageant is a thing of the past. However, the current plethora of pageants for babies, children, teenagers, and adult women through grandmothers would seem to contradict this position.

The sensationalism surrounding the mysterious 1997 murder of child beauty queen JonBenet Ramsey, who was portrayed in pictures not only as stunningly beautiful but dressed and made up to resemble a young woman in her twenties, points to a continuing fascination bordering on obsession with beauty at any age. The popularity of men's magazines, pornography in film and on the Internet, and television shows like the much-watched 1990s *Baywatch* all seem to indicate that the way women are viewed has not changed much. In this vein, then, perhaps the Miss America Pageant is the lesser of many evils.

The women's liberation movement argued the obvious: If beauty pageants were substantially more than girl-watching exercises, then there would be pageants for men, too.[78] Yet over the past few decades, a few male pageants have taken place, the most recent in the form of "reality television": *America's Sexiest Bachelor,* which aired on Fox in October 2000. However, none has garnered the level of interest that the Miss America Pageant has. Some critics argue that pageants and pornography have many parallels. These individuals believe that both institutions aid one another by denigrating and degrading the female body and instilling feelings of low self-esteem in women of all races and ages.[79] Other critics argue that the dearth of creative outlets contributes to the frustration and anxiety that we see among some young women—pageant and nonpageant contestants.[80]

For some, the death of the Miss America Pageant cannot come soon enough. Its history of racism, sexism, homophobia, and even xenophobia is clearly etched in their minds. Such ambivalence about the role of the pageant in American culture reflects the continuing conflict society experiences when female beauty is equated with competitiveness and must be judged. On another level, with minority contestants becoming commonplace and frequent winners, the pageant seemingly has moved beyond issues of race. And Heather Whitestone's win in September 1994 made an attempt to eradicate the myth that only "normal" contestants can become Miss America.[81]

As noted in the conclusion of our original article, "the conflict of the importance of inner beauty versus physical beauty as exemplified by the Miss America Pageant remains unresolved. Inclusion of the Miss America platform and promotion of the pageant as the largest provider of scholarships to women reflects society's struggle to remove physical beauty as a measure of a woman's worth."[82] The pageant's continued success may be determined by the pageant organization's ability and willingness to find new and innovative ways to address an everevolving, more inclusive beauty standard.

To that end, our contributors engage such issues as racial and political identity, ageism, regional diversity, economics, ethnicity, consumerism, adversity, history, and aesthetics to challenge us to examine in new and creative ways the aging, but enduring, icon of American beauty and femininity, the Miss America Pageant.

Notes

1. Richard Corliss, "Dream Girls," *Time* (18 September 1995): 102–105.
2. Leonard Horn, "Miss America Organization, 1998," www.missamerica.org.
3. Robin Morgan, former editor of *Ms.* magazine, quoted on a PBS television program discussing Miss America. "Miss America, The American Experience," 27 January 2002.

4. Miss America Organization officials forced 2002 Miss North Carolina winner, Rebekah Revels, to surrender her crown when her former fiancé, Tosh Welch, notified pageant officials that he had topless photos of her in his possession. Runner-up Misty Clymer was named Miss North Carolina and competed in the 2002 pageant. *New York Times,* 13 September 2002; www.wral.com, 9 September 2002, accessed 16 November 2002.

5. Erika Harold, Miss America 2003, became embroiled in a major controversy when, following her crowning, she announced that she planned to revert to her original platform of promoting sexual abstinence among American teenagers, much to the consternation of Miss America Organization officials. Christian conservative Harold noted that she would not be "bullied" by pageant officials and intended to adamantly speak out in support of her cause. "Miss America: The Politics of Chastity," *The Week,* 8 November 2002; www.abcnews.go.com, 15 November 2002.

6. *Journal of Popular Culture,* Summer 2000 issue. The article received the Russel B. Nye award by the journal for best article of the year, 2000–2001.

7. Jill Neimark, "Why Do We Need Miss America?" *Psychology Today* (October 1998): 40–43.

8. Kathy Peiss, *Hope in a Jar: The Making of America's Beauty Culture* (New York: Metropolitan, 1998).

9. Sarah Banet-Weiser, *The Most Beautiful Girl in the World: Beauty Pageants and National Identity* (Berkeley: University of California Press, 1999), 6.

10. Lois Banner, *American Beauty* (New York: Alfred A. Knopf, 1983), 268.

11. "Intercity Beauty Picked," *New York Times* (8 September 1921): 9. See also Elwood Watson and Darcy Martin, "The Miss America Pageant: Pluralism, Femininity and Cinderella All in One," *Journal of Popular Culture* 34, no.1 (Summer 2000): 105–126.

12. Banner, *American Beauty,* 276. Beginning as early as 1922, with Greta Garbo's film debut in *Luffarpetter,* through the heyday of swimming movies in the 1940s and 1950s—for example, films starring Esther Williams such as *Neptune's Daughter* (1949) and *Pagan Love Song* (1950)—beautiful women in swimwear have attracted filmgoers. Since that time, advertisers have incorporated attractive young women in swimsuits to sell all kinds of products from cosmetics to cars.

13. Ann Marie Bivans, *Miss America: In Pursuit of the Crown* (New York: Mastermedia, 1991).

14. Ibid., 12.

15. Banner, *American Beauty,* 269.

16. Ibid., 12.

17. "Miss America, The American Experience."

18. Frank Deford, *There She Is: The Life and Times of Miss America* (New York: Viking Press, 1971), 147.

19. Bivans, *Miss America.* 17.

20. Elaine Tyler-May, *Pushing the Limits: American Women 1940–1961* (Oxford: Oxford University Press, 1994), 25.

21. Deford, *There She Is,* 193.

22. A. R. Riverol, *Live from Atlantic City: A History of the Miss America Pageant* (Bowling Green, OH: Bowling Green State University Popular Press, 1992), 115–121.

23. Ibid., 195.

24. Candace Savage, *Beauty Queens: A Playful History* (New York: Abbeville Press Publishers, 1998), 100.

25. Susan Faludi, *Backlash* (New York: Anchor Books/Doubleday, 1992), 75.

26. Excellent accounts of the 1968 protest, including the infamous "bra-burning" incident, can be found in Ruth Rosen, *The World Split Open* (New York: Viking Penguin, 2000); Susan Brownmiller, *In Our Time: Memoir of a Revolution* (New York: The Dial Press/Random House, Inc., 1999); Rita Freedman, *Beauty Bound* (Lexington, MA: D.C. Heath and Company, 1995); Banner, *American Beauty;* and Faludi, *Backlash,* to name a few. It is interesting to note that at midnight following the 1968 pageant and the feminist protest to the pageant, the first Black Miss America Pageant was held in Atlantic City "as a direct protest of the pageant." Nineteen-year-old Saundra Williams was the first recipient of the title. See PBS television program, "Miss America, The American Experience," 27 January 2002, www.pbs.org/wgbh/amex/missamerica.

27. Savage, *Beauty Queens,* 108–109.

28. According to the Miss America Organization website, Miss America is the world's number-one provider of scholarships to women.

29. 1995 Miss America Pageant, www.missamerica.org

30. Gwen Florio, "Miss America Contestants vote 42–50 in Favor of Swimsuit Competition," (Knight-Ridder/Tribune News Service, 21 August 1995).

31. "And Miss Nicest Navel . . ." *Time* (4 August 1997): 17.

32. The last Miss America to be crowned wearing a bathing suit was Barbara Jo Walker, Miss America 1947.

33. Savage, *Beauty Queens,* 115.

34. Freedman, *Beauty Bound,* 89.

35. W. E. B. Du Bois, *The Souls of Black Folk* (Chicago: A. C. McClurg), 1903.

36. Maxine Leeds Craig, *Ain't I a Beauty Queen? Black Women, Beauty, and the Politics of Race* (New York: Oxford University Press, 2002), 45–64. K. Sue Jewell uses the image of "Mammies" to define black domestics, "Sapphires" to describe the "loquacious and headstrong" woman as exemplified by the role of Sapphire in the *Amos and Andy* television series, and "Jezebels" to portray the "bad-black-girl." K. Sue Jewell, *From Mammy to Miss America: Cultural Images & the Shaping of U.S. Social Policy* (New York: Routledge, 1993), 45–46.

37. Friedan's seminal work on women, *The Feminine Mystique,* was first published in 1963.

38. Banner, *American Beauty,* 274–276.

39. Ibid.

40. M. M. Manning, *Slave in a Box: The Strange Career of Aunt Jemima* (Charlottesville: University of Virginia Press), 1998.

41. There were a number of debates and articles written that expressed resentment that Bo Derek was receiving so much credit and attention for adopting a hairstyle that had been a major part of black female culture for centuries. See, for example, Paulette Caldwell, "A Hairpiece: On the Intersection of Race and Gender," *Duke Law Journal* 41, no. 397 (1991), and Kathy Russell, Midge Wilson, and Ronald Hall, *The Color Complex: The Politics of Skin Color among African Americans* (New York: Anchor, 1992).

42. Christopher Newfield, "What Was Political Correctness? Race, the Right, and Managerial Democracy in the Humanities," *Critical Inquiry* 19 (Winter 1993): 320.

43. Banet-Weiser, *The Most Beautiful Girl,* 18–19.

44. Ibid.

45. Ibid.

46. Ibid.

47. Jewell, *From Mammy to Miss America,* 35.

48. See Naomi Wolf, *The Beauty Myth* (New York: W. Morrow, 1991; reprint ed., New York: Anchor Books, 1992).

49. Elwood Watson, "Miss America Pageant Evolves with America," *Delaware State News* (16 September 1996).

50. Watson and Martin, "The Miss America Pageant," 105–126.

51. Lynn Norment, "Vanessa Williams Is Black, Brainy and Beautiful." *Ebony* (December 1983): 132–136.

52. Jewell, *From Mammy to Miss America,* 52.

53. "Black Leaders See a Victory of Hope," *Philadelphia Inquirer,* 19 September 1983.

54. Wilson, Russell, and Hall, *The Color Complex.*

55. Vanessa Williams's reign as Miss America provoked numerous commentaries from print media, radio, and black organizations and journalists.

56. Watson and Martin, "The Miss America Pageant," 113.

57. Susan L. Taylor, "For Vanessa," *Essence* (October 1984): 79.

58. "Miss America Explains How and Why She Says No to Sex," *People* (26 November 1984): 109–111.

59. 1987 Miss America Pageant, www.missamerica.org.

60. Lynn Norment, "Back-to-Back Black Miss America's," *Ebony* (December 1990): 46–49.

61. bell hooks, *Killing Rage: Ending Racism* (New York: Henry Holt Publishing, 1995).

62. Valerie Helmbreck, "Miss America's Changing Face," *Wilmington News Journal* (Wilmington, DE) 18 September 1990.

63. Nella Larsen, *Quicksand* (New York: Alfred A. Knopf, 1928).

64. A. Cleft Pellow, "Literary Criticism and Black Imagery," in *Images of Blacks in American Culture,* ed. J. C. Smith (Westport, CT: Greenwood Press, 1988), 151–154.

65. Toni Morrison, *The Bluest Eye* (New York: Holt, Rinehart and Winston, 1970).

66. Toni Morrison, *Jazz* (New York: Alfred A. Knopf, 1992).

67. Vanessa Dickerson, *Recovering the Black Female Body: Self-Representations by African-American Women* (New Brunswick, NJ: Rutgers University Press, 2001), 307–308.

68. Dorothy Roberts, *Killing the Black Body: Race, Reproduction and the Meaning of Liberty* (New York: Vintage, 1997).

69. Mary, interview in Banet-Weiser, *The Most Beautiful Girl,* 127.

70. Vanessa ShortBull, Miss South Dakota 2002, television interview, 2003 Miss America Pageant, 21 September 2002.

71. Leonard Horn, "Swimsuits: It's HER Choice, Not Ours, Not Yours," Knight-Ridder /Tribune News Service, 9 September 1997.

72. Freedman, *Beauty Bound,* 128.

73. Jane Jayroe, Susan Powell, and Shawntel Smith, Miss America 1967, 1981, and 1996 respectively, all attended Oklahoma City University.

74. Gerald Early, "Waiting for Miss America." *Antioch Review* 42, no. 3 (Summer 1984).

75. Sloan Wilson, *The Man in the Gray Flannel Suit* (New York: Simon and Schuster, 1955).

76. Freedman, *Beauty Bound,* vii.

77. Claudia Levy, "Margaret Cahill, First Miss America, Dies," *The Washington Post,* 3 October 1995.

78. Deford, *There She Is,* 10.

79. Joan Jacobs Brumberg, *The Body Project: An Intimate History of American Girls* (New York: Random House, 1997).

80. See Chapter 1, "The Beauty Myth," Wolf, *The Beauty Myth,* 9–19.

81. 1994 Miss America Pageant, www.missamerica.org.

82. Watson and Martin, "The Miss America Pageant," 123.

Part I

History

1

Bathing Suits and Backlash

The First Miss America Pageants, 1921–1927

Kimberly A. Hamlin

Girls are called incomprehensible. They have always been so since
first men looked at them—looked at them out of men's minds as
part of men's world. They will keep on being so, always, or until we
stop looking at them with men's eyes, speaking of them in men's
terms, and testing them by men's needs.

> Introduction to "Girls," by R.S.V.P.
> The *Atlantic Monthly* (April 1920)

When we hear the words "women" and "pageant" together, most
of us think of beauty pageants. This, however, was not always
the case. Prior to 1921, most Americans had never heard of a
"beauty pageant." In the 1910s, the most popular and well-known female
pageants were the elaborate, theatrical events created, produced, and performed
by the woman's suffragists. Hazel MacKaye, a leader in the suffrage movement,
believed that pageants were the most powerful and convincing way to bring the
equal rights campaign to the public. She wrote, "Through pageantry, we women
can set forth our ideals and aspirations more graphically than in any other way."[1]
Although pageants were a popular form of civic entertainment and reform agi-
tation throughout the Progressive Era, no one produced more effective ones

than the suffragists. In fact, scholars cite the suffragists' skillful use of pageants as one reason for the success of the Nineteenth Amendment in 1920.[2] Suffrage pageants consisted of a series of short scenes, or tableaus, that generally depicted important women in history, such as Joan of Arc or Florence Nightingale, and showcased women's contributions to the community as mothers, pioneers, and workers. Such tableaus suggested that women's suffrage was the next logical step in the march of progress. On stage, women portrayed historic figures or virtues such as "courage" or "justice," which helped to normalize the presence of women in the public sphere and gave the participants confidence in their abilities and role models to emulate. Scholar Linda Lumsden argues "the most fundamental function of pageants as suffrage assemblies was that they placed women at the center stage of history and civic life."[3] During the pageants and the parades that often accompanied them, the suffragist participants wore costumes or sashes across their chests emblazoned with slogans such as "Votes for Women." Indeed, women parading down major thoroughfares, or on stage, with their telltale white sashes are among the most memorable images of the suffrage campaign. Generally held in easily accessible public venues, such as parks or civic buildings, the suffrage pageants attracted a wide variety of attendees, many of whom simply came to be entertained.[4] Suffragists used pageants to persuade viewers, gain publicity, fortify adherents, and raise money. According to MacKaye, "for the purpose of propaganda, a pageant can hardly be surpassed."[5] By the mid-1920s, however, a very different type of all-female pageant had captured the public imagination and become a new symbol of American womanhood: the Miss America Pageant.

Unlike the suffrage pageants that preceded them in popularity and renown, the first Miss America Pageants pitted woman against woman and judged participants on physical attributes. Women did not participate as part of a larger political movement; contestants competed as symbols of their cities or states. Although they wore sashes that looked suspiciously like those donned by the suffragists, theirs proclaimed their state or city of origin, such as Miss New York, and their intent to compete against other women for the ultimate prize—the "Miss America" sash. The contestants' sashes did not represent their ideas and goals, as the suffragists' had; they sent the message that the contestant's personal identity was of no consequence. In contrast to the suffragists' pageants, the Miss America contest did not celebrate women's history, solidarity, or new opportunities, nor did it encourage feelings of liberation or agency among participants. Instead, it encouraged women to vie for male approval based on physical appearance and to view their looks as their most important assets. Despite the fact that these two types of female pageantry have little in common in terms of goals or purpose, they are linked by chronology and proximity in the public imagination. Furthermore, the Miss America Pageant would not have been possible without the earlier success of the suffrage pageants, which introduced the public to all-female pageantry, popularized pageantry in general, and, more important for this chapter, challenged prevailing views of acceptable gender roles.

Founded in 1921, the year after women gained the right to vote, the Miss America Pageant has become one of the most prominent and recognizable symbols of women in America. Through its uniform selection criteria and format, it has fostered the notion that there is such a thing as *the* ideal American woman. Generations of Americans have grown up watching the pageant on television, and it has generated a global industry in beauty contests for women and girls of all ages. *Pageantry* magazine lists a mind-boggling twenty-three national beauty pageants in the United States alone, not including Miss America, most of which have state preliminaries and subdivisions for Miss Teen, Miss, and Mrs. categories—titles for which thousands of women and girls compete each year.[6] The Miss America Pageant inspired these pageants, and it remains the gold standard. It was the first national beauty contest, and it is still the largest and the most prestigious, competitive, and well-known pageant.

Studying the origins of the Miss America Pageant tells us much about women in the 1920s and women in modern America in general. From its inception, the Miss America Pageant has been a site of contestation about what the ideal American woman should be. As will be discussed in greater detail later, male pageant creators sought to avoid the stigma of commercialism and fought the increasing presence of Hollywood, Broadway, and advertising executives who hoped to gain publicity and profit by casting Miss America in their shows or ads. Producers and advertisers knew that beautiful, scantily clad women sold tickets and products and, to them, the ideal Miss America would do just that. To pageant promoters and their audience, however, the ideal American woman was demure and interested only in marriage, not in a career or in seeking public acclaim for herself. In short, the early Miss America Pageants, from 1921 to 1927, provide a window through which to view the struggle to define women's proper place in society at a time when traditional gender roles were in upheaval.

In *The Invention of Tradition,* historian Eric Hobsbawm argues that we must study invented traditions, "set[s] of practices, normally governed by overtly or tacitly accepted rules and of a ritual or symbolic nature, which seek to inculcate certain values and norms of behaviour by repetition," because they are "important symptoms and therefore indicators of problems which might not otherwise be recognized, and developments which are otherwise difficult to identify and date." In other words, "they are evidence."[7] The invention of the Miss America Pageant, one of America's most popular and enduring traditions, is evidence of a pervasive postsuffrage backlash and America's anxiety over changes in gender roles wrought by women's participation in politics and public life, the emergence of the flapper, and the growing commercialization of beauty.[8]

Most histories of the Miss America Pageant describe its inception as the At-lantic City Hotelmen's Association's clever ploy to extend the tourist season past Labor Day, and many explain its playful structure and content as part and par-cel of the culture of the Roaring Twenties.[9] The relaxed spirit of the decade may have allowed for such an event to take place, but the rhetoric of the pageant and the type of women selected as Miss America testify to the overall conservatism of the event and the widespread desire to reinstate a modest, asexual, domestic woman as the American ideal, an ideal recently complicated by, to name a few, Freud, World War I, and suffrage. By tracing the pageant's inception, structure, and reception, and, most important, by looking critically at the winners of the 1920s pageants, this chapter makes the case that we might instead view the pageant as a revolt, conscious or otherwise, against women's increased indepen-dence and presence in the public sphere.

Beauty contests were not new in 1921, the year of the first Miss America Pageant. In fact, a Miss United States competition was held in Rehoboth Beach, Delaware, in 1880, but its promoters decided it was not profitable enough to sponsor again in subsequent years.[10] Between the 1880s and the 1920s, numerous seaside towns, carnivals, and museums held photographic or in-person beauty contests, but these events were small-scale, local, and often frowned on by the middle and upper classes.[11] There was something special about the historical mo-ment that transformed Atlantic City's Inter-City Beauty Contest, as the Miss America Pageant was first called, into an enduring national phenomenon and cul-tural tradition. What was it about the 1920s that made the Miss America Pageant an acceptable form of family entertainment whereas earlier bathing beauty con-tests were considered lowbrow and bawdy? What was it about these early pageants that ingrained the Miss America Pageant into our national identity as an impor-tant, patriotic annual event?

The 1920s are preserved in popular imagination as the decade in which the hemlines went up and the old order came crashing down. Books, movies, and cartoons depicting the 1920s showcase young men and women drinking in speakeasies, smoking cigarettes, and dancing the Charleston. Memoirs such as that of *Harper's* journalist Frederick Lewis Allen *Only Yesterday: An Informal His-tory of the 1920s,* glorify such stereotypes. As Allen recalled, a "revolution in morals and manners" was under way.[12] According to him, the women of the twenties wanted freedom, "not from men but to attract men." Women strove to be "youthful, light-hearted companions" or "pals" to men.[13] Perhaps the best-known symbol of women in the 1920s is the flapper. Young, single, urban, and free from the confines of corsets, long hair, and ankle-length skirts, the flapper helped define the age. Yet, in looking through popular magazines and newspa-pers of the 1920s, it becomes clear that there was something much more com-plicated going on with women beyond bobbed hair and shorter skirts.[14]

Armed with their newly won suffrage and fresh from working to support World War I, American women of the 1920s appeared more prominently and more regularly in the public sphere than at any previous time in their history. For example, in the early 1920s, the *New York Times* covered many women's firsts, including a woman running for the U.S. Senate on a "Women First" platform; women serving on juries for the first time; and a group of women in Tennessee establishing the first "all feminine" bank.[15] Frequent reports of women working, voting, and running for office, combined with images of the independent, carefree flapper, deeply upset the balance of gender relations and precipitated a cultural backlash against women.

Survey any popular magazine of the 1910s and 1920s and one is sure to find articles, cartoons, and poems grappling with changes in domestic life and gender roles. In 1911, author Helen Hay Wilson alerted her readers to the coming backlash: "At present a kind of reaction is setting in. The cult of the simple life and the cry of 'Back to the land!' are reinforced by a further cry of 'Back to the home!' The domestic heroine has reappeared in fiction, the domestic type has reappeared—if indeed she ever disappeared—in real life."[16] America's debate about changing gender roles was so pervasive by 1920 that *The Atlantic Monthly* devoted an entire issue to the topic. In that issue, "R.S.V.P." denied the possibility of expanded opportunities for girls: "In every generation, a girl's physical structure will foster this preoccupation [with people] and urge her to be what girls have always been—beloved sisters, incomparable friends, hostesses and entertainers, knitters of the human family into firm unity."[17] That same year, author Rhoda Broughton proclaimed "[n]o check stands in the way of [the girl of 1920] guiding every faculty of her being into whatever channel she feels the inclination or the ability to direct them." Contrary to generations of her predecessors, "[e]nnui and unemployment are practically non-existent for her," and she will never have to experience "[t]he intense dreariness of the afternoon of life."[18]

In the midst of this cacophonous debate, a dominant voice emerged. It told women that, despite their newly won suffrage, growing presence in the workforce, and progress toward personal liberation, the ideal place for them was in the home. Advertisements, books, magazines, newspapers, and movies all carried the message. As historian Lois Banner explains, "the premise that women had achieved liberation gave rise to a new antifeminism, although it was never stated as such. . . . [I]t involved the creation of a new female image, certainly more modern than before but no less a stereotype and still based on traditional female functions."[19] Corporations and government officials launched a veritable public relations campaign to popularize this new image and lure women back to the home. For example, President Woodrow Wilson signed a bill authorizing Mother's Day in 1914, when suffrage loomed on the horizon, reminding the nation of women's primary role.[20] One historian refers to the 1920s as an "early version of the feminine mystique" because popular media, government, and advertising agencies presented a unified message that "women should stay home to pursue domestic tasks and to consume commercial goods."[21] Indeed, consuming goods and purchasing new, time-saving appliances was one of the primary ways in which advertisers attempted to convince women, who often controlled the family's purse strings, that their place was in the home. For instance, a two-page advertisement for Sellers Kitchen Cabinets claimed that these cabinets keep "modern housewives . . . young and beautiful" and that they have "helped many, many women preserve their charm—to conserve their health—to increase their ability to enjoy life."[22] Advertising doubled in volume during the 1920s and glamorized household appliances, cleaning products, and cosmetics, telling readers that these were the most important things with which a woman could be concerned.[23]

- In concert with the traditional images of women promoted by government and advertising, and in stark contrast to images of female politicians, professionals, and flappers, the Miss America Pageants of the 1920s celebrated small, passive, nonthreatening women with little or no interest in remaining in the public eye. To pageant promoters, judges, and audiences, a young, long-haired, docile girl was the American ideal. Compared to other images of middle-class white women (which all the contestants were) in popular culture, such as flappers, office workers, or suffragists, the first Miss Americas projected an overall persona of innocence and tradition. Entrants displayed this innocence by arriving at the pageants with their mothers; eschewing makeup, alcohol, and tobacco; denying professional or personal interest in the pageant or anything else; and highlighting their attendance at church. Indeed, the 1920s' winners were the smallest, youngest, and least vocal entrants ever to be crowned Miss America. The press and the public alike lauded the first Miss Americas for their "unbobbed hair," "unpainted faces," and refusal to smoke cigarettes. Judging from the immediate national popularity of the pageant, this image of womanhood appealed to people from coast to coast. By consistently selecting the contestant who least resembled a "flapper" or "new woman," the pageants of the 1920s promoted a standardized and retrograde ideal of womanhood and sent important messages to women and men across the country.

Understanding the volatility of gender roles in the 1920s, it should come as no surprise that the September 9, 1921, edition of the *New York Times* featured two seemingly incongruous articles: "Uncorseted [woman], is Man's Equal" and "1,000 Bathing Girls on View in Pageant: 150,000 See Picked Beauties in One-Piece Suits in Atlantic City's Fall Event."[24] The first article discussed medical findings that "women are developing endurance and muscular activity almost equal to men's by discarding their waist armor." The second article shifted the focus from women's agency and equality to women's objectification; it reported that the girls "were judged on their shapeliness and carriage, as well as beauty of face." Just as women liberated themselves from the corset, a new and even more oppressive tradition asserted itself: the bathing suit competition. The innocuously titled "Fall Event" was in fact the first-ever Miss America Pageant. In 1920, H. Conrad Eckholm, owner of Atlantic City's Monticello Hotel, persuaded the Business Men's League to sponsor a Fall Frolic in the hopes of extending the summer tourist season. That September, the first annual Fall Frolic took place to modest success. The hotel owners, buoyed by the belief that they had an idea with great potential, formed a committee to explore expanding the Frolic in 1921. By February 1921, they agreed that the upcoming event would include, among many other attractions, a bathing beauty contest. A local reporter on the committee suggested that the winner be called "Miss America."[25]

Unofficial pageant historian Frank Deford writes, "the formal pageant appears to be a modern creation with no obvious antecedents."[26] Banner, however, traces the roots of beauty pageants back to community festivals, most notably May Day celebrations and their selection of a queen. She also links the popularity of photographic beauty contests held by newspapers and the rise of fairs and carnivals featuring displays of beauty to the hotelmen's decision in 1921 to host a beauty pageant.[27] P. T. Barnum popularized the photographic beauty contest in the 1850s, and, by the end of the nineteenth century, newspapers across the country used them to boost sales.[28] The photographic beauty contest invited readers to submit photos of beautiful local women and selected a winner from the photos. These gimmicks proved lucrative for the newspaper and, at the same time, allowed the contestants to keep their middle-class decency intact by never appearing on display in person. By 1920, bathing beauty contests were common, although not always reputable, forms of seaside entertainment, particularly in working-class resorts. Atlantic City businessmen were keenly aware that they needed to package the pageant in a way that would be acceptable to the middle- and upper-class patrons they wanted to attract. To solicit entrants for an event of questionable moral status, pageant promoters approached the newspapers in their trading areas and urged them to solicit pictures of beautiful girls. In a decade struggling to accept women's agency, the fact that contestants could not nominate themselves or volunteer to participate also may have been appealing.

Such a subterfuge did not assuage all critics of beauty contests. On August 13, 1921, the *New York Times* reported that a congressman from Oklahoma had introduced a bill to ban photographic beauty contests. The congressman accused modern women of thinking more of their looks than of their homes and proposed that any newspaper editor who promoted such a contest face a jail sentence.[29] This proposal brought the congressman a few fleeting moments in the limelight. Later that month, the *Times* published an editorial about him entitled "Congressmen Should Be Literates." The *Times* railed, he "spells like a child of six or a next to wholly illiterate farmhand and . . . he constructs sentences in a way that has no merit except originality." The editor went on to suggest that the congressman seek employment in a less conspicuous post in Oklahoma.[30] Although the editors did not address the merits of the congressman's bill to outlaw beauty contests, there were no subsequent articles on it, and the *Congressional Record* lists only that the bill was introduced. There does not appear to have been any debate or vote on it. Regardless, the Atlantic City beauty contest proceeded accordingly, although controversy surrounding it mounted over the years.

Pageant promoters contacted newspapers from around the mid-Atlantic region, and eight young women representing cities as far west as Pittsburgh and as far south as Washington, D.C., arrived in Atlantic City on September 6, 1921.[31] Miss New York, Virginia Lee, an early favorite, arrived with the other contestants and was presented with an "engraved certificate of freedom of the city" by Atlantic City's mayor.[32] Female contestants were divided into two categories: professional and amateur. The amateur section consisted of the women who had won their local newspaper's beauty contest. Professional denoted women working as dancers, actresses, or models. This section received far less publicity, and pageant organizers discontinued it in the 1930s. Originally the amateur and professional winners competed against each other for the title of Miss America. The organizers' decision to divide the women into two categories and the fact that only amateur beauties ever became Miss America exemplifies their desire to give the pageant a wholesome image and reinstate a more traditional woman, not one working as an actress or a model, as the nation's ideal. Furthermore, by dividing the women into two categories and selecting only "amateur" women as queens, audiences and judges could simultaneously objectify women on stage and denounce acting and related professions as options for women.

In contrast to pageants in subsequent decades, the first Miss America contest was merely one event during the weeklong Fall Frolic. There were also bathing suit competitions between men, young people, and clubs. Even the police officers dressed in comic bathing attire. Additional festivities included rolling chair parades, car races, swimming expositions, and other community events.[33] The *New York Times*'s coverage of the event led with "[e]ight miles of rolling chairs and wheel floats passing before an assemblage of 150,000 along the boardwalk" and devoted only a fraction of the article to the beauty contest.[34] According to these reports, the appeal of the first Fall Frolic was its communitywide participation and optimism. The beauty contest was not initially the centerpiece of the event, nor were women the only ones who appeared in their bathing suits. The structure of the bathing beauty review and the kind of femininity celebrated by the pageant, however, so captured the public's attention that organizers greatly expanded the beauty contest over the years, and soon it was the only Fall Frolic event of any consequence.

The standards by which judges selected the first Miss America foreshadow later trends in the pageant and testify to the overall tenor of the event. Although mature and sophisticated Virginia Lee of New York captured the professional beauty title and was favored to beat out the amateur contender in the final round, the five male judges, all artists, selected "sweet little" Margaret Gorman of Washington, D.C., as the first Miss America.[35] Gorman was also the audience's choice. An anonymous person had submitted then-fifteen-year-old Gorman's picture to the *Washington Herald*'s beauty contest. The reporters who went to her house to inform her that she had won the preliminary contest recalled finding her at a nearby playground shooting marbles in the dirt. She had no previous pageant experience and no idea that someone had sent her picture to the paper. Besides being the smallest and the youngest contestant in 1921, she also had the longest hair; a bob would have been wholly unacceptable. At five foot one inch and 108 pounds, with measurements of 30–25–32, Gorman is still the most petite Miss America on record.[36] From descriptions of Gorman's appearance and stature, it is apparent that the judges were not interested in celebrating the new, emancipated women of the 1920s but in promoting images of the girls of yesterday: small, childlike, subservient, and malleable. As former judge and informal pageant historian Frank Deford notes, Gorman's victory "set a precedent . . . the judges will almost never vote for the one girl who exhibits the most brazen femininity."[37] Labor leader Samuel Gompers praised Gorman. "She represents the type of womanhood America needs," he raved, "strong, red-blooded, able to shoulder the responsibilities of homemaking and motherhood. It is in her type that the hope of the country rests."[38] What it was about Gorman's diminutive frame that convinced Gompers she could shoulder much of anything is unclear; what is clear, however, is that the type of woman America needed was not a suffragist, a professional, or a flapper.

Many commentators suggested that Margaret Gorman had been chosen because of her resemblance to movie star and "America's sweetheart" Mary Pickford. Deford cites a local newspaper account which claimed that Gorman was crowned due to her "Pickford-like beauty."[39] Mary Pickford became famous playing wide-eyed, innocent adolescents. She was also one of Hollywood's shrewdest businesspeople, but her attempts to break out of youthful roles were largely unsuccessful.[40] As Banner explains, Mary Pickford was "neither a sex symbol nor a bathing beauty, her image was the perfect foil for any presumed celebration of sensuality behind the bathing beauty queen of the United States."[41] Beyond legitimizing the pageant and allaying middle-class reservations about it, Gorman's selection and her similarities with Pickford testify to the pageant's conservative and reactive nature.

The official pageant picture of Gorman shows her in her winning one-piece bathing suit with her stockings rolled below her knee. Ironically, as Gorman and her parents traveled from Washington, D.C., to Atlantic City, Louise Rosine, a thirty-nine-year-old novelist from Los Angeles, sat in an Atlantic City jail for appearing on the beach in much the same garb. Atlantic City ordinances required female bathers to wear stockings to avoid any display of bare skin. While at the beach on a record hot day, Rosine rolled down her stockings and was arrested for refusing to cover herself when confronted by a police officer. Reporting on the incident, the *New York Times* headline read, "Bather Goes to Jail; Keeps Her Knees Bare."[42] Rosine allegedly refused to "roll 'em up" when ordered to do so by a beach policeman; instead, she argued, "the city has no right to tell me how I shall wear my stockings. It is none of their darn business. I will go to jail first." After Rosine delivered a "lusty blow" that "nearly knocked him down," the officer was happy to oblige her.[43] She spent the next several days in jail with only her bathing suit and a blanket. Louise Rosine's arrest speaks to the ways in which the Miss America Pageant was not an example of the general decline of Victorian morality in the 1920s but an attempt to assert a repackaged form of restrictive Victorian gender roles. If the pageant was a manifestation of the Roaring Twenties and expanded opportunities for women's self-expression, then officials would have viewed Rosine's bathing attire with the same wink and smile with which they greeted the rolled-down stockings of Margaret Gorman.

By the turn of the twentieth century, bathing and swimming were popular pastimes, but Americans continually debated and legislated acceptable beach attire.[44] Rosine's arrest is just one example of the many ways in which officials, community leaders, and municipalities from coast to coast attempted to deal with the growing problem of bathing suits that revealed skin. Newspapers of the early 1920s frequently ran articles describing the controversy surrounding the new, one-piece bathing suit popularized by the pioneering swimmer Annette Kellerman. Kellerman's suit lacked much of the cloth and constraints of earlier suits and was better for swimming. Even though it is modest by modern standards, many considered the suit shocking at the time because it exposed women's bare limbs. Illustrations of bathing suits in *Vogue* magazine promoted suits like Kellerman's, and even skimpier versions, claiming that these suits allowed greater flexibility.[45] Advertisements for the new one-piece suits also ran in mainstream publications such as *Harper's,* but many public officials and citizen's organizations resisted the encroachment of the more revealing swimsuits.[46]

Atlantic City's bathing suit ordinances caused quite a stir throughout the summer of 1921. Many young women argued for one-piece suits without stockings because they were much less cumbersome for swimming. Yet older women, led by the League of Women Voters, waged a letter-writing campaign extolling the city for its strict enforcement of bathing attire rules.[47] In fact, Atlantic City hired additional beach patrols, separate from lifeguards, to police the beaches for scantily clad women and the "bald beach lizards" who ogled them.[48] Contestants in the 1921 bathing review were allowed to wear the new one-piece bathing suits, even though such attire was technically illegal on Atlantic City's shores. This contradiction did not go unnoticed in the community. When the mayor announced that "Annette Kellerman's," as the one-piece suits were called, would be allowed at the bather's review, a Mrs. John W. White wrote him a letter asking how it was that these banned suits would "now not only be permitted but invited on our boardwalk for thousands to look at."[49] Apparently, it was more acceptable to Atlantic City officials for women to parade in front of judges and spectators in their bathing suits than to swim in the ocean in them. The debate over appropriate bathing attire demonstrates how complex gender relations were in the 1920s and how divisive the rules regarding them could be. The bathing suit debates also foreshadow larger controversies that would surround the pageant in subsequent years.

Bathing suit controversy aside, Atlantic City's intercity beauty contest was so popular that it gained in currency and prominence as plans for the 1922 Fall Frolic solidified. The hotel owners had such high hopes for the 1922 Frolic that they doubled the budget and invited "a prominent newspaper in every large city in the United States" to send beauty contestants.[50] Word of the successful 1921 pageant had spread, and fifty-seven young women from as far away as Los Angeles and Seattle arrived to participate in 1922's enlarged, three-day-long Miss America Pageant. The 1922 pageant inaugurated local preliminaries to select contestants as well as the evening gown competition. In keeping with the tradition of the 1921 pageant, the beauty contest was only one component of a week-long celebration featuring the rolling chair parade, which included city officials, townspeople, and police officers dressed up in their bathing suits or as clowns.[51] Such ancillary activities served to legitimize and desexualize the pageant, even though the bathing beauty competition was the main event.

By all accounts, the 1922 Frolic was a huge success. An estimated 67,000 people took the train to Atlantic City for the Saturday festivities, and over 250,000 people attended in total.[52] The contestants themselves also gained in attention and exposure. Testifying to the growing national prominence of the pageant and foreshadowing later conflicts, the Universal Film Company made test films of each entrant in the 1922 contest.[53] By 1922, many women made careers as actresses, dancers, and models, all of which required the display of faces and, often, bare limbs. The pageant, however, went to great lengths to distance itself from these industries as it continued to divide contestants into professional and amateur categories and eschewed links with Hollywood or

Broadway. The pageant structured itself very much as an antidote to the expansion of careers for women on stage or screen and selected as winners only those contestants who did not, at least at the time of their victory, espouse such careers. By emphasizing the winners' unbobbed hair and unpainted faces, the pageant's rhetoric also distanced it from associations with professional women who were known to wear makeup and who often had bobbed hair. In 1922, no contestants went on to work for Universal or any other movie company, and it was not until 1925 that a Miss America accepted a Hollywood offer.

Although contemporary commentators noted that Miss America 1922, Mary Katherine Campbell of Ohio, did not look like Margaret Gorman, the two had much in common.[54] Like Gorman, Campbell was the youngest of the contestants that year. Pageant bylaws required that entrants be at least sixteen, but Campbell later admitted to being just fifteen at the time of her victory. She was so young and naive that when she learned she had won the preliminary Miss Columbus title, she asked her mother "they said [I won] because of my figure. Mother, what's a figure?" To which her mother replied, "[t]hat's none of your business."[55] Campbell did have a larger, more athletic build than Gorman, but she was lauded for her youth and innocence and for wearing a size three shoe.[56] Campbell recalled that there was no formal interview, but that the contestants' personalities were a factor. Her wholesome qualities must have shown through because the judges selected her over a slate of arguably more polished, more poised, and more sophisticated young women. Again, judges and observers noted her innocence and traditional style. The *New York Times,* for example, reported "Miss Philadelphia and Miss Saint Louis had bobbed hair, while Miss America had an abundance of long-tresses."[57] Campbell was such a favorite that she returned to recapture her title in 1923, defeating both Miss America 1921 and the woman who would be crowned Miss America 1924.

Atlantic City historian Charles Funnell notes that the promoters of the early pageants "tended to select girls with conservative hair styling who would not identify Miss America with flaming youth. Bobbed hair handicapped any entrant, for it was thought to be bold in tone, and judges were convinced that the traditional long hair of the Victorian woman was an essential part of 'natural beauty.'"[58] In 1922, pageant directors noted with pride that fifty-five of the fifty-seven entrants had unbobbed hair.[59] Another commentator observed that all but two of the local Atlantic City women who appeared as attendants in various parts of the Fall Frolic had bobbed hair, while all but two of the contestants had long hair. To investigate this contrast, the judges surveyed more than a hundred photos of Atlantic City women involved with the pageant, found that all of them had bobbed hair, and concluded that "the selection of women to be sent to the national contest had been made with loaded dice."[60] Long hair was a necessary attribute of Miss America, but it was not a popular look among the majority of young women who were eager to take advantage of the decade's expanding opportunities for female expression. Although long hair was the most often cited criteria for Miss America, it was part of a longer list of desirable traits. One judge told a reporter that the ten "essential" qualities in Miss America were: form, carriage, health, features, simplicity, character, personality, training, adaptability, and distinctiveness.[61] This list is divided between physical attributes and personality or character traits inferred from those attributes. (There was no formal interview process during the 1920s and only informal opportunities for the contestants to speak to the audience or the judges.) These criteria and the consistencies in the judges' selections affirm that to them beauty was not an objective aesthetic standard. The judges were looking for the contestant whose looks and persona radiated a particular type of womanhood—innocent, traditional, and nonthreatening—and whose image would convey certain behavioral codes to the rest of America.

By the time Mary Katherine Campbell returned to Atlantic City in 1923 to defend her title successfully, the Miss America Pageant was a national event. That year seventy-six young women competed in the contest and an estimated 300,000 people attended.[62] Legendary artist Norman Rockwell was among the panel of male judges who were, in keeping with tradition, all artists. Each day, the Associated Press sent out 200 words of copy on the pageant, and wire reports were radioed around the nation.[63] The *New York Times* expanded its coverage to include images and descriptions of the contestants' outfits and biographical information, including a full paragraph on Campbell.[64] Other national newspapers began to cover the event as well. The *Chicago Daily Tribune,* for example, ran a photo of South Dakota contestant Elizabeth Thompson and a photo of the winner two days later.[65]

As the pageant's popularity increased, so, too, did protests against it and other beauty contests. Immediately following the 1923 pageant, the Ocean City Camp Meeting Association, a Christian group, adopted a resolution condemning Atlantic City's bathing review. The resolution warned: "the danger lies in taking girls of tender years and robing them in attire that transgresses the limit of morality. The effect on them and the publication of their photographs in the newspaper are to be highly deplored. The saddest feature of the affair is the willingness of a few businessmen to profiteer on the virtues of those tender years."[66]

Later that fall, screen idol Rudolph Valentino staged a beauty contest in New York City featuring eighty-eight of the prettiest girls from the United States and Canada.[67] Reports of this event brought a flood of complaints to the *New York Times.* The paper responded in an editorial entitled "This, too, Was Once 'Un-American.'" The editorial reads in part: "People with old-fashioned notions on the subject of feminine delicacies and proprieties are wondering what sort of young women they are who thus submitted themselves to inspection and comparison. . . . It would not do, because it would not be true, to say that no decent girl would exhibit herself this way, but certainly none would do it whose instincts were even a little nice or fine. . . . But even for the old-fashioned person of mossy and archaic notions there is one source of satisfaction to be derived from this episode. The winner of the first prize was a girl who confronted her judges with her charms unassisted by any touch of paint or powder!"[68]

Based on the *Times*'s use of the past tense "was once" and its characterization of those who opposed beauty pageants as possessing "mossy" and "archaic" notions, we can assume that by 1923, beauty pageants had edged their way into mainstream American culture. If Americans had to accept the growing popularity of beauty pageants, at least they could take comfort in the knowledge that they only crowned women who did not wear makeup. The following spring, the Trenton, New Jersey, chapter of the Young Women's Christian Association (YWCA) charged that the pageant "exposed the young women participants to serious perils," adopted a resolution condemning the pageant, and brought the issue to the national YWCA convention and seventy-five other organizations "interested in the welfare of young women."[69] Three days later, the *Times* editorialized in support of the YWCA's resolution: "Strong sympathy and enthusiastic approval are deserved by the resolutions condemning 'beauty contests.' . . . [the contestants] have learned to mistake notoriety for fame, their estimate of relative values has been utterly distorted, and of true modesty they can have but traces left. A more reprehensible way to advertise Atlantic City or any other town could not be devised by the devil himself."[70] The tone of this editorial differs greatly from one the previous year that argued, in effect, that beauty contests were an inescapable facet of modern life, but it did not preclude the *Times* from covering in great detail the subsequent Miss America Pageants. In addition to the *Times*'s condemnation, the Newspaper Publishers Association issued a bulletin advising its members not to sponsor the local contests anymore because they were providing Atlantic City with the "most flagrant use of free publicity in history." Despite this stern warning and increasing protests, no papers backed out and a record eighty-three women from all across the country entered the 1924 pageant.[71]

By 1924, the Miss America Pageant was a national phenomenon, and the bathing beauty contest eclipsed all other events at the Fall Frolic. Organizers extended the 1924 pageant to five full days, and the contestants had a more rigorous schedule than ever before. Even though their activities multiplied, the bathing review remained the contestants' "big test."[72] Unfortunately for Margaret Gorman and Mary Katherine Campbell, both of whom returned to Atlantic City in 1924 hoping to recapture the crown, refusing to wear cosmetics or bob their long hair was not enough to guarantee them victory. Early on, the people's favorite appeared to be Miss Philadelphia, Ruth Malcolmson, who had been a finalist the previous year. Deford explains that Malcolmson was "cut in the classic mode. Her mother was her chaperone. She sang in her Lutheran Church . . . had never been to a hairdresser's in her life, and used no makeup except lipstick."[73] Again, he does not describe Malcolmson's physical attributes, such as hair or eye color, only those that attest to her traditional, wholesome qualities. The *New York Times* noted that Malcolmson had "long golden brown curls" and that only one of the five finalists wore "bobbed hair" while the others "glor[ied] in flowing tresses."[74] At eighteen, Malcomson was older than her predecessors, but she was the youngest of all the finalists that year.[75]

Unlike the previous two winners, Malcolmson had already graduated from high school and was able to take advantage of the many theatrical and advertising offers that now accompanied the title. Campbell, Miss America 1922 and 1923, received offers to be in three films, two musicals, as well as circuses and vaudeville shows, but she returned to school in Ohio. Likewise, Malcolmson declared that she was not interested in entering show business. She agreed to watch a few Ziegfeld Follies' rehearsals but turned down offers to perform with them. Malcolmson did make appearances at hospitals, charity events, and institutions around Philadelphia, where she remained a local celebrity for several years.[76]

Deford argues that the first three winners are "prototypes of the dominant strain" of winners. That is, they were "shy . . . with no sustaining interest in pageants or any other form of publicity; but for this one incidental burst of fame [they are] never again in the public eye." He goes on to claim that most winners settled down, married, and lived happily ever after.[77] His summary of the typical Miss America testifies to the conservative vision of American women that the early pageant promoters attempted to ingrain in American popular culture. The early Miss America Pageants popularized the image of the traditional Victorian woman who wore her hair long and espoused no personal ambitions or aspirations other than to be a good wife and mother as an example for the nation to see and emulate.

It was not long, however, before contestants began using the title "Miss America" to their benefit. In 1925, the largest crowd yet, some 300,000 spectators, came to Atlantic City to watch the crowning of Miss America 1925, Fay Lanphier, who participated as Miss California. She had been a finalist the previous year competing as Miss Santa Cruz. Lanphier was the first Miss America from the West, the first to make a Hollywood movie, and the first to profit financially from the title.[78] Aside from the requisite long hair, Lanphier differed from the earlier winners in that she was nineteen years old, worked as a stenographer, and used the title for personal and professional gain. Deford explains that she was the first of the other kind of winner, "the Hollywood dreamer," but that "she soon ended up as an unknown housewife just like her predecessors."[79]

The *New York Times* reported that all contestants in the 1925 pageant were "gathered . . . into a room and . . . told to sign a contract" that required each girl to appear in a film by the prominent Hollywood Film Studio Famous Players-Lasky should she win. It is unclear whether this was done with the pageant promoters' blessing, but many of the contestants resented having to sign this contract. One contestant, Miss Walker of Pittsburgh, resigned from the pageant because she did not want to appear in a movie if she won. She told reporters that she "did not come down to be in a motion picture. I came down [*sic*] in a contest for Miss America. This whole thing reeks of commercialism."[80] Lanphier, however, did not object to the contract and after her victory immediately went to Hollywood to begin filming *The American Venus*. This movie was not successful and Lanphier's contract was dropped, but she did earn $50,000 on a sixteen-week personal appearance tour.[81] Lanphier's use of the title called attention to the paradox of commercialism in the pageant: Promoters founded the pageant to bring revenue to Atlantic City businesses but steadfastly fought the label of "commercial" by discouraging contestants from profiting from the title.

By 1925, many elements of the pageant were blatantly commercial. Pageant officials scolded one contestant in the rolling chair parade for attaching a sign advertising a powder puff to her chair. Also, the *Times* noted that the parade featured advertisements for cosmetics, the railroad, and a telephone company.[82] The most controversial element in the 1925 pageant, however, was the increased presence of so-called professional beauties. Miss America 1924, Ruth Malcolmson, refused to preside over the 1925 festivities, as was customary, because she resented the entry of Miss Katherine Ray, a New York showgirl, and the selection of Earl Campbell, Ray's employer, as a judge.[83] The other former Miss Americas refused to fill in for Malcolmson citing similar objections. Other contestants voiced concerns that "professionals," stage actresses or models from New York City, and Hollywood producers were taking over the pageant. In addition to Malcolmson and Walker, another contestant dropped out in protest over the entry of a professional beauty. Amid the charges of increasing commercialization of the pageant and its contestants, Atlantic City mayor Edward Bader announced publicly that he favored discontinuing the event.[84] Despite city leaders' concerns, the pageant gained in national popularity and lived on for two more years before being suspended indefinitely in 1928.

On the eve of the 1926 pageant, the *New York Times* published an editorial "for the benefit of a more or less palpitant [*sic*] nation" informing readers that the contestants had arrived safely in Atlantic City. The editors went on to decry the commercialization of the pageant as evidenced by the Atlantic City Chamber of Commerce's prominent participation in it: "Thus is symbolized the marriage of the beautiful and the useful with an emphasis that no doubt gladdens the heart of the stout missionaries who have labored so valiantly for the conversion of materialistic America to the gospel of beauty."[85] The editors' convictions aside, the *Times* extensively covered the 1926 pageant and its winner, Norma Smallwood of Oklahoma. With her retrograde looks, Smallwood, aged eighteen, beat out seventy-two other contestants for the title. The *Times*'s subheadline proclaimed "Winner's Hair is Unbobbed," and the text made what was by now a requisite mention of Smallwood's hair: "The new American beauty queen exemplifies the movement away from bobbed hair. Miss Smallwood's hair is unbobbed and brown."[86]

Following her victory, Smallwood received a cookstove and a marriage proposal from a New England professor. She took the stove but turned down the proposal explaining that husbands "are not absolutely essential just now."[87] Unlike previous winners, yet foreshadowing later trends, she made an estimated $100,000 in product endorsements during her reign. Soon thereafter, however, Smallwood married Thomas Gilcrease, a wealthy oil magnate, who insisted she give up her public life.[88] In 1934, Smallwood divorced Gilcrease and opened a beauty business with her mother. Prior to her high-profile divorce, Smallwood was the source of controversy in 1927 because she refused to come to Atlantic City to pass on her crown unless she received a $600 appearance fee. Pageant organizers refused her demand, and Smallwood instead accepted a paid invitation to crown a beauty queen at a county fair, fueling organizers' concerns about the increased commercialization of the pageant. From its very inception, the pageant was commercial, but its wholesome rhetoric and consistent type of winners allowed both the contest and the contestants themselves to remain free from the stigma of commercialism for the first four pageants. The actions of Miss Americas 1925 and 1926, however, precluded any further obfuscation about the commercialism inherent in the pageant.

Much to the pageant promoters' relief, the 1927 contest signaled a return to the "original sweet mold" of winner.[89] Lois Delander, Miss Illinois, was a sixteen-year-old honor student. She had previously won a medal for knowing Bible verses and boasted "her lips had never touched coffee or tea."[90] The *New York Times* headline read, "Beauty Show Victor Is Not a Smoker."[91] In a telling description of the finalists and their relative purity, the *Chicago Daily Tribune* reported, "none of the beauties used cosmetics in any form . . . all from the south [have] long, dark tresses, and . . . most of the others have forsaken or eschewed bobbed locks . . . among other defects marked against contestants were 'gold teeth' and 'plucked eyebrows.'"[92] Hair was still very much an issue in 1927, as the *Daily Tribune* noted that Delander had "unbobbed hair" not once but twice in its coverage of her victory.[93] She also had no desire to go on the stage. Shortly after being crowned, she spoke about losing time in school and immediately returned home.

By 1927, Miss America was not only a national icon of ideal womanhood but also a tremendous source of hometown pride. The day after her victory, Delander's parents drove her home to a welcoming party so extravagant that it "surpassed . . . all previous welcomes accorded celebrities . . . in Joliet [Illinois]." The local paper reported that Delander was a "modest, wholesome, level-headed type of girl who can handle the beauty crown gracefully."[94] Following her victory, "Lois went on to college and then, like so many other Miss Americas, was happily married and never heard from again."[95]

Delander's youth, lack of interest in a stage or film career, long hair, and traditional behavior marked her as the sure winner, especially after the turmoil of the previous two years. Her victory, however, did not allay concerns about the escalating commercialization of the pageant or the public aspirations of some contestants. Following the 1927 contest, two protests made headlines. First, the Atlantic County Federation of Church Women sent a protest to the City Commission and pageant directors claiming "we are persuaded that the moral effect on the young women entrants and the reaction generally is not a wholesome one."[96] A few days later, in an address to the Atlantic City chapter of the Catholic Daughters of America, Bishop William Hafey of Raleigh, Maryland, condemned the pageant as an "exploitation of feminine charm by money-mad men."[97] Shortly after the 1927 festivities concluded, the hotel association of Atlantic City entertained proposals to discontinue the Miss America Pageant.[98] Although the pageant had grown steadily in both popularity and profitability since 1921, the hotel owners claimed that it was bringing negative publicity to Atlantic City and discouraging middle- and upper-class patrons from attending. Yet press reports indicate that while small-scale attacks on the pageant, such as those just listed, persisted, it was, by and large, embraced by mainstream America.

The main difference between the pageants of the early 1920s and those of the latter half of the decade was not so much an increase in commercialism but the fact that contestants started to profit from the title and seek public acclaim for themselves. Julian Hillman, president of the Hotelmen's Association, summed up the group's reasoning for discontinuing the pageant in 1928: "there has been an epidemic recently of women who seek personal aggrandizement and publicity by participating in various stunts throughout the world, and the hotelmen feel that in recent years that type of women [sic] has been attracted to the Pageant in ever-increasing numbers."[99]

Thus, the pageant ended up encouraging what it had attempted to throttle—the rise of independent, ambitious women in the public sphere. The pageant always had been about parading young women in their bathing suits in order to attract business, and it always had been profitable. What it had not been until the mid-1920s was a vehicle by which women could gain financial independence and notoriety. As contestants began to capitalize on the profit and fame the title "Miss America" could bring them, Atlantic City leaders suspended the pageant indefinitely.

Far from being a liberating experience for women or an outgrowth of their expanded freedom of expression, the Miss America Pageants of the 1920s were actually a struggle between two equally limiting, yet opposing, views of appropriate female roles and appearances. One, represented by pageant promoters, judges, and, presumably, the hundreds of thousands of Americans who watched the annual contests, trumpeted the event as an opportunity to promote images of the traditional, wholesome girl with no aspirations for the stage or public life. This girl was characterized by long hair, youth, innocence, and domesticity and was epitomized in the winners of the majority of the earliest pageants.

The second view of ideal femininity, represented by Hollywood, Broadway, and advertising, sought to capitalize on the relaxing standards of female display by using women to sell tickets and products. This contingent worked to convince women that their most marketable and important assets were their looks and their figures, fostered superficial competition among women, and encouraged women and men alike to view women's bodies as objects to be critiqued. Although distinct from efforts to reinstate a wholesome, domestic feminine ideal, the widespread commercial objectification of women in the 1920s also can be seen as a backlash against women's increasing personal and political agency. The winners of the 1925 and 1926 pageants represent this second, competing ideal, which was antithetical to the pageant organizers' plans yet inextricably linked to it. In trying to replace images of flappers and suffragists with a more traditional vision of American femininity, the promoters of the Miss America Pageant also eased the way for the commodification of American women and reified the importance of the bathing suit contest, both literally and figuratively, for generations to come.

In the 1920s, just as women achieved unprecedented personal, professional, and political power, the Hotelmen's Association of Atlantic City stumbled on something that Hazel MacKaye and the suffragists already knew: namely, that pageants are a highly effective form of propaganda. Instead of welcoming women into politics and the professions, the Miss America Pageant encouraged women to compete against each other for a crown and then return home to live quietly ever after. The first Miss America Pageants praised and represented only those young women who looked nothing like flappers or suffragists and who posed little or no threat of emerging in the public sphere. That such an image of womanhood was, by all accounts, unanimously agreed on by promoters, fans, and judges and celebrated across America testifies to its broad-based appeal. In the 1920s, crowning a passive, traditional, "un-painted," and "unbobbed" girl soothed a nation struggling to accept the changing gender roles brought about by suffrage, world war, and the flapper and provided a cookie-cutter version of America's ideal woman.

Although the Miss America Pageant was temporarily suspended in 1928, something about its brand of conservative femininity piqued the nation's interest. The pageant was revived in the 1930s and has continued to be one of the most prominent symbols of women in America. As the *Woman's Journal,* a suffrage newspaper, explained the power of pageantry: "An idea that is driven home to the mind from the eye produces a more striking and lasting impression than any that goes through the ear."[100] Over the years, especially since it began to be broadcast on national television in 1954, the Miss America Pageant has become one of the most culturally ingrained and accepted ways through which people learn to perceive women as objects and symbols. It gives us the numeric language to evaluate contestants ("she's an 8.5"), much as products are evaluated in publications like *Consumer Reports,* and an annual forum where we can hone our skills of discernment. In addition, the structure of the event encourages viewers to see women, contestants or otherwise, as a series of parts ("nice smile, but thick ankles and bad hair"). Women, in turn, often internalize this objectification and judge themselves according to these superficial criteria.

In other words, beauty pageants are not about beauty. They are about power. The work of French cultural theorist Pierre Bourdieu, in particular, provides the critical framework and vocabulary necessary to understand the ways in which the body is a site of political contestation and the subtle yet pervasive ways the sex-gender system asserts itself through society's preoccupation with female appearance. To those who argue that women willingly participate in beauty pageants and that this is somehow empowering, or at least rewarding, for them, Bourdieu would reply: "it only has to be pointed out that this use of the body remains very obviously subordinated to the male point of view."[101] Bourdieu shows that even though some women elect to participate in beauty pageants, beauty pageants do not benefit women. To the contrary, this indicates that women have so internalized their role as bearers, not makers, of meaning that they privilege it over other more self-actualizing roles. The sashes contestants wear declaring their state or city of origin epitomize women's symbolic function in beauty pageants. This is in no way a critique of contestants themselves; it is an indictment of the overall system in which beauty pageants exist and prosper. As Bourdieu explains, the fashion-beauty complex does "no more than reinforce the effect of the fundamental relationship instituting women in the position of a being-perceived condemned to perceive itself through the dominant, i.e., masculine, categories."[102] Beauty pageants, thus, are not necessarily meaningful in and of themselves, but they are evidence of larger, more insidious power inequities. One shudders to think how Hazel MacKaye and the other women who bravely donned the sashes of suffrage would respond if they knew that their version of female pageantry has long since been forgotten and that, today, white satin sashes are best known as the markers of those nameless bathing beauties representing America's ideal woman.

Notes

1. Hazel MacKaye, "Wake Up Woman!—To This Man-Made World," n.d. Percy MacKaye Papers, Baker Library, Dartmouth College, Hanover, NH. Quoted in David Glassberg, *American Historical Pageantry: The Uses of Tradition in the Early Twentieth Century* (Chapel Hill: University of North Carolina Press, 1990), 135.
2. See Linda J. Lumsden, *Rampant Women: Suffragists and the Right of Assembly* (Knoxville: University of Tennessee Press, 1997), 96, 106–108, and 147, for a discussion of how suffrage pageants hastened the passage of the Nineteenth Amendment.
3. Ibid., 147.
4. For a comprehensive discussion of suffragists' pageants see ibid., 96–113. See also Glassberg, *American Historical Pageantry,* 135–136, 152.
5. Hazel MacKaye, "Pageants as a Means of Suffrage Propaganda," *Suffragist* 28 (November 1914): 6. Quoted in Lumsden, *Rampant Women,* 101.
6. "Links—National Competitions," *Pageantry* (17 December 2002), Internet www.pageantrymagazine.com/links.html.
7. Eric Hobsbawm introduction to Hobsbawm and Terence Ranger, eds., *The Invention of Tradition* (New York: Cambridge University Press 1983), 1, 12.
8. Similarly, theater scholar Jennifer Jones uses René Girard's "theory of culture in which all rituals can be explained by tracing their roots back to an act of generative violence" to argue that the Miss America Pageant originated to "reestablish and reinforce traditional gender boundaries" at a time when the flapper and the new woman threatened to displace long-standing beliefs about gender roles. According to Jones, "one woman's coronation in the Miss America pageant [*sic*] may be viewed as a ritualized violent act disguised as a ceremony, whose real purpose is to banish disorder by intensifying differences within the community" (101). Jones, "The Beauty Queen as Deified Sacrificial Victim," *Theatre History Studies* 18 (June 1998): 99–106.
9. For example, historian Charles E. Funnell argues, "[o]n the most basic level, the Pageant was a pleasure event, and although it belonged to a well-established trend in the culture, it had the nice timing to appear in a notably hedonistic decade." Funnell, *By the Beautiful Sea: The Rise and High Times of That Great American Resort, Atlantic City* (New York: Alfred A. Knopf, 1975), 148. For additional discussion of the pageant's relation to the culture of the 1920s, see, for example, Frank Deford, *There She Is: The Life and Times of Miss America* (New York: Viking Press, 1971), 108–128; Sarah Banet-Weiser, *The Most Beautiful Girl in the World: Beauty Pageants and National Identity* (Los Angeles: University of California Press, 1999), 33–35; Ann Marie Bivans, *Miss America: In Pursuit of the Crown, The Complete Guide to the Miss America Pageant* (New York:

Master Media Limited, 1991), 8; and A. R. Riverol, *Live from Atlantic City: The History of the Miss America Pageant Before, During and After and in Spite of Television* (Bowling Green, OH: Bowling Green State University Popular Press, 1992), 1–13.

   For the most comprehensive history of the pageant's origins, see Lois Banner, *American Beauty* (New York: Alfred A. Knopf, 1983), 249–270. Banner traces the roots of the event to earlier community festivals that selected queens and to the rise of modeling and photographic beauty contests. She argues that "the history of beauty contests tells us much about American attitudes toward physical appearance and women's expected roles. Rituals following set procedures, beauty contests have long existed to legitimize the Cinderella mythology for women, to make it seem that beauty is all a woman needs for success, and, as a corollary, that beauty ought to be a major pursuit of all women" (249). For an unofficial institutional history, see Deford, *There She Is*. See also Riverol, *Live from Atlantic City*. For feminist interpretation of the pageant's origins, see Jones, "The Beauty Queen as Deified Sacrificial Victim."

10. Deford, *There She Is*, 108–110.

11. Banner, *American Beauty*, 255–260.

12. Frederick Lewis Allen, Only Yesterday: An Informal History of the 1920's (New York: Harper & Row, 1931), 73–101.

13. Ibid., 262–263.

14. See, for example, Edward S. Martin, "The Girl That Is to Be," *Harper's* 128 (April 1914): 915; Helen Hay Wilson, "On the Education of Daughters," *Harper's* 123 (November 1911): 780; R.S.V.P. "Girls," *Atlantic Monthly* 125–2 (April 1920): 490; Elizabeth Breuer, "What Four Million Women Are Doing," *Harper's* 147 (December 1923): 116; Wilson Follett, "The Soulful Sex," *Atlantic Monthly* 125–2 (June 1920): 736; Anne Winsor Allen, "Boys and Girls," *Atlantic Monthly* 125–2 (June 1920): 796; Alexander Black, "Is the Young Person Coming Back?" *Harper's* 149 (August 1924): 337; and Margaret Culkin Banning, "A Great Club Woman," *Harper's* 149 (November 1924): 744.

15. See, for example, "Woman Seeks Senatorship on 'Women First' Platform," *New York Times*, 9 September 1920: 1; "Prosecutor Saddened by Women on Jury; 'Frightful Evidence Unfit for Their Ears,'" *New York Times* (10 September 1921): 1; or "Women Establish a Bank," *New York Times* 5 September 1920, 20 (this edition also features a humorous article in the book review section on the prospect of the first woman president).

16. Wilson, "On the Education of Daughters," 180.

17. R.S.V.P., "Girls," 491.

18. Rhoda Broughton, "Girls Past and Present," *Ladies' Home Journal* 37 (September 1920): 36.

19. Lois Banner, *Women in Modern America: A Brief History* (New York: Harcourt Brace Jovanovich, 1974), 142.

20. Anne Ruggles Gere, *Intimate Practices: Literacy and Cultural Work in U.S. Women's Clubs, 1880–1920* (Chicago: University of Illinois Press, 1997), 139.

21. Glenda Riley, *Inventing the American Woman: A Perspective in Women's History, 1865 to the Present* (Arlington Heights, IL: Harlan Davidson Inc., 1986), 86.

22. Advertisement for Sellers Kitchen Cabinets, *The Saturday Evening Post* 195–2 (9 September 1922): 98–99. Other examples include: "Win Freedom from

Dudgery with the HOOSIER," advertisement for Hoosier kitchen cabinets, *The Saturday Evening Post* 195–2 (2 September 1922): 71; a full-page drawing in the "Wife" issue of *Life* magazine depicts a beautiful woman with a halo over her head with the caption "A guardian angel o'er his life presiding, / Doubling his pleasures, and his cares dividing." *Life* 77 (12 May 1921): 679; and an ad for Lorain Oven Heat Regulators, which asks: "Why do the cakes in bakeshop windows always look so much more appetizing than your own?" *The Saturday Evening Post* 195–2 (9 September 1922): 143.

23. Banner, *Women in Modern America,* 143.
24. "Uncorseted, Is Man's Equal," *New York Times* (9 September 1921): 5; "1,000 Bathing Girls on View in Pageant," *New York Times* (9 September 1921): 15.
25. Deford, *There She Is,* 110–112.
26. Ibid., 108.
27. Banner, *American Beauty,* 256–266.
28. Ibid.
29. "Seeks Beauty Contest Ban," *New York Times* (13 August 1921): 11.
30. "Congressmen Should Be Literates," *New York Times* (27 August 1921): 8.
31. Deford, *There She Is,* 112.
32. "Beauties at Atlantic City," *New York Times* (7 September 1921): 13.
33. Deford, *There She Is,* 114.
34. "1,000 Bathing Girls on View in Pageant," *New York Times* (9 September 1921): 15.
35. Deford, *There She Is,* 114; Riverol, *Live from Atlantic City,* 14.
36. Deford, *There She Is,* 113.
37. Ibid., 114.
38. "Inter-City Beauty Picked," *New York Times* (8 September 1921): 9.
39. Deford, *There She Is,* 117.
40. David Robinson, *Hollywood in the Twenties* (New York: A. S. Barnes and Company, 1968), 145–146. See also Banner, *Women in Modern America,* 162–163.
41. Banner, *American Beauty,* 268.
42. "Bather Goes to Jail; Keeps Her Knees Bare," *New York Times* (4 September 1921): 4.
43. "Keeps Her Knees Bare in Atlantic City Jail," *New York Times* (5 September 1921): 5
44. For a detailed discussion of the controversies surrounding swimwear and their relation to beauty pageants, see Angela J. Latham, "Packaging Women: The Concurrent Rise of Beauty Pageants, Public Bathing, and Other Performances of Female 'Nudity,'" *Journal of Popular Culture* 29, no. 3 (1995): 149. See also Riverol, *Live from Atlantic City,* 8–9.
45. Christina Probert, *Swimwear in Vogue since 1910* (New York: Abbeville Press, 1981), 16–29.
46. "Spring and Summer Styles Meet and Blend," *Harper's* 148 (December 1923-May 1924), advertising section in back of volume, unnumbered pages.
47. Angela Latham, *Posing a Threat: Flappers, Chorus Girls and Other Brazen Performers of the 1920's* (Hanover, NH: University Press of New England, 2000), 72–73.
48. "Bars Beach 'Lizards,'" *New York Times* (27 May 1921): 14. Quoted in ibid., 75.
49. Ibid., 70.

50. Deford, *There She Is,* 115.

51. Ibid., 115–116; Banner, *American Beauty,* 267–269.

52. Riverol, *Live from Atlantic City,* 23.

53. Funnell, *By the Beautiful Sea,* 148.

54. Banner, *American Beauty,* 269.

55. Deford, *There She Is,* 116.

56. Ibid.

57. "1922 Prize Beauty Is Winner Again," *New York Times* (8 September 1923): 8.

58. Funnell, *By the Beautiful Sea,* 149.

59. Ibid.

60. Ibid., 149–150.

61. "Fall Carnival Holds Sway," *New York Times* (6 September 1923): 28.

62. Deford, *There She Is,* 119; Riverol, *Live from Atlantic City,* 23.

63. Deford, *There She Is,* 118–119.

64. See, for example, "1922 Prize Beauty Is Winner Again," *New York Times* (8 September 1923): 8.

65. "Seeks Beauty Prize," *Chicago Daily Tribune* (6 September 1923): 4; photo of Mary Katherine Campbell, *Chicago Daily Tribune* (8 September 1923): back cover.

66. "Attacks Bathing Review," *New York Times* (11 September 1923): 15.

67. "88 'Beauties' Arrive," *New York Times* (27 November 1923): 2; "Beauties Dazzle Hulbert," *New York Times,* 28 November 1923, 20; "Paintless Girl Wins," *New York Times* (29 November 1923): 30.

68. "This, Too, Was Once 'Un-American,'" *New York Times* (30 November 1923): 14.

69. "Y.W.C.A. Opens War on Beauty Contest; Calls Atlantic City Parade Peril to Girls," *New York Times* (18 April 1924): 21.

70. "Criticism Well Deserved," *New York Times* (21 April 1924): 16.

71. Deford, *There She Is,* 120.

72. "'Miss Philadelphia' Wins Parade Prize," *New York Times* (5 September 1924): 7.

73. Deford, *There She Is,* 121.

74. "Philadelphia Girl Gets Beauty Crown," *New York Times* (7 September 1924): 9.

75. Ibid.

76. Deford, *There She Is,* 123.

77. Ibid.

78. Ibid., 124.

79. Ibid., 124.

80. "Two More Spurn Beauty Pageant," *New York Times* (10 September 1925): 29.

81. Deford, *There She Is,* 125.

82. "'Miss California' Wins Beauty Title," *New York Times* (12 September 1925): 6.

83. "Two More Spurn," 29.

84. "'Miss California' Wins," 6. '

85. "The Pride of the Cities," *New York Times* (9 September 1926): 22.

86. "Western Girl Wins Miss America Title," *New York Times* (11 September 1926): 15.

87. "Prefers Stove to Husband," *New York Times* (13 September 1926): 10.

88. David Randolph Milsten, *Thomas Gilcrease* (San Antonio, TX: Naylor, 1969), 137. Courtesy of the Center for American History, University of Texas at Austin.

89. Deford, *There She Is,* 127.

90. Ibid.

91. "Beauty Show Victor Is Not a Smoker," *New York Times* (11 September 1927): 31.

92. "Midwest Girls in Finals for Miss America," *Chicago Daily Tribune* (9 September 1927): 31.

93. "Illinois Maid Wins Crown of Miss America," *Chicago Daily Tribune* (10 September 1927): 15.

94. "Home City Plans Grand Welcome to Miss America," *Chicago Daily Tribune* (11 September 1927): 8.

95. Deford, *There She Is,* 128.

96. "Women Open Fight on Beauty Pageant," *New York Times* (18 November 1927): 12.

97. "Bishop Condemns Beauty Pageant," *New York Times* (30 November 1927): 10. Despite much searching, I have been unable to find any explicitly feminist protest of the pageant. Most protests come from religious groups and focus on female morality and virtue. The only protest I came across that could be considered feminist was a 1927 play written by Mae West. The *Wicked Age,* or the *Contest,* was essentially a satire of modern beauty pageants. West's play was not published, so I must rely on secondhand sources for a description of it, but, by all accounts, it was a brazen attack on the increased commercialization of the female body. West decried the exploitation of women in beauty contests, an avenue of exploitation of which women themselves were not in control. Carol Ward, *Mae West: A Bio Bibliography* (New York: Greenwood Press, 1989), 15–16, 140–141.

98. "Beauty Pageants Opposed," *New York Times* (18 September 1927): 27.

99. Deford, *There She Is,* 129–130.

100. "Why the Pageant?" *Woman's Journal* (15 February 1913): 50, quoted in Lumsden, *Rampant Women,* 103.

101. Pierre Bourdieu, *Masculine Domination* (New York: Cambridge University Press, 2000), 29.

102. Ibid., 68.

2

Miss America, Rosie the Riveter, and World War II

Mary Anne Schofield

When the day's work is done, is our usefulness to be judged if we appear bathed, coiffured and smartly groomed? Or will it serve a greater purpose if we appear tear-stained and worn? After all, it's the men we try most to please; let's ask them. Would we help them more if, when they are about to perish for freedom's sake, we showed ourselves to them worn with sorrow and dejection? O, let's lift our heads and send them off with iron in our hearts, a smile on our red lips and a bloom in our cheeks. I say: Thank God for cosmetics and the other harmless foibles. I, as one American woman, think these inventions—of man's lesser intelligence, shall we say— serve their purpose well.

> —Mrs. Horace L. Harrison in "Glamour as Usual. A Reply,"
> *New York Times Magazine*, 26 April 1942

In October 1943, a writer for the *Women's Home Companion* observed: "American men, bless them, expect their women to be (a) useful or (b) beautiful, but seldom both at once. To many of them there's the type of girl they dream about when they're growing up and the type they marry. Or in reverse order, there's the kind who is capable in an emergency and the kind who's nice to have around when there's moonlight . . . the girl who can handle a crane like a man and the girl who is too pretty to learn . . . the girl the boys overseas are engaged to and the girls whose pictures they use to adorn the walls of their tents. Grease paint and black velvet are the magic brew of fascination, but a gal whose face may be charmingly daubed with engine grease and black oil is the kid the boys have got used to ignoring."[1] This conundrum of glamour and grime, of Miss America and Rosie the Riveter, defines the America of 1941 to 1945 with its conflicting worlds of beauty pageants, defense factories, cosmetic advertising, and scrap drives. How and why was it possible, almost imperative, for the World War II ideology of the United States to support both the glamour girl of the beauty pageant and the grimy girl of the factory swing shift?

The answer becomes, as social historian Michael Renov succinctly states, "the object of a remarkable degree of calculation and social engineering"[2]; in essence, the existence of both icons during the 1940s defined the cultural production of representational forms used in virtually every vehicle of communication and entertainment that promoted the war aims of the United States. The durability of this campaign can be seen as late as 1980 when director Connie Field made *The Life and Times of Rosie the Riveter,* using clips from both the defense industry shipyards and from the government propaganda film, *The Glamour Girls of '43.* Clearly, the continued pairing of the two icons demonstrates the success of the wartime campaign.

It was a marketing campaign managed as adroitly as any battle plan devised by the military or the government. A year earlier, in 1942, a poll of "sailors, soldiers and marines" conducted by the *Ladies' Home Journal* to find out "What Is Your Dream Girl Like?" resulted in this "blueprint for a dream girl, 1942 model":

> She is short, rather than tall—the "pocket-size girl" seems to reach as high as the average man's heart. She is healthy and vital, may even be a trifle plump. No languid beauties for these lads! She is devoted to home and children. Although she can take part in at least one outdoor sport, and likes a moderate amount of dancing. Business ability and braininess run a mighty poor second to a talent for cooking. Her figure and her disposition are more important than her face. Too much make-up is a worse hazard than bowlegs, and untidiness gets a black look from practically every one of those able-bodied males. . . . A college education isn't necessary, and most young men would prefer not to have their wives work after marriage unless an emergency made it desirable. . . . All in all, I would like to have a girl be a square shooter.[3]

Elizabeth Field, a square-shooting journalist herself, recorded in the *Independent Woman* that the "Glamour Girl is going out. The Working Girl is coming in!" Unlike the soldiers', sailors', and marines' dream girl, according to Field, the "girl of 1942 wears blue jeans or slacks, a steel helmet, safety boots, and carries a dinner pail. On her chest, her identification badge of labor. Big as life! She wears it with more pride than if it were a five-thousand dollar diamond brooch."[4] This "Working Girl in coveralls or blue jeans, look[ed] as beautiful, probably to her male coworker as any Garbo . . . and [was] much healthier!"[5]

So in 1941, 1942, and throughout the war years, exactly which type of woman was the "dream girl" so desired by the serviceman? By the American advertising and government propaganda machine? Was it Rosie the Riveter, or was it Miss America? Was she "useful," or was she "beautiful"? "Can a woman be begrimmed one minute and bewitching the next? . . . Is the girl who steps like a veteran into a production soldier's shoes—dumb, dull and dowdy, more interested in rivets than lipstick?"[6] Or, as many in the cosmetic advertising industry assured the woman of these years, was it possible to be both: "American women are learning how to put planes and tanks together, how to read blueprints, how to weld and rivet and make the machinery of war production hum under skillful eyes and hands. But they're also learning how to look smart in overalls and how to be glamorous after work. They are learning to fulfill both the useful and the beautiful ideal."[7]

In their article, "The Miss America Pageant: Pluralism, Femininity, and Cinderella All in One," Elwood Watson and Darcy Martin argue that "the pageant, at any given time in its history, for the most part, reflects the values and beliefs of the greater American society, particularly in its view of women."[8] If this is an accepted truism, then the years 1941 to 1945, those of America's involvement in World War II, offer a unique position to observe not only the position of the American woman during the war years but also the historical significance of this position in the postwar years, a debate that continues unabated to this day among historians and literary critics, sociologists and economists alike.[9] How was it possible, they ask, for the nation to support two such extraordinarily different views of femininity and womanhood during World War II? How does the five-foot-four-inches, 130-pound Miss America compete with a riveting Rosie wielding a welding torch and other appropriate shipbuilding or airplane constructing equipment? Did the increase of Rosies affect the definition of American femininity during the war years, thereby creating a crisis in American womanhood?

The answer is no; the advertising and propaganda campaign waged by the cosmetic industry, popular culture, and the government allowed America's women to be both beautiful and useful, a feminine beauty and a wench wielding a rivet.

This uniting of both icons became the topic of articles in the popular magazines of the day. Journalists Wilhela Cushman, Elizabeth Field, Nell Giles, Fannie Hurst, Steve King, James Lynch, and Virginia Bennet Moore, for example, ably examined the paradox of the begrimed beauty.[10] Labeled "hot-money mammas, adult delinquents, home wreckers, good workers, and bad workers,"[11] these Rosies, according to *Ladies' Home Journal* contributor Nell Giles, made up more than 3 million replacement troops in industries after the Pearl Harbor attack.[12] Joining the assembly lines, the women moved from one stereotypic look to another. Steve King, for example, reported that "Betty" was just too attractive in her sweater-girl look; "Suppose one of the boys looks at you instead of his work and drops a punch press on his hand. . . . Without a murmur, Betty changed into coveralls." King continued: "She was perfectly willing to co-operate on behalf of somebody else—a man, especially—where she rebelled at regulations that interfered with her personal vanity."[13]

But femininity and vanity were still part of women's identity, the war notwithstanding; during these years, American women learned to combine this new, needed-in-the-workforce-power with their beauty to get the job done. As Steve King reported in *American Magazine* in 1942: "They know that the old clinging-vine stuff works as well in a factory as on a parlor sofa. Listen to a cute blonde named Irene: 'When a girl lets her foreman know she can handle the job without his help, she might as well go home and stay there. I manage to get into trouble once or twice a day, just so the foreman can help me out. That makes him feel manly and superior—and friendly. Men want their women to be efficient—but not *too* efficient.'"[14]

Targeted by the advertising industry and told that overalls and makeup, glamour and the factory assembly line could mix: they applied lipstick and powdered their noses before riveting. They learned to be beautiful, attractive, and efficient Rosies and pro-active beauty queens. And they did so because the advertising campaigns of the public and private sector, the government and the cosmetic industry, supported the propaganda machine that said that femininity and war work went together. In a word, the American beauty had to work and Rosie had to be beautiful. (It is interesting to note that, during the war years, the cosmetic industry, like the pageant, provided a place for women to succeed.)

Two things happened simultaneously in the wartime culture. The United States government supported the Miss America Pageant during the war years, thus allowing the icon of femininity to represent wartime women, and Norman Rockwell, with his *Saturday Evening Post* cover of May 29, 1943, stylized the other side of wartime women with his portrait of Rosie the Riveter. The beauty queen becomes a warrior and the woman warrior becomes a beauty queen.

The two icons meet in a lipstick ad. In the *Ladies' Home Journal* of August 1943, Tangee ran an ad for lipstick that declared "Beauty is her badge of courage." The ad article read: "For the first time in history woman-power is a factor in war. . . . It's a reflection of the free democratic way of life that you have succeeded in keeping your femininity—even though you are doing a man's work! If a symbol were needed of this fine, independent spirit—of this courage and strength—I would choose a lipstick. . . . A woman's lipstick is an instrument of personal morale that helps her to conceal heartbreak or sorrow; gives her self-confidence when it's badly needed; heightens her loveliness when she wants to look her loveliest. No lipstick—ours or anyone else's—will win the war. But it symbolizes one of the reasons why we are fighting . . . the precious right of women to be feminine and lovely—under any circumstances."[15]

In a stimulating article, feminist critic Page Dougherty Delano observes that the "props of make up and fashion which are the staples of Miss America, those very props that sexualize and limit the female, are also the same props that allow for visibility and assertiveness when used by Rosie the Riveter."[16] Makeup, she continues, "was a sign of an intensified sense of [female] self during World War II."[17] And it is just this sense of female self that the two icons represent. The beautifully made-up woman was the very thing that men were fighting for. Women in wartime, so the cosmetic industry said, had a right to be beautiful and feminine, and every product, from face cream to lipstick, would enhance the woman worker's femininity and morale iconography. The beauty queen and the riveter both paint on a "war face," which cosmetics industry leader, Elizabeth Arden, described "as 'vividly alive—vital—adventurous—radiant with spirit—above all vibrantly healthy—and natural.'"[18] Journalist Pete Martin, writing "Right Face" for *The Saturday Evening Post*, summarized the meeting of the two faces, Rosie and Miss America, and the saving of face by touting the necessity of lipstick and face powder to all the women in war.[19]

Both the Miss America Pageant and the Office of War Information (OWI), orchestrated by the wartime New Deal, were about visual culture and about its insertion into and within the dominant ideological formation of the feminine icon. Cultural critic Michael Renov argues that the half decade, 1941 to 1945, "constituted a unique moment in the history of representational forms in America,"[20] a period that has never been duplicated again in the annals of American cultural life. Miss America was a visual symbol that predated America's entry into World War II. In the early history of the pageant, for example, photographs of the beauty contestants were submitted as visual representations of the women. And Rockwell's *Saturday Evening P*ost cover visualized Rosie. With her compact, lace hankie, rouge and lipstick, Rosie the Riveter encapsulates the conundrum of these two visual wartime icons. Rockwell's portrait of Rosie is symbolic of the ambiguity and ambivalence in the presentation of wartime roles for women in America. Feminist critic Melissa Dabakis argues that the Rosie the Riveter icon "formed a part of a discourse, a constellation of beliefs, images, and representations, which did not simply reproduce the experience of women but sought to shape that experience"[21]; the image both encourages the number of stereotypic, defense-working Rosies, women who were paid for their work, while also trying to limit the number and keeping women in their nondefense positions, and the ongoing Miss America Pageant limited the numbers of beauty queens but sought to increase the number of women supporting the war effort. And although statistics demonstrate that two-thirds of wartime women workers were employed prior to the attack on Pearl Harbor,[22] the agencies controlling the visual culture, the hegemonic middle-class males, seemed unaware of the success of their advertising campaign; they were unaware that they had, albeit temporarily, given women a voice in their usually male-controlled wartime world. Historian Maureen Honey examines the persuasive abilities of American advertising and concludes that one of the results of this creation "of an ideological framework for the employment of women in male-identified blue-collar jobs" was the simultaneous acknowledgment that women could perform men's jobs while also preserving the essentials of their femininity, which resulted, oddly enough, in "a narrowing rather than an expansion of women's sphere."[23] Initially designed and engineered to attract, define, and redefine women's wartime role, both campaigns constructed a monolithic image of white, middle-class womanhood during the war. The OWI used three strategies to recruit women: good wages, work that was pleasant and not taxing, and glamour. The Miss America Pageant offered scholarship money, work that was pleasant such as war bond tours, and glamour. The war created, fortified, and publicized gender roles and codes; the paradox, however, is the iconic beauty queen and the monolithic Rosie, created by the government and the advertising industry, operate against the hegemonic order, as the public and the private feminine world coalesce. In advertising, the two conflicting images existed side by side during the war years: There was, according to Maureen Honey, "the strong dependable patriot who could run the nation and the innocent vulnerable homemaker who depended upon soldiers to protect her way of life."[24] The Atlantic City runway and the defense factory assembly line provide a stage for the selling of American wartime womanhood: Miss America and Miss Rosie become the quintessential morale boosters for the ideology of America's participation in the war. And they did so by allowing Rosie the Riveter, the icon that should have contradicted the Miss America Beauty Queen/feminine self-cum-happy homemaker, into actually contributing to the final exaltation of the beauty queen and the elimination of the strong, competent, wage-earning Rosie.

Live from Atlantic City

The OWI decided to use the immense popularity of the Miss America Pageant for wartime propaganda. Ignoring a precedent for no pageant during wartime (it had been suspended from 1928 to 1932 and again in 1934 because of protests from conservative church groups), the official online site of the Miss America Organization records that in response to the war situation, "Pageant leaders developed a regional network of volunteers, and for the first time, it expanded to include a contestant from every state in the nation"[25]; previously cities had been sending contestants to represent them, not states. In 1940, the pageant was incorporated as a nonprofit civic corporation with a board of directors (eighteen business leaders from Atlantic City elected annually that replaced the former), and in 1940 Convention Hall, the current site of the pageant, was built; in 1941, however, it was taken over by the Army Air Force and became a training site. In response to the war situation, the pageant became more entertainment (hence morale-boosting) oriented as it included a Navy Maneuvers, Mardi Gras, and fireworks; a dance in the Convention Hall ballroom had been added in 1940. In 1942, the first pageant after the Pearl Harbor attack, was held in the Warner Theater. And for one month in 1942, "even the glittering lights of the Boardwalk were dimmed when it was suspected that Nazi submarines lurked offshore."[26] Suspected Nazis and extreme budget cuts, from $50,000 to $16,000, did put a crimp in the pageant organization, but never on its portrayal of American womanhood. For example, in order for the 1943 show to go on, officials went to the War Finance Department to get approval to continue and got it, for the pageant was considered a major opportunity to sell war bonds. The 1943 pageant staged patriotic themes with a "Stage Door Canteen," a "Parade of Allies," and, of course, a rousing chorus of "The Star Spangled Banner," in which all thirty-three contestants enthusiastically participated. During the war years, Miss America went on war bond tours and traveled with the United Service Organizations (USO); contemporary Miss Americas also have traveled with the USO to entertain United States troops in the Vietnam War and both Gulf wars.

Miss America became a working woman. In 1941, Rosemary LaPlanche from Los Angeles, California, was one of the youngest women to compete, and proved to be a very popular Miss America. She traveled extensively with the USO and sold war bonds and was credited with selling $50,000 worth of bonds in one day. She went on to make motion pictures with RKO films during the war years and by the late 1940s even had her own radio show. Jo-Carroll Dennison from Tyler, Texas, Miss America of 1942, used her crown as a springboard into the entertainment field working in the Golden Age of television.

The 1943 Miss America, Miss California, Jean Bartel, went on a three-month bond-selling tour to fifty-three key American cities and sold over $2.5 million in Series E bonds—80 percent of which were sold to women; she sold more bonds than anyone else in the United States during that year. Her success became the idea behind the Miss America Scholarship Fund.

Miss America of 1944, Venus Ramey, earned a Special Citation from the United States Treasury Department for her efforts in selling war bonds and was very active in the political system after her year's reign; she also worked on suffrage bills from Kansas and Missouri to Washington, D.C. She became the first Miss America to run for public office as a member of the Kentucky House of Representatives. And she was painted on the nosecone of a B-17 bomber of the 301st Bomb Group of the United States 15th Air Force, stationed at Foggia, Italy, during the last months of the war. The 301st dubbed Venus Ramey "the girl we'd most like to bail out with over a deserted Pacific isle."[27]

And Miss America of 1945, Bess Myerson, still holds a unique position in the Miss America annals. Not only was she the first, but she is still the only Jewish Miss America. She came from the Bronx in New York, not from the usual small, conservative towns of the majority of pageant winners; she was the daughter of Russian immigrants. She had entered the pageant to earn money for graduate school music studies. She was beautiful and she was independent. Just four weeks into her reign, Myerson realized that the majority of sponsors were not going to allow a Jewish woman to endorse their products, so she challenged the anti-Semitism of the age by telling the pageant she was no longer interested in being their spokesperson and, instead, worked for the Jewish Anti-Defamation League, thus setting the stage for the contemporary social platform requirement that became a part of the pageant since 1989.

At the same time, Lenora Slaughter, pageant director from 1935 to 1967, saw the pageant as a way to change women's lives by targeting a female population, those between eighteen and twenty-five years of age, who were not connected with any commercial interests by providing educational money. Miss America moved from beauty icon to educated worker. Initially Slaughter raised $5,000 in scholarship funds, and the 1945 pageant was the first organization in the country to offer college scholarships to its winners. (Today the Miss America Pageant is the leading provider of educational scholarships for women.)

The Miss America Pageant officials, then, took the crisis of the war years and turned the events to the benefit of the pageant, ultimately transforming Miss America "into an emblem of patriotism and national pride"[28]; she became "enshrined in the nation's imagination as America's ideal woman."[29] Selling war bonds and boosting troop morale was the tangible contribution the pageant made, but why did the Miss America Pageant continue during these war years? Was it strictly to raise the American morale, as Watson and Martin argue? Did Americans want to see women not only out of their kitchen and aprons but out of their factories and overalls as well? (Do not forget that even though one portion of the pageant was the evening gown competition, the most popular event remained the bathing suit parade.). How do we reconcile and understand the coexistence of riveters and beauty queens? Of welders and bathing beauties? Lois

W. Banner argues that "[d]espite pretensions to intellect and talent, physical beauty remained the overriding feature of the ideal American beauty,"[30] which would clearly place the continued existence of the pageant during World War II as a national need to control and maintain the status quo of the male objectification of the female body. The pageant allowed men to know what they were fighting for.

Did the pageant allow women workers to know what they were fighting for as well? The defense worker did not find herself displayed on the airplane's nosecone, but without Rosie, there would be no nosecone to decorate with the Miss America beauty. Was Rosie visible only as the invisible plane builder? Clearly, there could not be nosecone art without the Rosies, and yet they were never pictured on their creations. Why?

The answer lies in the collusion of the two icons. Rosie made the planes; Miss America decorated them. Rosie squeezed her body into infinitesimally small spaces in the interior of the plane so that the Miss America beauty could be symbolically displayed on the phallic-shape nose of the plane. Both women left their private domains of domesticity for the public world of defense work, advertising images, and the increasingly open sexuality of wartime America.

Sex erupted into the public discourse through such media as the advertising industry, the cosmetics industry, and the fashion industry, but most especially with the Miss America Pageant because, first and foremost, the Miss America Pageant was and is about beautiful, young female bodies. As Banner noted: "Even when later pageants added a talent division and gave scholarships as prizes, the review of the contestants in bathing suits was still the most important part of the competition."[31] It was not until 1948, post–World War II, that a Miss America was crowned not wearing a bathing suit. The Miss America Pageant objectified the beautiful feminine body; the advertising campaign for Rosie the Riveter manipulated the female worker's body. Both became symbols of American life, freedom, patriotism, and the raison d'être of war. World War II might not have had its specific Helen of Troy, but every American serviceman was fighting for some woman—mother, wife, sweetheart—just as each Rosie was fighting for her father, brother, husband, or sweetheart. Bodies, male and female, were drafted for the duration.

Live from the Defense Factory

Although the Miss America Pageant targeted the eighteen- to twenty-five-year-old single white female, the advertising campaign to attract Rosies targeted a different age group. But both were made to look feminine. Some defense industries—for example, Lockheed Martin—even offered lunchtime fashion shows for the female workers so they could look like a riveter on the assembly line but dream about the after-work look of the beauty queen.[32]

Statistics show that the actual number of Rosies was a small percentage of women workers during the war. Melissa Dabakis notes:

> Eighteen million women entered the work force during the war years, six million for the first time. Three million worked in defense plants, but the majority worked in traditional women's occupations. Of women workers, 50 per cent had at least five years' experience, 30 per cent ten years. What was clear from these figures was that most women had already been in the work force and had converted to wartime jobs; what was new was the influx of middle-class married women into the workplace. Women who performed skilled industrial tasks, among them welding and running a drill press, were small in number and among the elite. They formed a special cadre of women workers whose skilled status and high pay made them clearly visible to the American public. Most women, however, worked in tedious and poorly paid jobs such as room clerk, waitress, elevator operator, maid, and cook.[33]

And historian Elizabeth Fox-Genovese further increases the conundrum of women in the wartime workplace by noting that the high-profile women and those targeted by the beauty pageant campaign were not in the majority of the actual workers: "While women 20 to 24 years of age increased their labor forces participation by 14 percent, and those of 25 to 44 years of age increased their labor force participation by 28 percent, women 19 and under and women 45 and older increased their participation in the labor force by more than 60 percent. Immediately following the war, there was a drop in the absolute numbers of women employed in all age groups, but between 1940 and 1950 the only age group that experienced a drop in the percentage of women in the labor market was that of the 20-to–24-year-olds."[34]

So who is the winner—Miss America or Rosie the Riveter? Or was there even a contest created by the government and the advertising industry? Perhaps the answer is best found in the observations of Margaret Barnard Pickel, who had been in both the ultra-feminine beauty world and that of the factory, who was both a beauty and a Rosie; she wrote in 1944: "It is splendid to look back and see what women have accomplished, how many doors they have opened, how many fields of usefulness they move in. Perhaps it was the indomitable refusal of the early feminists to admit that anything was impossible for women that broadened the roads women now travel. In principle women may now do anything they want to. . . . Many women feel that the world is all before young women, and that the woman of the present and the future can take her solitary way through Eden."[35]

She wrote to dispel such "paradise-gained" visions; Pickel remarked, "What women will have to do is to make the best of what the post-war world turns out to be. We can be better prepared for it if we forget our wishes and consult probabilities."[36] She continued: "By and large women will not be, any more than they have been in the past, the movers and shakers of the world beyond the horizon. Is it too hard for women to be instead the helpers and servers? . . . women can profit by bringing to their work the qualities that are essentially feminine,"[37] and she went on to designate teaching, homemaking, interior decorating, landscaping, and health care professions as the workplace focus of women; further women will be needed in their nurturing and nursing capacity to deal with the care and rehabilitation of the wounded veterans. Women should not live on illusions, and the long and the short of it is, according to Pickel, that one should put one's money on "the sudden appearance of Mr. Right, mounted figuratively, if not literally on a white horse."[38] Pickel obviously had read the tone of the times correctly, for Miss America of 1947, Barbara Walker, declared to the judges that the only contract she wanted was a marriage contract; she was married in June of her reigning year.

So the first postwar Miss America returns to the private, domestic sphere. The returning veterans force the majority of the Rosies out of their public workplace and back into the domestic domain. Fox-Genovese articulates the ambiguity when she examines the rather long shadow cast by Rosie the Riveter: "The demands of wartime production drew women in unprecedented numbers into work notably factory work, which had previously been reserved for men. Most of us also know, however vaguely, that with the advent of peace women left those jobs to return to the bosom of their families. The public accounts are a little imprecise about whether women were pulled out of their newfound employments by the lure of domesticity or whether they were pushed out of them by returning veterans who were reclaiming their positions. But confusion about the cause notwithstanding, it is clear that as early as 1947 the image of the woman in coveralls, with her curls caught up in a bandana, had been replaced by the image of the young suburban wife with a cinched waist and billowing skirts."[39]The cinched waist and the billowing skirt is another version of the beauty queen; her runway is now the sidewalk to her front door.

Conclusion

The existence of the Miss America Pageant and the simultaneous movement of women into the defense industries during the war years speak to the possible defeminization of women that could have occurred because of the movement of Rosies to the defense factories. But the advertising campaigns and government propaganda made sure that, throughout the period, women were constantly reminded that they *were* women. The existence of the pageant during the war years allowed for a quicker and easier return to normalcy at the end of the war, for the greatest desire of the postwar years was a return to stability and continuity. The continuance of the Miss America Pageant allowed for this transition to happen seamlessly. During the war years, the pageant acted as a way to reshape the Rosies into a Miss America image so that femininity still reigned supreme. Rosies wore lipstick, carried compacts, and went to lunchtime fashion shows.

The triumph of Miss America over Rosie the Riveter is the triumph of the doctrine of normalcy, economic security, and social order. It is about the restoration of the "American Ideal" no matter how engineered and calculated. It is the return to the family, the domestic sphere, prosperity, and two washes in the morning and a bridge party at night, according to social historian Ruth Schwartz Cohan.[40]

The fact that records, statistics, and the like are sketchy about Rosie the Riveter—who she really was, what her background and her life before and after the war years was—proves that the Miss America icon was the superior one for the American war years. Miss America did not go from the runway to the workforce no matter how much the cosmetic and fashion industry tried to reconcile the two platforms. Instead, she detoured into the bedroom and the nursery. And she did it in record-breaking time. As historian Elaine Tyler May recorded: "Over one million more families were formed between 1940 and 1943 than would have been expected during normal times. And as soon as Americans entered the war, the birthrate began to climb. Between 1940 and 1945 it jumped from 19.4 to 24.5 per 1,000 population."[41]

In the final analysis, cultural critic Sarah Banet-Weiser best articulated the place of the Miss America Pageant during the war years when she noted that beauty pageants "are actually a kind of feminist space where female identity"[42] can be constructed. Historians would like us to believe that World War II actually changed the position of American women. But truth to tell, by examining the duality of the two images of Miss America and Rosie the Riveter, it is clear that a transformation did not take place. The icon of femininity triumphed in the postwar years as America returned to normalcy.

Notes

1. Virginia Bennet Moore, "Begrimmed—Bewitching or Both," *Woman's Home Companion* (October 1943): 80.
2. Michael Renov, "Advertising/Photojournalism/Cinema: The Shifting Rhetoric of Forties Female Representation," *Quarterly Review of Film and Video* 11 (1989): 1.
3. Louise Paine Benjamin, "What Is Your Dream Girl Like?" *Ladies' Home Journal* (May 1942): 28.
4. Elizabeth Field, "Boom Town Girls," *Independent Woman* (October 1942): 296.

5. Ibid., 298.
6. Moore, "Begrimmed—Bewitching or Both," 80.
7. Ibid.
8. Elwood Watson and Darcy Martin, "The Miss America Pageant: Pluralism, Femininity, and Cinderella All in One," *Journal of Popular Culture* 34, no. 1 (Summer 2000): 106.
9. See Karen Anderson, *Wartime Women: Sex Roles, Family Relations, and the Status of Women during World War II* (Westport, CT: Greenwood Press, 1981); D'Ann Campbell, *Women at War with America* (Cambridge, MA: Harvard University Press, 1984); William Henry Chafe, *The American Woman: Her Changing Social, Economic, and Political Roles, 1920–1970* (New York: Oxford University Press, 1971); William Henry Chafe, *The Paradox of Change: American Women in the 20th Century* (New York: Oxford University Press); Susan M. Hartmann, *The Home Front and Beyond: American Women in the 1940s* (Boston: Twayne Publishers, 1982); Maureen Honey, *Creating Rosie the Riveter: Class, Gender and Propaganda during World War II* (Amherst: University of Massachusetts Press, 1984); Ruth Milkman, *Gender at Work: The Dynamics of Job Segregation by Sex during World War II* (Urbana: University of Illinois Press, 1987); Leila Rupp, *Mobilizing Women for War: German and American Propaganda, 1939–1945* (Princeton, NJ: Princeton University Press, 1978); and Doris Weatherford, *American Women and World War II* (New York: Facts On File, 1990).
10. See Wilhela Cushman, "Now It's Woman's Work," *Ladies' Home Journal* (May 1942): 28–29; Field, "Boom Town Girls"; Nell Giles, "What About the Women?" *Ladies' Home Journal* (May 1942): 23, 157; Fanny Hurst, "Glamour as Usual?" *New York Times Magazine* (29 March 1942): 10–12; Steve King, "Danger! Women at Work," *American Magazine* (September 1943): 40–41; James C. Lynch, "Trousered Angel," *Saturday Evening Post* (10 April 1943): 23, 84, 87; and Moore, "Begrimmed—Bewitching or Both."
11. Giles, "What About the Women?" 23.
12. Ibid.
13. King, Danger!"118.
14. Ibid.
15. Constance Luft Huhn, "War, Women and Lipstick," *Ladies' Home Journal* (August 1943): 73.
16. Page Dougherty Delano, "Making Up for War: Sexuality and Citizenship in Wartime Culture," *Feminist Studies* 26, no. 1 (Spring 2000): 41.
17. Ibid.
18. Pete Martin quoted Elizabeth Arden in his article: Martin, "Right Face," *The Saturday Evening Post* (March 1943): 49.
19. Ibid., photo.
20. Renov, "Advertising/Photojournalism/Cinema," 3.
21. Melissa Dabakis, "Gendered Labor." Norman Rockwell's Rosie the Riveter and the Discourses of Wartime Womanhood," in *Gender and American History Since 1890,* ed. Barbara Melosh (London: Routledge, 1993): 185.
22. Renov, "Advertising/Photojournalism/Cinema," 7.
23. Maureen Honey, "The 'Womanpower' Campaign: Advertising and Recruitment Propaganda During World War II," *Frontiers* 6, nos. 1–2 (1981): 50.
24. Ibid., 53.

25. See www.missamerica.org/history/1940.html.
26. Watson and Martin, "Miss America Pageant," 109.
27. Barney Oldfield, "Miss America and the 301st Bomb Group," *Air Power History* 37, no. 2 (1990): 41–44.
28. www.missamerica.org.
29. Ibid.
30. Lois W. Banner, *American Beauty* (Chicago: University of Chicago Press, 1983), 270.
31. Ibid.
32. Sherna Berger Gluck, *Rosie the Riveter Revisited: Women, the War, and Social Change* (New York: New American Library, 1987), 31.
33. Dabakis, "Gendered Labor," 186.
34. Elizabeth Fox-Genovese, "Mixed Messages: Women and the Impact of World War II," *Southern Humanities Review* 27 (Summer 1993): 238.
35. Margaret Barnard Pickel, "A Warning to the Career Woman," *New York Times Magazine* (16 July 1944): 19.
36. Ibid., 20.
37. Ibid., 33.
38. Ibid.
39. Fox-Genovese, "Mixed Messages," 235–236.
40. See Ruth Schwartz Cohan, "Two Washes in the Morning and a Bridge Party at Night: The American Housewife Between the Wars," *Women's Studies* 3 (1976): 147–172.
41. Elaine Tyler May, "Rosie the Riveter Gets Married," in *The War in American Culture,* ed. Lewis A. Erenberg and Susan E. Hirsch (Chicago: University of Chicago Press, 1996), 137.
42. Sarah Banet-Weiser, *The Most Beautiful Girl In the World: Beauty Pageants and National Identity* (Berkeley: University of California Press, 1999), 24.

3

Miss America, National Identity, and the Identity Politics of Whiteness

Sarah Banet-Weiser

*I*n September 1945, Bess Myerson became the first Jewish woman to win the Miss America title. Fifty years later, in September 1995, Heather Whitestone became the first woman with a disability (she is deaf) to win the crown of Miss America. Although the historical contexts of both of these formative moments differ considerably, both demonstrate how the pageant privileges whiteness. For Bess Myerson in 1945, the pageant's emphasis on whiteness revolved around the discourse of assimilation and Americanization. With World War II providing a nationalist backdrop to the Miss America Pageant, and the complicated terrain of U.S. anti-Semitism and the increasing national realization of the Holocaust operating as political context, the pageant's cultural politics of whiteness offered a particular kind of logic to the selection of a Jewish woman as Miss America.

In 1995, the material and cultural politics of whiteness continued to hold sway over the Miss America Pageant, although the way in which whiteness was "waged" was slightly different.[1] The mid-1990s in the United States were characterized by public recognition of "identity politics," ostensibly a politics and practice that recognized specific racial, ethnic, and cultural difference. However, the reality of identity politics during this historical moment in the United States is not the celebration of difference, but rather the flattening out and diffusion of racial identity in ways that "accept" difference while not posing a threat to the dynamic power of whiteness. Thus, while on one hand public rhetoric lauded the "color-blind" public policy that supposedly structured U.S. laws and government, on the other, this very same policy contributed to the maintenance of racism through what cultural scholar George Lipsitz has called the "possessive investment in whiteness."[2] This conservative reading of identity politics functions to privilege an ideology of innocent white victimhood (where injustices and other "injuries" such as work-related privileges and college admissions occur because one is white, in a historical context that embraces cases of reverse discrimination) rather than celebrate "difference." Against this setting, the supposed innocence of whites, claimed by conservatives to be apparently unfairly disadvantaged in many realms of life, became a privileged discourse. These, then, were the conditions for the crowning of Heather Whitestone, Miss America 1995, who through her white body became a liberal heroine by overcoming the "obstacle" of her disability to win the pageant, affirming in the conservative parlance of the day that "differences" should really make no difference.

These two moments in the history of the Miss America Pageant are instructive in illuminating some of the ways in which whiteness functions in popular culture. The recognition of these two moments, fifty years apart in the history of the pageant, clearly does not represent a historical investigation of the Miss America as an entire institution. Rather, through the stories of two individual Miss Americas, Bess Myerson and Heather Whitestone, we witness how a utopian fantasy of national identity, structured by whiteness, is produced in two very different historical moments. These moments reveal much about how American popular culture produces representative bodies and, specifically, how these two moments in the Miss America Pageant contribute to a broader national politics that consolidates whiteness as a dominant ideology.

The politics of whiteness, as much recent scholarship has demonstrated persuasively, exists as a normative power in the sense that it presents itself as the "normal" state of affairs. It also exists as an institutionalized structure of government regulations and policies, cultural privilege, and political entitlement.[3] Cultural scholar Richard Dyer has pointed out that power embodied as normal "works in a peculiarly seductive way with whiteness, because of the way it seems rooted, in commonsense thought, in things other than ethnic difference."[4] In other words, whiteness becomes an entitled form of privilege precisely through its invisibility *as* racial privilege and its forcefulness as the (unraced) "normal." Dyer continues: "In the realm of categories, black is always marked as a colour (as the term 'coloured' egregiously acknowledges), and is always particularizing; whereas white is not anything really, not an identity, not a particularizing quality, because it is everything—white is no colour because it is all colours."[5] Thus whiteness becomes the unmarked standard, not even recognized as "race," but rather most often in the universal terms of liberal personhood.

The status of whiteness as what Lipsitz calls "the unmarked against which difference is constructed" has historically structured racism in the United States.[6] However, as Lipsitz has argued, racism changes with history: "Political and cultural struggles over power have shaped the contours and dimensions of racism differently in different eras. . . . Racism has changed over time, taking on different forms and serving different social purposes in each time period."[7] The Miss America Pageant lies squarely within "political and cultural struggles over power" as it is dedicated to defining the ideal American woman at any given time period. This ideal, historically and currently, has been bounded by whiteness; even as the pageant accommodates "difference" (as in women who identify or who are identified as different from white women), whiteness remains the standard against which all other racial categories are measured. In this way, examining two different historical moments in the pageant, 1945 and 1995, can reveal some of the ways in which racism changes depending on cultural conditions. Lipsitz points out: "Contemporary racism has been created anew in many ways over the past five decades, but most dramatically by the putatively race-neutral, liberal, social democratic reforms of the New Deal era and by the more overtly race-conscious neoconservative reactions against liberalism since the Nixon years."[8] The Miss America reigns of Bess Myerson and Heather Whitestone fall within these time lines; Myerson became Miss America in the midst of the New Deal era and the overt ideologies of assimilation and Americanization, and the Miss America Pageant in which Whitestone participated was situated within the race-conscious decade of identity politics that characterizes the 1990s. In this way, the pageant not only reinforces American society's investment in whiteness, but also the dominant liberal definition of Americanness, or national identity. In other words, whiteness is a crucial element in the foundation of the language of liberal individualism, and as such it ideologically encourages the American public to think in individualistic terms rather than to understand "the disciplined, systemic, and collective group activity that has structured white identities in American history."[9]

Woman as Nation

By all accounts, the Miss America Pageant takes its claim of national representation quite seriously. Indeed, the pageant sees itself as a forum for promoting a kind of eternal feminine code for the "typical" American woman—a woman living in a nation that prides itself on the coherence of its internal differences—even as it defines typicality according to white, middle-class norms and even as those norms change. The woman who is crowned Miss America each year conforms to this "typicality": Appealing to the rhetoric of equal opportunity, Miss

America contestants are an inclusive group, alienating no one, and providing clear evidence that the liberal system of meritocracy is alive and well in the United States. Of course, the implicit connection of whiteness and national identity to equal opportunity rhetoric (i.e., where typicality translates to whiteness, and the ordinary is that which is not marked by race) illustrates not an *erasure* of identity markers (which may gesture toward equality), but rather a kind of national identity politics that privileges whiteness.[10]

Historically the Miss America Pageant has been an interesting display of ideological musings and concerns about national identity, sustaining its position on whiteness by projecting a national utopic vision of "typicality" and the ordinary. Although the particularities of what is regarded as typical changes in history, the utopic fantasy that the typical also is racially coded as white has enjoyed remarkable longevity within not only pageant history but also more broadly in U.S. history. The "typical" American woman, as represented by the Miss America Pageant, largely lacks apparent identity markers and appeals to a liberal rhetoric of personhood. The space of the Miss America Pageant thus becomes one in which we are all, simply, "persons," flattening out the spectrum of varying political characteristics. Within this space, traditional markers of identity—race, class, and ethnicity—are reshaped so that they better accommodate the politics of whiteness that structure the entire event. The politics of identity that structure the pageant make an overt connection between these politics and the larger politics of national identity within the United States. In other words, it is not simply that the Miss America Pageant defines the "typical" woman within the bounds of whiteness, but also that the pageant presents this definition of typicality as a *national* identity for all women.

Many feminists have called our attention to the fact that, for women, national identity often is defined within the domestic, private sphere, rather than the more obvious nationalist cultural site of the military, where soldiers are called on literally to give up their lives for their nation, or the public sphere, where the social and political contours of the nation are discussed continually. As cultural scholar Lauren Berlant has argued, to clearly see the way in which women both constitute and are constituted by national identity, we need to investigate realms outside the traditional purview of national discourse, in the spaces of the everyday: in the family and the household, in the education of children, and in all those places that, as Berlant argues, "can be counterposed as 'the local' to the national frame of abstracted citizenship and power."[11] The domestic sphere and the discourses of privacy that structure domesticity are the primary spaces in which women organize their national identity. As cultural scholars Lynn Spigel, Eileen Tyler May, and others have demonstrated, in the post–World War II era, ideals and desires of family and national coherence took shape within domestic life, and women's national role as guardian of this domestic sphere was a key element of this utopic fantasy.[12]

The beauty pageant has an interesting relationship to the domestic ideology that structures women's national identity in the United States. On one hand, the pageant is quite public in the sense that the contestants perform on a stage in front of a nationally televised audience. Yet on the other hand, the performance of femininity the contestants offer is one that is devoted to women as domestic beings, dedicated to home, family, and the maintenance of dominant ideology regarding traditional gender roles. The resulting cultural event is a beauty pageant that insists on defining itself as unpolitical, as it remains a highly political practice.[13] The nationalist sentiment of the beauty pageant does not necessarily take into account dynamic social and historical contexts of national struggles, nor does it account for the formation of nation-states; rather, it produces the formation and operation of what Berlant calls the "National Symbolic."[14] The pageant spectacularly performs every element of the National Symbolic for a collective national subjectivity: It constitutes icons and heroes, it functions as a metaphor for the collective nation, and it offers a classic liberal narrative of individualism (i.e., overcoming obstacles, pulling oneself "up by the bootstraps," etc.) as the appropriate life trajectory.

In this sense, the pageant represents what might be called the "political space of the nation," representing a shift from the conventional national realm of law and citizenship to a relation that links "regulation to desire, harnessing affect to political life through the production of 'national fantasy.'"[15] It is within this space of representation, desire, and fantasy—the space of the beauty pageant— where "the idea of the nation works, figuring a landscape of complacency and promise, inciting memories of citizenship, but bringing its claims and demands into the intimate and quotidian places of ordinary life."[16] The Miss America Pageant produces images and narratives that articulate dominant expectations about who and what "American" women are (and should be) at the same time as it narrates who and what the nation itself should be through promises of citizenship, fantasies of agency, and tolerant pluralism. Therefore, the beauty pageant provides the United States with a site to witness the gendered construction of national identity—in its doubled sense, as both a statement of the *gendered* nation and the feminine body of *nationalist.*

The beauty pageant is not simply, then, about the feminine body, but also about the feminine national(ist) body. Because the pageant interweaves discourses of femininity with discourses of the nation, the body of a beauty pageant contestant is constituted metaphorically, where the individual contestant "stands in" for the larger nation.[17] But on the other hand, the construction of this metaphor makes a statement about the individual citizen, where the array of bodies on a beauty pageant stage serve as visual testimony for ascribing political subjectivity: Each woman "represents" the abstract characteristics of membership in the national imaginary of the U.S., and all are positioned as regional identities that then function to "map the nation."

The pageant contestants thus "prove" the diversity of the American public, representing both the promise and the fantasy of citizenship. The curious focus on the dialectic between the public and the private—a public liberal identity embodied within individual, private contestants—fleshes out the mutually constitutive character of the feminine body, female liberal citizenship, and the national body. The pageant invites a reading of the body both as a symbol of the national social body and as the individual liberal citizen. The 1945 Miss America Pageant, where the contestants were not merely beautiful bodies but patriotic subjects in the midst of a world war, was precisely the setting for this kind of reading.

Bess Myerson: Miss America 1945: "You Can't Be Beautiful and Hate"

In 1945, the Miss America Pageant underwent significant transformations. Most notably, this was the first year that the pageant offered academic scholarships as prizes. (It now is the largest scholarship organization exclusively for women in the United States.) With a scholarship firmly in place, the vision of the Miss America board of directors concerning who Miss America ideally should be became less of an abstraction and more of a real possibility. The women who entered the 1945 Miss America Pageant were quite different from those first contenders for the crown who entered "bathing beauty" contests on the beaches of Atlantic City in the early 1920s; they were beautiful, and they were feminine, but they were also active agents in a volatile political culture.[18]

The 1945 Miss America contestants experienced their adult lives in the midst of a world war. The femininity performed on the stage of the pageant was constructed in explicitly nationalist terms; with Rosie the Riveter as their symbol, and "We Can Do It" as their motto, the 1945 contestants were both acutely aware of and participants within the political context of World War II. Bess Myerson, the first and only Jewish Miss America, was crowned. In her memoirs, she recalls this moment: "Thousands and thousands of [panorama pictures of the contestants] were produced. . . . A fellow I know from camp wrote to me that he saw one in Okinawa. Another fellow saw one in Berlin. We couldn't have realized it, standing on the bleachers, sucking in our bellies, fixing our smiles, but we were at that moment becoming the cheesecake that followed the flag."[19] Although Myerson claims that she and the other contestants "couldn't have realized" what they were doing, it is clear that these women were at least acutely aware of their bodies as representations (as well as being aware of the disciplinary practices required to conform to this representation). "Becoming the cheesecake that followed the flag" is both a statement and an action laden with meaning about what the American flag represents. Myerson's remark situates female bodies as specific embodiments of the abstract meaning of the flag and clearly calls our attention to the way in which icons of femininity are constitutive of national meaning and sentiment.

Through a relentless focus on the body—sucking in bellies and fixing smiles—the production of the 1945 Miss America contestants' identity circulated far beyond the intentions of the contestants; the gaze at that moment was not just the judges' but encompassed all U.S. soldiers. And the gaze was focused most intensely on Myerson. Explicitly acknowledged as a Jewish intellectual, she performed her identity around a series of narratives circulating around the nation: Beautiful, talented, she was also the daughter of immigrants, and she represented the thousands of people for whom American soldiers were fighting. In short, she was living proof of the reliability of the American dream. Although much of the specific knowledge of the Holocaust was not yet commonplace in U.S. culture during the 1945 Miss America Pageant, it was clear that Jewish identity was at the center of the war. Myerson's Jewish body became a specific symbol for displacing a nation's troubles, anxieties, and guilt.[20] The question is, how—through what social and cultural discourses and practices—did Myerson, during that particular moment, reassure the nation that it possessed a coherent identity?

Managing Americanness: Bess Myerson and Ethnic Assimilation

In the 1930s and 1940s, the gendered definition of national identity was culturally inscribed in many realms of American society. One significant realm centered on the ideological efforts to assimilate new immigrants as newly American—at the same time as Jim Crow society pushed racial "others" outside the norm ever more vigorously. As cultural historian Michael Rogin has argued, during the 1930s and 1940s, the notion of Americanization and the melting pot strongly resonated with vaudeville and film audiences. The Miss America Pageant was part of a process that, along with movies and vaudeville performances, "turned immigrants into Americans."[21] With the nativism of the 1920s receding, the decades of the 1930s and 1940s celebrated the supposed melting pot of America, and popular as well as political culture effectively performed and articulated this version of national discourse.

However, as Rogin (among others) has astutely documented, melting pot ideology moves ethnic persons from a "racially liminal position to a white identity."[22] In other words, those persons who could be considered "racially liminal" are precisely those who, through their visually white skin, can become white morally and emotionally. This group included (at different moments during this general era) Irish Americans, Italian Americans, German Americans, and Jewish Americans. The discursive construction of the "white middle class" that would form the bulk of suburban commodity culture of the 1940s, 1950s, and 1960s was based on the dilution of ethnic identity of some groups; as Lynn Spigel has argued, "the prefabricated postwar suburbs encouraged a flattening out of religious identities and also leveled ethnicity to the extent that the communities allowed second-generation European immigrants to sever their national and ethnic ties with urban neighborhood networks."[23] George Lipsitz similarly charts this movement to the suburbs through an examination of the Federal Housing Agency's policies on housing loans: "The Federal Housing Act of 1934 brought home ownership within reach of millions of citizens by placing the credit of the federal government behind private lending to home buyers, but overtly racist categories in the Federal Housing Agency's (FHA) 'confidential' city surveys and appraisers' manuals channeled almost all of the loan money toward whites and away from communities of color."[24] Thus, as is well known, dominant melting pot ideology and the privileges and entitlements (such as suburban housing and FHA loans) that accompany this ideology welcomed only a select group of citizens, who were identified in specific contrast to people of color. Jewish Americans were increasingly part of this group.

Bess Myerson became a nationally symbolic figure within the context of the various cultural discourses and practices that Spigel and Lipsitz chart. World War II was a transformative moment for solidifying the ethnic, rather than racial, identity of Jewish Americans. As Rogin has argued, Jewish assimilation in the U.S. was about transforming immigrants into Americans while at the same time retrenching the identity of African Americans and other nonwhite ethnic groups as those that could not be assimilated.[25] And Karen Brodkin, in her work *How Jews Became White Folks,* points out: "Ethnic pluralism gave rise to a new construction of specifically Jewish whiteness. It did so by contrasting Jews as a model minority with African-Americans as culturally deficient."[26] During World War II and the postwar period, the U.S. witnessed a refiguring of Jewish identity that focused on the successful assimilation of Jews into American society specifically against the backdrop of blackness and working-class status.

Much of this "refiguring" took place publicly, within the fields of entertainment, in radio programs and television shows like *The Goldbergs,* in the newly established movie mogul industry on the U.S. West Coast, and in the Miss America Pageant with the crowning of Bess Myerson. Newly considered white, with a specific unique cultural heritage, immigrant Jews in the U.S. "were Americanizing themselves through their place in popular entertainment."[27] As Lipsitz has discussed, the popular radio program *The Goldbergs,* which later became a television program, featured a working-class Jewish family who moved from the Bronx to the middle-class suburb of Haverville, symbolically charting the journey of millions of Americans from their immigrant past to the newly consolidated American dream of the suburbs and middle-class consumer culture.[28] Bess Myerson also symbolically occupied this place; her role as Miss America confirmed the rhetoric of melting pot ideology and reinforced the promise of assimilation. Through her commitment to disciplinary practices that constitute white femininity, her education at Julliard and her success as a talented pianist, and her immigrant history, Myerson was deemed by pageant judges to be an appropriate representative of the national body.

But perhaps even more important, her white femininity conformed to dominant ideology regarding the current political context. Propagandists mobilized beauty queens such as Myerson as symbols that justified overseas fighting in World War II. As historian Robert Westbrook has argued, "for those who had no personal pin-ups of wives or girl friends to plaster to the machines of war, the studios in cooperation with the state provided surrogates like Betty Grable. Grable, far and away the most popular pin-up of the war, was offered to soldiers less as an exotic sex goddess than as a symbol of the kind of woman for whom American men were fighting."[29] Myerson, like Grable, provided both U.S. soldiers and the broader American public with a model of femininity that fit perfectly with dominant U.S. nationalist ideology of the day. Her white ethnicity did not threaten the national vision of white femininity, and her Jewish identity justified and legitimated the presence of U.S. soldiers overseas.

Nonetheless, despite the facts that Myerson represented what was considered an "appropriate" Jewish identity and her status as "different" worked to consolidate rather than threaten whiteness, she was still the target for anti-Semitism in her role as the ideal American woman. For example, unlike all other previous Miss Americas, Myerson was often denied entry into country clubs, sponsors frequently reneged on traditional Miss America arrangements, and some private citizens refused to allow her to visit their sons in veteran's hospitals.[30] Perhaps as a response to these tensions, during her reign Myerson not only went on the usual vaudeville and modeling tours, but was also a participant in the Brotherhood Campaign with the Anti-Defamation League (ADL). She gave speeches for the ADL during the entire year of her reign, drawing on her identity as both Jewish and Miss America.[31] Her motto, "You can't be beautiful and hate," was offered to high school students, housing project residents, and others on the tour of the Brotherhood Campaigns. In her first speech for the ADL, she said, "Miss America represents all America. It makes no difference who she is, or who her parents are. Side by side, Catholic, Protestant, and Jew stand together . . . and we would have it no other way. . . . And all those things are important in Atlantic City—or anywhere else where real Americans take your measure and pass judgment."[32] In an overtly political move, Myerson explicitly attempted to use her status as a national feminine representative as a means through which evidence of the success of assimilation can be—and is—realized.

Thus, despite her whitened ethnicity and despite her commitment to the conventional understandings of what it meant to be "American," there were experiences that could not be contained within Bess Myerson's representational form—there were things that she could *not* do that other Miss Americas could. In other words, there was clearly an excess to her meaning as Miss America, demonstrated by her rhetorical strategy of "You can't be beautiful and hate." This sentiment forced her audience to conceptualize femininity, nationhood, and tolerance as mutually constitutive categories of identity. Myerson was positioned as a symbol for a nation that was clearly fraught with racial and ethnic tension, guaranteeing that some of these tensions would be brought to bear during her reign as Miss America. Indeed, one reason why she could not "resolve" these tensions is that, at that particular historical moment, she was, along with other immigrants and other Jewish Americans, part of the shifting national discourse on Jewish American identity.

Televised Femininity

Bess Myerson marks the end of one visual regime in U.S. popular culture and the beginning of another. In 1945, being crowned Miss America was a reminder to the American public of the triumph of an American liberal individualism and of the merits of the melting pot. After 1945, however, the Miss America Pageant was on its way to a different kind of stage: a nationally televised one. The advent of television shifted the culture of the visual to one in which the camera provided, among other things, what seemed to be iron-clad evidence of diverse womanhood. Indeed, the widely circulated image of the taxonomic array of feminine bodies that is now the most recognizable sign of the Miss America Pageant is possible only through the technology of television. Clearly, the politics of whiteness that structured the crowning and reign of Bess Myerson remain evident and powerful, and the assimilationist politics that structured her identity as Miss America continue to be a motivating element of dominant U.S. nationalist ideology. However, in the late twentieth-century this nationalist ideology was also connected to a different sort of politics, one that emerged through the commodity and entertainment cultures of which television is a crucial part. That is, a kind of national identity politics resulted through the positioning of the mass media as a national public sphere and changed what Americans can and do fantasize about. The televised nation (which is, after all, perhaps the most readily available relationship with the "nation" that most Americans have) shifts what can be visualized as crucial components of national identity.

Indeed, as cultural scholars Horace Newcomb and Paul Hirsch have argued, television is a "cultural forum," one in which national issues are often represented. As they put it: "In its role as central cultural medium [television] presents a multiplicity of meanings rather than a monolithic dominant point of view. It often focuses on our most prevalent concern, our deepest dilemmas. Our most traditional views, those that are repressive and reactionary, as well as those that are subversive and emancipatory, are upheld, examined, maintained, and transformed."[33]

This cultural scrutiny that television offers structures the contemporary Miss America Pageant. What changed from the time of Bess Myerson's reign to contemporary conceptualizations of feminine national identity are the social practices of vision itself. The relentless focus on the visual that legitimates television's ubiquitous presence in the lives of contemporary Americans allows us—indeed insists—that we collapse identity with representation. Historian Benedict Anderson theorized the nation as an "imagined community" where citizens "imagine" themselves as part of a vast nation: Since it is virtually impossible to know every member of a nation, we come to know our fellow members through the media—newspapers, television, and the like. Thus, the nation is not as powerful physically or geographically as it is within the imagined possibilities of its members. In the cultural context of the mass media, however, the nation goes beyond the point of merely being imagined; it is a community that is embodied through televised representation.[34] Through what cultural theorist Robyn Weigman calls "economies of visibility," television democratizes both accessibility to and availability of national identity. It positions representational politics—as opposed to political representation—as the heart of national identity.[35]

In the 1990s, the representational politics of national identity reinvented themselves within the terms and boundaries of a postindustrial, highly massmediated political context, and symbols of the nation are embedded in the fantasies of television, among other places. Although the cultural context of both Myerson and Miss America 1995 Heather Whitestone are about accommodating difference, and both demonstrate the effectiveness and efficiency of the beauty pageant stage for these strategies of accommodation, the technology of television allows the pageant and the pageant audience to indulge in the fantasies offered by the spectacle in a directly visual manner. Indeed, if the commodity and entertainment cultures of twentieth-century and early twenty-first-century America provide the setting for asking questions about national identities, then it is through a regime of the visual that these questions are both posed and answered.[36]

One of the responses to queries and confusions about national identity in the 1990s was an insistence on white victimhood. During that decade, public discourse continually circulated stories about the various ways in which white people were "discriminated" against *because* of their whiteness, as in "reverse discrimination." In other words, the mass-mediated "public" sphere of television attends to representations of difference and diversity as the vitality and vibrancy of American national identity, but always within the context of whiteness. The cultural conditions of the time supported this ideology, including: the anti-immigrant Proposition 187 and the anti–affirmative action Proposition 209 in California; the increase in the number of charges of "reverse racism," where whites claimed to be unfairly judged because of minority presence; the publication and mainstream success of books such as Charles Murray and Richard Herrnstein's *The Bell Curve* and Dinesh D'Souza's *The End of Racism;* and the O. J. Simpson case as a widely discussed example of "black racism."[37] The 1990s were a decade where "race" was translated as a kind of diversity and difference that must be disciplined and domesticated in order to ensure national "coherence," and identity politics became a dominant form of identification for whites as well as people of color.

During that decade, popular entertainment culture became a prevailing site for the articulation of these kinds of identity politics, as well as the context for contemporary politics. Theorist Wiegman goes on to wonder: "What does it mean . . . that the visual apparatuses of photography, film, television, and video . . . serve as our primary public domain, our main shared context for the contestations of contemporary, cultural politics? And perhaps more important, what does it mean that within these technologies the body is figured as the primary locus of representation, mediation, and/or interpretation?"[38] In the context of beauty pageants, Wiegman's query points to the notion that pageants provide a public domain for demonstrating America's cultural trust in the objectivity of observation and collapse of identity with representation. Indeed, the visual supremacy of popular culture makes it an ideal site to fetishize the visual body as "difference," even as it erases the social and political structures and practices that both facilitate and diminish this very same difference. Within the beauty pageant, for example, the inclusion of racially diverse contestants since the late 1980s increasingly has posed the problem of constructing representations of a unified and singular national identity while acknowledging difference. Popular discourses like television attempt to resolve this contradiction by relying on classic liberal stories about individual achievement and pluralist tolerance.

Television, then, serves as the main representational domain in late-twenti-eth-century and early twenty-first-century U.S. culture; it not only provides the context of producing and performing a national identity, but also functioned ac-cessibly and visually as a display of the "proper"—in terms of race, class, sexual-ity, and the like—national body. This medium molds dominant understandings and definitions of who can become, who can act, and who can commodify themselves as "Americans."[39] It is also the site for tension, disruption, and re-membering collective and individual struggles—simply, television is one ele-ment of mass entertainment culture that constitutes subjects.[40] In the context of the Miss America Pageant, the women who participate pose as particular com-modities: they position their bodies and their personalities to "sell" an idealized version of American citizenship and American life. In 1995, a particularly suc-cessful Miss America in this regard was Heather Whitestone.

Heather Whitestone: The Difference that Makes No Difference

> Heather's becoming Miss America has enabled her to pursue an even more worthy dream—to be a bridge between two worlds, so that hearing and deaf people throughout our country and around the earth will have a better understanding and appreciation for each other and for what we can learn from one another.
>
> —Daphne Gray, Mother of Heather Whitestone, Miss America 1995

Heather Whitestone, Miss America 1995, was the first deaf Miss America and an exemplary model for a new face of America. Through her innocence (gained apparently through her inability to hear), she earned a place of civic virtue and situated by the pageant and the pageant's audience as special evidence that tes-tified to the success of a liberal America. Because of her disability, she was uniquely marked both by difference and the privilege of whiteness, and her ac-complishment on the pageant stage "proved" the myth of meritocracy. The lib-eral ideology of equal opportunity, in fact, structures the many ways in which whiteness is a privileged ideology of the pageant. For example, the statement "Anyone can do it if they try" continues to be the rhetorical driving force of the pageant, even as the standardized practices of femininity required to enter the event—slim body, "good," long hair, European facial features—are ever more vigorously and viciously regulated. With Heather Whitestone, the pageant proved once again to the American public that it was committed to equality and the ideals of meritocracy. Deaf since she was eighteen months old, Whitestone,

Miss Alabama 1994, wowed the pageant's audience with her ballet routine and her response to the onstage interview questions.

What interests me about the Whitestone crowning is not so much her deafness itself, but what her deafness signified to the American audience about the cultural conditions that produced her selection as a logical choice for Miss America. How did her "difference," a physical disability, work culturally to consolidate dominant conventions and conceptions of whiteness and national identity in that particular historical moment? Moreover, what kind of citizenship did American society idealize through the 1995 Miss America Pageant, where both the material stage of the event and the virtual stage of the nation were characterized by a peculiar multicultural vision and conservative pluralist politics?

Whitestone's deafness was very clearly an issue of anxiety and confusion during her participation in pageants. According to her mother, her family was determined to raise her as an active participant in the oral-centric world, and therefore Whitestone interacted only sporadically in the deaf community. (She attended a school for the deaf between the ages of eleven and fourteen.) She did not learn sign language until she was an adult, because her mother, Daphne Gray, wanted her to practice speech and not rely on sign language until her oral speech was perfected.[41] Whitestone once participated in a Miss Deaf Alabama pageant but apparently felt alienated and confused when she was given the cold shoulder because of her inability (interpreted as unwillingness) to sign. As her mother tells it, the Whitestone family viewed sign language as a second language, one intended to bolster—not replace—her primary language of spoken English. For the Whitestones, the deaf community was positioned as many minority communities are: as subcultures, conceptualized only in terms of the distance of their relationship from the norm, or from hegemonic, and in this case, oral-centric, culture. Whitestone's mother commented that if and when Whitestone learned sign language, she "figured she'd [Whitestone] then have the best possible chance to access both worlds—the hearing world *all of us live in* and the smaller deaf world with its own rich and unique heritage."[42] As many if not most in the deaf community will argue, "all of us" do not live in the hearing world. This construction of a larger world all of us live in as encompassing a smaller one, exotic (and often erotic) in its "rich and unique" heritage, is a familiar strategy of reducing the threat that a subculture or minority culture poses to the dominant culture. The disabled community, like communities of people of color, thus exists on the periphery of the dominant culture.[43]

Because Whitestone has some hearing and thus is physically capable of speaking, her family believed that the "best choice" for her was the choice to live in the hearing world. As her mother commented, "I see it as an advantage if deaf people can speak. Then you can communicate in both worlds." Whitestone herself said, "Maybe God wants me to be a bridge between the two worlds."[44] For the Miss America Pageant, then, Whitestone was an exemplary spokesperson for those people who are marked by "difference": She accommodated the dominant world by subsuming or obscuring her own difference. Her difference indeed makes no difference; she echoed the oft-heard query of the mid-1990s, "Why can't we all just get along?"[45] In fact, she not only asked us to "get along," but she, as the bridge between two worlds, facilitated our friendship.

The pageant is just the site for this negotiating between different worlds. After several years during which the pageant vehemently insisted that it was not a racist production, Whitestone was crowned as a final testimony to the nation that the pageant encourages difference. Her whiteness, of course, underscored and legitimated her disability; it also represented the triumph of a reactionary, anti-affirmative action and anti-immigrant "multicultural" U.S. society in the mid-1990s. These kinds of complicated negotiations between dominant and marginal cultures are perhaps most seamlessly and satisfyingly resolved in popular culture, which endlessly recycles liberal stories of meritocracy and equal opportunity.

By making invisible the social technologies that produce difference, these liberal stories result in the retrenchment of a national identity defined by white middle-class norms. For Heather Whitestone, the pageant's privilege of the rhetoric of "personhood" proved to be an entry into an event that previously dismissed women with disabilities as too weak to represent the nation. Her statement to the interview judges focused on this point; she said at the interview, "I want to be Miss America, and I want to graduate from college. But I know each of you has a question in mind, and I want to answer it for you right now: Can a profoundly deaf woman fulfill the duties of Miss Alabama and Miss America? To this I say, yes. I can do it! Because I realize that everything is possible with God's help. I don't see my deafness as an obstacle, but as an opportunity for creative thinking."[46] Translating difference into "an opportunity for creative thinking" relies on a liberal ideology that suggests that eradicating racism and other prejudices is as simple as an attitude adjustment or a mere tinkering with already established ideological frameworks.

This rhetoric colludes perfectly with the dominant ideology of the Miss America Pageant, where it is expressed either through liberal agency—"I'm a person, I can do what I want"—or through success stories in a meritocracy—"I just keep telling myself: you can do it, and here I am!"—or even through appropriated feminist language—"No, I don't feel exploited, I feel like a winner."[47] For example, Miss New York 1991, Marisol Montalvo, a contestant in the September 1991 Miss America Pageant perhaps best expressed how successful the deployment of the power liberal discourse of personhood can be. The only African American finalist in the pageant, she responded to a question about multicultural society in the U.S.: "It is so important that if we want to stop the problem of racism that is so prevalent in our country we all have to view ourselves as Americans. Not as Hispanic Americans or Afro Americans—we have to take a look at ourselves as one nation because our ethnicity makes us special, and we need to understand each other instead of beating down each other and acting superior. We're one people and we have to start acting like one people: Americans!"[48] Not surprisingly, this contestant shifted the problem of racism from a social, institutionalized problem to one involving the efforts of the individual: If we would all just adjust our attitudes and think of ourselves as Americans, racism presumably would be eradicated. In this way, she echoed conservatives who argue that if we would merely stop obsessing about our racial and sexual identity and remember that the best sources of individuality and social cohesion are a "shared history, a common culture and unifying values," we could return to the golden age of liberal personhood and erase identity politics from our social and political landscape.[49] Of course, the erasure of identity politics is not *actually* the goal—only identity politics that benefit communities of color is seen as damaging to the nation's coherence. However, as Lipsitz has so persuasively argued, the "possessive investment in" whiteness is also a form of identity politics. The ways in which whiteness functions as an invisible standard against which all other racial categories are measured (and found wanting), and the fact that "whiteness never has to speak its name, never has to acknowledge its role as an organizing principle in social and cultural relations" is precisely how identity politics works.[50] The Miss America Pageant participates in this dynamic, even as it situates Whitestone's universalism as the erasure of "messy" and particular identity characteristics.

In other words, as is so often the case, even while Whitestone denied that her difference limits her (thus reinforcing the dominance of the speaking world), it is precisely her deafness that marked her as extraordinary. She situated herself—and was situated by the pageant—as an inspiration because she overcame "obstacles" as a classic liberal heroine should. But simultaneously, she profited from the possessive investment in whiteness through her active erasure of identity characteristics that mark her as different. She does not sign, and she does not use an interpreter. She went to a deaf school only to learn what was absolutely essential for her to "pass" in the hearing world. By embedding her deafness in liberal doctrine—as an obstacle to overcome—she accommodated the pageant's construction of universalized femininity even as her body was testimony to its diversity.

For example, Whitestone's talent performance perhaps best exemplified her symbolic status as a liberal heroine. She chose as her ballet routine "Via Dolorosa" (the story of the crucifixion of Christ), and initially she wore a yellow dress tinged with red to symbolize Christ's blood (she later changed her costume to an all-white dress). But more than the choice of the song and its symbolism, or the actual outfit she chose, her ballet routine demonstrated her commitment to liberalism and individual transcendence: She performed a dance where the music was the most important element, yet she could not hear. She triumphed over convention by becoming purely somatic, feeling the beats through her feet and interpreting the music through her faith. Not surprisingly, hosts Kathie Lee Gifford and Regis Philbin made much of her amazing ability to feel the beats through her feet, and the focus on the pageant's attention on Whitestone centered on the fact that she was able to dance *at all;* with the other contestants, the focus was placed on the method and skill demonstrated through the dance, song, or other routine. Her talent, then, was intensely centered on her deafness, but with a particular focus: Deafness was an obstacle Whitestone had "overcome," and her ballet routine was the required evidence of that triumph.

Another way in which Whitestone performed the liberal story of accommodation was through her official issue platform, which she named the STARS program, for Success Through Action and Realization of your dreams. Insisting on the platitude "anything is possible," her issue platform focused on her deafness as a way to insist that difference is truly what one makes of it. One can strategically use it to "get ahead," which was the familiar argument at the time against federal programs and propositions such as affirmative action and other civil rights initiatives that intend to rectify a historical and social structure of discrimination. Or one can, as Whitestone did, develop a program detailing how to succeed against the odds. The program itself is merely a reiteration of liberal doctrine: Try hard, believe in yourself (and in God), be determined.[51] But although her story and her platform were hardly novel, they were situated in an important way in the mid-1990s U.S. social and cultural politics. Her crowning as Miss America occurred within the context of increasing national anxiety about marginalized communities, an anxiety fueled by the potential threat these communities pose to dominant society and culture. Her STARS program enthusiastically performed this ideology: The narrative of good attitude and hard work that will bring success references apparently faulty and politically wayward federal programs such as affirmative action. One consequence of these very public struggles over personal meaning is the conservative reading of them in which identity markings such as race and gender are clearly unproductive and only create cultural, political, and individual dilemmas. Rather than focus on these marks of difference, we should all merely conduct ourselves as "persons." The question, however, becomes one of *how* this works, if contemporary desires to do away with the dilemmas of race and gender are culturally sanctioned. How do particular kinds of race privilege support the notion of "personhood," for surely that is not an identity that all Americans historically have enjoyed. The desire to all act as "persons" is represented as a particular social need—the need not only to address problems of difference differently, but also to, in fact, evade these problems altogether.

Heather Whitestone was the Miss America Pageant's answer to this dilemma. The strategies she used for self-representation not only were a way of constructing personal identity, but also were tailor-made for television. Television was a particularly appropriate medium for the demonstration of Whitestone's identity because it functions so well as an equalizer; difference is obscured and, at the very least, flattened out and made to seem insignificant. Again, I do not mean to suggest that Whitestone's disability was not a "true difference," or that she should not be admired for her accomplishments. I do mean to suggest that at her particular moment in U.S. cultural history, Whitestone functioned as an exemplary spokesperson on the apparent dangers of identity politics precisely because her whiteness was not particularized as an identity characteristic. Whitestone truly followed a utopic fantasy about the liberal, postindustrial, multicultural world: She presented her identity as a deaf person as one that could be tried on and taken off almost at whim, and it is this ability (or perhaps it is merely the belief or the hope that all marginalized peoples have this ability, regardless of their markers of difference) that transforms accommodation into inspiration or assimilationist into liberal heroine. In this way, her deafness functioned much as race does in the rhetoric of the "color-blind" society, which, as legal scholar Neil Gotanda has argued, relies on the ability of the law initially to recognize the racial identity of a person and then promptly to forget it. This process of recognizing only then to erase works to create all of us as "persons," equal before the law, and thus dismisses any overt identity claims of individuals outside of this basic characterization. Of course, this ideology refuses to recognize that "personhood," historically and currently, has specifically signified *white* personhood.[52]

Indeed, Whitestone was an especially interesting celebrity for the press because of this complicated self-presentation. Of course, the fact that she was the first Miss America with a disability meant that the press focused on her intensely. For example, columnist Barbara Lippert wrote about Whitestone's selection as an exemplary choice but also queried the judges' motivation in selecting a deaf contestant. Lippert wrote, "What does it mean that at a time of identity crisis for both genders, we seem able to reclaim the standards of American purity, innocence and fairness only by focusing on people with disabilities?"[53] What I find especially interesting about her comment is her recognition of the Miss America Pageant as an apparently unique site in which to "reclaim the standards of American purity, innocence, and fairness" in a time of what Lippert calls a gender identity crisis. Part of the cultural climate of 1995, as I have mentioned, was a conservative desire to eliminate difference as a viable category of identity—at least when it came to employment, education, and politics. The year 1995 was a banner one for reclaiming American purity.

This was also the year that *Forrest Gump* won the Oscar for the best movie of 1994. At its heart, this film was about the disavowal of history—especially the disavowal of the history of racial formations and social protests as they structure U.S. society. Forrest Gump becomes a national icon through this disavowal, through his vulnerability, his purity, and his innocence. He wipes the slate clean, and as Wiegman has pointed out, the film argues that through the embrace of his injured body we are healed—we can each disavow our own injuries and heal our own injured body.[54] In other words, it is the guilt of dominant white America that is healed. He is, as Berlant (and others) have argued, simply "too stupid to be racist, sexist, and exploitative; this is his genius and it is meant to be his virtue."[55]

We can see how Heather Whitestone occupies a similar position—and as Miss America, she symbolized the ideal American woman, the corollary to the ideal American man that is Forrest Gump. Unlike Gump, she is not stupid, but she represented an ideal of purity at a time when the national imaginary, or the imagined community of the nation, was one of whiteness and victimhood. This national imaginary of white injury—and in particular the injury that comes from *being* white—produced Heather Whitestone as Miss America, who denied domination by representing a kind of purity through her nonhearing body—and in fact was purely somatic as she danced her ballet routine, hearing no music but instead feeling the beats through the vibrations in the floor. At this historical moment, Whitestone's purity and innocence trumped identity politics, even as, through her whiteness, her identity was assured precisely because of these politics.

Whitestone's family constructed her deafness as a sort of innocent shield by which she was protected from the cruelties of the world, including the deaf world. Her inability to hear shielded her from the cruel gossip and speculation of the pageant world and enabled her not only to avoid answering questions about her capabilities as a national representative, but also to determine the site and audience for those questions. So, her lack of hearing allowed her to experience the world as one without overt, personal cruelty. As her mother comments, "She doesn't pick up on nuances and innuendoes. Her hearing impairment actually proved an advantage, a natural cocoon, sheltering Heather from the air of tension and conflict."[56] Although the focus of this comment is on gossip, representing a disability as a cocoon gives credence to Whitestone's representation as pure, someone, like Forrest Gump, who simply does not see (or hear) negativity or cruelty in the world. Through this self-representation, Whitestone reaffirms the power of whiteness as an invisible standard. In a cultural climate that insists on the erasure of difference as meaningful identity characteristics, Whitestone's performance as Miss America profits from the identity politics of whiteness.

There She Is

The Miss America contestant's body, through her disciplined physique, her commitment to virtue, and her testimony to stability, represents a well-managed collective *white* American body. Through the display of female bodies and the insistence of an ideology of whiteness, the beauty pageant transforms a culture's anxiety about itself—its stability as a coherent nation—into a spectacular reenactment and overcoming of that very anxiety.

It is through the performance of the local and the national that those women crowned Miss America also perform the abstract character of white liberal personhood within a particular national imaginary. Bess Myerson and Heather Whitestone were seen by the Miss America audience as individuals in terms of their race, ethnicity, culture, and commitment—even as they represented a more universal vision of white femininity. This vision, in turn, constitutes what Frank Deford, a journalist and former Miss America judge, called "good old Miss America," who "still talks like Huckleberry Finn, looks like Patti, LaVerne, and Maxine, and towers over the land like the Ozarks. She really is the body of the state, and the country is in her eyes."[57]

Notes

1. David R. Roediger, *The Wages of Whiteness: Race and the Making of the American Working Class* (London: Verso, 1992).
2. George Lipsitz, *The Possessive Investment in Whiteness: How White People Profit from Identity Politics* (Philadelphia: Temple University Press, 1998).
3. Richard Dyer, *The Matter of Images* (London: Routledge, 1993); Lipsitz, *Possessive Investment in Whiteness;* Cheryl I. Harris, "Whiteness as Property," *Harvard Law Review* 106, no. 8 (June 1993).
4. Dyer, *The Matter of Images,* 142.
5. Ibid., 142.
6. Lipsitz, *Possessive Investment in Whiteness: How White People Profit from Identity Politics,* 1.
7. Ibid., 4–5.
8. Ibid., 5.
9. George Lipsitz, "The Possessive Investment in Whiteness: Racialized Social Democracy and the 'White' Problem in American Studies," *American Quarterly* 47 (September 1995): 383.
10. I am grateful to Robyn Wiegman for pointing out the way in which the politics of whiteness work in this context.
11. Lauren Berlant, *The Queen of America Goes to Washington City: Essays on Sex and Citizenship* (Durham, NC: Duke University Press, 1997), 27.
12. See Lynn Spigel, *Make Room for TV: Television and the Family Ideal in Postwar America* (Chicago: University of Chicago Press, 1992); Elaine Tyler May, *Homeward Bound* (New York: Basic Books, 1988).

13. Geoff Eley and Ronald Grigor Suny, eds., *Becoming National: A Reader* (New York: Oxford University Press, 1996), 27.

14. Lauren Berlant describes the National Symbolic as: "the order of discursive practices whose reign within a national space produces, and also refers to, the 'law' in which the accident of birth within a geographic/political boundary transforms individuals into subjects of a collectively-held history. Its traditional icons, its metaphors, its heroes, its rituals, and its narratives, provide an alphabet for a collective consciousness or national subjectivity: through the National Symbolic the historical nation aspires to achieve the inevitability of the status of natural law, a birthright." Berlant, *Anatomy of a National Fantasy: Hawthorne, Utopia, and Everyday Life* (Chicago: University of Chicago Press, 1991), 20.

15. Ibid.

16. Eley and Suny, *Becoming National,* 28.

17. For more along these lines, see Lisa Lowe, *Immigrant Acts: On Asian American Cultural Politics* (Durham, NC: Duke University Press, 1996, 18. The beauty pageant constructs and maintains a particular configuration of the female citizen through the imagined promise of citizenship, the fantasy of female agency, and the deferral of inequalities in the public realm to the apparently level playing field of culture. In this sense, the pageant is about the coherence of a national body, but because pageants are about real as well as imagined bodies, about visual and cultural representation, they "erupt in culture," as Lowe points out. Lowe, *Immigrant Acts,* 3.

18. Susan Dworkin, *Miss America, 1945: Bess Myerson's Own Story* (New York: Newmarket Press, 1987).

19. Ibid.,105. During this time, the pageant initiated what was to become an intimate relationship with the military—not only were photographs of the contestants sent to soldiers overseas, but Miss America and her runners-up traveled on USO tours to entertain the troops. In addition, the 1945 contestants participated in a swimsuit parade for the wounded veterans at various hospitals, a practice that continues to this day, especially with the smaller, local franchises of the Miss America Pageant.

20. I am not arguing that Myerson bore the burden of this kind of displacement alone. On the contrary, at this particular historical moment, as Michael Rogin has argued, many forms of entertainment and popular culture "served the Americanization plot." Rogin, *Blackface, White Noise: Jewish Immigrants in the Hollywood Melting Pot* (Berkeley: University of California Press, 1996), 62. The Miss America Pageant, with its dual emphasis on respectable femininity and national identity, was one of those forms, and it found a particularly effective representative of its claims in Bess Myerson.

21. Ibid., 60.

22. Ibid. See also Eric Lott, *Love and Theft: Blackface Minstrelsy and the American Working Class* (New York: Oxford University Press, 1993); Roediger, *Wages of Whiteness;* Lipsitz, *Possessive Investment in Whiteness.*

23. Spigel, *Make Room for TV,* 6.

24. Lipsitz, *Possessive Investment in Whiteness,* 5.

25. Rogin, *Blackface, White Noise.*

26. Karen Brodkin, *How Jews Became White Folks & What That Says About Race in America* (New Brunswick, NJ: Rutgers University Press, 1998), 144.

27. Rogin, *Blackface, White Noise,* 64.
28. George Lipsitz, *Time Passages: Collective Memory and American Popular Culture* (Minneapolis: University of Minnesota Press, 1990).
29. Robert Westbrook, "Fighting for the American Family: Private Interests and Political Obligations in World War II," in *The Power of Culture: Critical Essays in American History* by Richard Wightman Fox and T. J. Jackson Lears (Chicago, IL: University of Chicago Press, 1993), 212.
30. Dworkin, *Bess Myerson, 1945.*
31. Ibid., 192.
32. Ibid., 196.
33. Horace Newcomb and Paul M. Hirsch, "Television as a Cultural Forum" in *Television: The Critical View,* 5th ed., Horace Newcomb, ed. (New York: Oxford University Press, 1994), 506.
34. Benedict Richard O'G. Anderson, *Imagined Communities: Reflections on the Origin and Spread of Nationalism* (London: Verso, 1983).
35. Robyn Wiegman, *American Anatomies: Theorizing Race and Gender* (Durham, NC: Duke University Press, 1995).
36. For more on this, see ibid.
37. For a discussion of the California propositions, see Lowe, *Immigrant Acts,* and Lipsitz, *Possessive Investment in Whiteness.* For more on the O. J. Simpson trial, see Darnell Hunt, *O. J. Simpson Facts and Fictions: News Rituals in the Construction of Reality.* (Cambridge: Cambridge University Press, 1999). Charles Murray and Richard Herrnstein, *The Bell Curve: Intelligence and Class Structure in American Life* (New York: Free Press, 1994). Dinesh D'Souza, *The End of Racism.* (New York: Free Press, 1996).
38. Wiegman, *American Anatomies,* 3.
39. Lowe makes this argument in general in *Immigrant Acts.*
40. For more on this, see Marita Sturken, *Tangled Memories: The Vietnam War, the AIDS Epidemic, and the Politics of Remembering* (Berkeley: University of California Press, 1997).
41. Daphne Gray, *Yes, You Can, Heather!: The Story of Heather Whitestone, Miss America 1995* (Grand Rapids, MI: Zondervan Publishing House, 1995).
42. Ibid., 159; emphasis added.
43. Here I do not intend to conflate a minority disability culture with a minority nonwhite culture; there are clearly differences in power relations, resources, and historical contingencies. Nonetheless, there are similarities. Perhaps one of the most significant characteristics that the deaf culture and the African American, Latino, or Asian American cultures in the United States have in common is the way in which they are situated as part of a dominant liberal story that is told in many ways and through many different approaches about what it means to be American. This story insists that all citizens parcel their identities into components, so that we are all "persons" before we are deaf or before we are gendered or before we are raced. In that sense, the construction of Heather Whitestone's deafness is an interesting but subordinate cultural component of her identity shares characteristics with the way in which racial and ethnic cultures are positioned as peripheral to and less significant than dominant "unmarked" culture.
44. Gray, *Yes, You Can, Heather!,* 173.

45. This became the unofficial "anthem" of the civil uprisings (at least for some groups) around the beating of Rodney King in Los Angeles in 1992.

46. Gray, *Yes, You Can, Heather!*, 214–215.

47. Personal interviews with author, 1990–1994.

48. Miss America Pageant, September 1991, telecast, NBC.

49. George Will, "The New Face of America," *Time*, special issue, Fall 1993.

50. Lipsitz, *Possessive Investment in Whiteness*, 1.

51. Gray, *Yes, You Can, Heather!*

52. Neil Gotanda, "A Critique of 'Our Constitution Is Color-Blind,'" *Stanford Law Review* 44, no. 1 (1991).

53. Barbara Lippert, "Cleavages and Causes," *Glamour* (December 1994): 211.

54. Wiegman, *American Anatomies*.

55. Berlant, *Queen of America*, 183.

56. Gray, *Yes, You Can, Heather!*, 213.

57. Frank Deford, *There She Is: The Life and Times of Miss America* (New York: Penguin Books, 1978).

Part II

Gender, Race, and Identity

4

The Rhetoric of Black Bodies

RACE, BEAUTY, AND REPRESENTATION

Valerie Felita Kinloch

What is the significance of a national organization that promotes Americanness, but often fails to reflect the racial composition of a diverse American nation? How has its history of excluding black people helped reinforce negative cultural images of blackness? These questions point toward the complex and changing place beauty occupies in American culture in the midst of the nation's changing ethnic composition. Despite gains within the past few decades, people of color are still not sufficiently represented in such pageants, which leads to an examination of the following: What female bodies are encouraged or allowed to participate in the pageant? Whose construction of beauty and the beautiful body defines America and its national identity? And what happens with the female bodies that are premarked with nonnational and nonrepresentational beauty?[1]

Bearing these questions in mind, this chapter draws on the growing body of research on pageants, beauty, race theory, and feminist critiques[2] and examines the racial dynamic of the Miss America Pageant and how this dynamic affects public understanding of what constitutes the American ideal of female beauty. This chapter focuses on black bodies competing in a traditionally white event that has disfranchised black people from the pageant's inception in 1921 to the tumultuous 1960s, when the first Miss Black America Pageant was held. Power, race, and national standards of beauty can best be under-stood, according to scholar Stephen Haymes, by "look[ing] critically at the re-lationship between black cultural identity and white consumer culture."[3] The cultural denigration of black bodies results in part from the tension between the actual and the imagined constructions of women, beautiful women, and white female beauty standards.

Returning to "Black Is Beautiful"

The Miss America Pageant, in one way, represents the racist politics of identity through symbolic meaning making: historically it has rewarded the beauty of white bodies and disregarded the beauty of black bodies. In resisting the racist domination and racial constructions perpetuated by a white culture, black people in general and black women in particular often help perpetuate racist stereotypes of their bodies by participating in an oppositional culture: We straighten our hair, bleach our skin, flatten our figure, and re-create identities that uphold white beauty and values disassociated from black beauty. The legacy of whiteness as the standard of beauty and "the beautiful" informs how many black women see them-selves through other people's eyes. Beauty acts as a primary agent of acceptance and "American" representation, and at the same time intensifies the desire of many black women to become a part of western standards of beauty. The problematic nature of this desire to possess western beauty standards lies in the inherent con-ception of what and who is beautiful: the epitome of western beauty being tall with long limbs, golden skin, and long hair. This type of beauty is highly com-mercialized in beauty magazines, across billboards, and in state and national pageants. Its dominance undermines the beauty that is black, that belongs to black people, and that embodies black values, rites of passage, and communities.

In her 1986 study, *Beauty Bound,* psychologist Rita Freedman writes: "The mind does not remain a blank slate for very long. An idealized image of beauty is soon etched upon it. In our culture, this image is built on a Caucasian model. Fairy-tale princesses and Miss Americas have traditionally been white. This fair image weighs most heavily on the brown shoulders of minority women who bear a special beauty burden. They too are taught that beauty is a feminine im-perative. They too set out in search of it, only to discover that failure is built in for those whose lips smile too thickly, whose eyelids fold improperly, whose hair will not relax enough to toss in the wind, whose skin never glows in rosy shades."[4] In the dominant public sphere, the democratic and capitalistic society that relentlessly classifies people by sex, race, and age, nonwhite women, ac-cording to Freedman, are excluded from representations of beauty, and "black women speak of feeling downright ugly at some point in their lives."[5] Freedman conceptualizes American standards of both beauty and womanhood, standards that draw attention to the nonconforming physical features of black women. In addition, the idealized image of beauty as being patterned after a white model, to use Freedman's words, reinforces the cultural denigration of black bodies. The continued denigration of black forms of beauty (different skin tones, hairstyles, and body shapes) in favor of institutionalized white forms of beauty means that the black body will continue to be perceived as inferior and in need of constant alteration. Many black women, after decades of being told "Black Is Beautiful," are still influenced by white conceptions of beauty.

The relationship between black women proclaiming that "Black Is Beautiful" and being influenced by white standards of beauty becomes complicated because black women's relationships with themselves and one another are multifaceted. The 1960s Black Power revolution challenged black people to "decolonize" their minds and dispense with their sense of inferiority instilled by the history of oppression and white supremacy. Black women wore Afros, celebrated different shades of blackness, and embraced their striking black features. In her 1994 text, *Outlaw Culture: Resisting Representations,* feminist scholar bell hooks addresses the process of decolonization as a way to resist insulting values of a white culture by insisting that black people see themselves outside of such values. To do so, they must "establish a politics of representation which would both critique and integrate ideals of personal beauty and desirability informed by racist standards."[6] This politics of representation holds the promise of providing a number of things: It would allow black people to define beauty outside of the dominant paradigm of blonde hair and white skin; it would encourage a return to the "Black Is Beautiful" campaign by giving positive visibility to black skin, bodies, features, hair, and culture; and it would encourage black people to maintain their own look and uphold their cultural, social, familial, and historical rituals and practices in the public realm, such as in beauty pageants.

Establishing a Politics of Representation

The Miss America Pageant still prohibited the participation of black contestants during the 1960s, a period significantly marked by the civil rights movement. As a result, black communities sponsored the 1968 Miss Black America Pageant in Atlantic City on the same day of the Miss America Pageant and the feminists' demonstration against the pageant.[7] The pageant took place immediately following the Miss America Pageant telecast. The first annual Miss Black America Pageant established what hooks refers to as a politics of representation in its critique of the absence of black women in the Miss America Pageant. Other women of color had participated in the Miss America Pageant by the early

1950s, including Native American Mifaunwy Sunatona, Miss Oklahoma 1941, "Irma Nydia Vasquez, a young woman of Hispanic ancestry from Puerto Rico, and Yun Tau Zane, the first Asian contestant, as Miss Hawaii,"[8] the latter two having participated in 1948 Miss America Pageant. Yet the absence of black participants continued under the direction of Lenora Slaughter, the pageant's "benevolent dictator"[9] from 1935 to 1967. After becoming director, Slaughter, a former businesswoman who worked at the St. Petersburg, Florida, Chamber of Commerce during the 1920s and early 1930s, commented, "Contestants must be of good health and of the white race."[10] The racist construction of beauty and of power devalues the physical nature of black women and their historical connection with oppression. The racist stereotypes of black women as "ugly, monstrous, undesirable,"[11] as hooks explains, were challenged when eighteen-year-old Saundra Williams, a college student, was crowned the first Miss Black America. In her excitement, she said, "With my title, I can show black women that they, too, are beautiful."[12] Then in 1969, Dr. Zelma George, director of the Cleveland Job Corps for Women, was appointed the first black judge of the Miss America Pageant; the next year, Cheryl Browne of Iowa became the first black contestant in the pageant's history.

These events are important as black people struggle against white supremacy: they signify the intensity of black women's victimization, and they challenge descriptions of the body as a machine of erotic desires. Racial theorist Karla Holloway, in *Codes of Conduct: Race, Ethics, and the Color of Our Character,* discusses how the effects of racism and sexism force black people to critically understand their bodies in relation to public perceptions of black bodies. She states, "Contemporary events that publicly exhibit the black woman's body—in literature, film, academic conferences, or Senate chambers—are evidence that black women's bodies are a conflicted site."[13] As "a conflicted site," or a contested terrain, the black body complicates white beauty standards and further disrupts the control of white supremacy. This disruption, however, occurs at a price: "African-American women have learned well how and when to hide our bodies. . . . the history of racist and sexist aesthetics has made us hate our hair and mask our bodies, and has encouraged the desperation of Kotex on our heads—or sedate teal blue dresses. At what cost this dissembling? When we mask in these ways, we actually, and perversely, privilege the gaze of others. The bodies that emerge when others control our images are disfigured and fragmented."[14] Consider, for example, how the Miss America Pageant controls and disciplines women's bodies, particularly black women's bodies. During the swimsuit competition, which accounts for "15 percent of each contestant's total score,"[15] contestants parade across the stage in high heels, tracing an invisible figure-eight design, displaying how their bodies meet and/or exceed the standards of the beautiful American body.

Their bodies thus become signs of nationalism and racial wholesomeness be-cause "Miss America must be provocative but wholesome, a pretty but pure vestal virgin, like Cinderella."[16] Particularly during the swimsuit competition, the body becomes a spectacle: "parading in front of a panel of judges, is in fact about feminine achievement—or, more precisely, the achievement of femi-ninity,"[17] and femininity has for so long been construed as an achievement only afforded to white women. Therefore, the discourse of power in feminine acts, such as swimsuit competitions and the Miss America Pageant, engages in a denigration of black bodies because nationalism and racial wholesomeness have always been imagined as white. From slavery to dominant social narra-tives and onward, the black female body always has been denigrated, eroti-cized, and objectified by white culture, viewed as a site of pleasurable danger, indiscriminate promiscuity, poverty, and abuse. To dismantle this view, black people must imagine their bodies as feminine and beautiful even though pub-lic events will continue to mark the black body as a site of contestation. Both hooks and Holloway advocate that we discuss how the iconization of certain beauty forms disfigures black bodies; engage in public discourses about skin color, beauty standards, and representation in regards to internalized racism; and fight against the denigration of blackness. The purpose of this process of interrogation is best summed by Stokely Carmichael's 1967 argument[18]: "Black people in the United Sates must raise hard questions, questions which challenge the very nature of the society itself: its long-standing values, beliefs and institutions. To do this, we must first redefine ourselves. Our basic need is to reclaim our history and our identity from what must be called cultural terrorism, from the depredation of self-justifying white guilt. We shall have to struggle for the right to create our own terms through which to define our-selves and our relationship to the society, and to have those terms recog-nized."[19] Cultural critic Cornel West in *Prophesy Deliverance! An Afro-American Revolutionary Christianity* develops this argument further as he outlines the challenges confronting black people: "The two basic challenges presently confronting Afro-Americans are those of self-image and self-determination. The former is the perennial human attempt to define who and what one is, the sempiternal issue of self-identity, the later is the political struggle to gain significant control over the major institutions that regulate people's lives."[20] These two issues addressed by West, that of self-image and self-determination, were the guiding principles behind the 1960's adoption and popularization of the phrase "Say It Loud: I'm Black and I'm Proud," for black people identified a need to redefine the parameters of beauty, image, self-esteem, and self-love. Carmichael and West's arguments prove that black people, systemically, must create what hooks calls "radical Black subjectivities" in deconstructing how white supremacy and the values of a white consumer culture denigrate black identities and bodies. This deconstruction can lead to a better understanding of why and how the black female body has had a long history of rejection and experience with victimization by the Miss America Pageant.

Historian Sarah Banet-Weiser provocatively talks about this history by pointing to the contradictions of femininity in the absence of contestants of color. She notes that "pageants are forced to confront contemporary demands that they reflect racial and ethnic diversity."[21] Nevertheless, this reflection and inclusion of difference is difficult, given that the Miss America Pageant historically has represented the ideal beauty of whiteness and to alter this ideal is to assault "the traditional function of pageants as sites for the control of nonwhite identities through the enforcement of dominant, universal norms of beauty."[22] This assault would, further, lead to the public questioning of nationalism and race, which are not but have for so long been perceived as fixed variables by a dominant white culture. Why were black women excluded from participation in the Miss America Pageant from 1921 to 1970? Why did the National Association for the Advancement of Colored People (NAACP) sponsor the first Miss Black America Pageant on the same night of the Miss (White) America Pageant in 1968? Why, in the fall of 1966, did the student body at Howard University in Washington, D.C., powerfully chant, "Umgawa, Black Power, Umgawa, Black Power" after the crowning of Robin Gregory, the university's first queen to wear an Afro, to speak of race relations, and to defy the traditionally accepted role and look of a queen? Because black people, from the early feminist protests to the Black Power revolution to the cheering of the first black Miss America, Vanessa Williams, established a politics of representation and radical black subjectivities to combat racist stereotypes of black as not beautiful or queenly while advocating for complete acceptance of being black and proud and being black and beautiful.[23]

Our First Black Miss America: Vanessa Williams and the Disruption of Whiteness

When Vanessa Williams was crowned Miss America 1984, I recall the tears of joy from black women in my family. For them, Williams signified the truth that black womanhood could indeed represent the national identity of America. Although they realized that the struggle for voice and acceptance was definitely not over, they felt a sense of accomplishment: "The crowning of Vanessa Williams is widely understood by pageant culture as the year that the Miss America Pageant shed, once and for all, its stubborn and notorious racist past."[24] Nevertheless, the crowning and decrowning of Williams represented the political climate of the 1980s, the New Right, and Reaganism in that she was "a test-site"[25] for the quickly developing multicultural society that was America. Furthermore, the crowning of Williams disrupted the pageant's long history of excluding black women as participants. In 1923, the first black people to appear in the Miss America Pageant were men and women depicted as slaves who performed a musical selection; the first black contestant, Iowa's Cheryl Brown, entered the pageant in 1970; in 1980, Miss Arkansas, Lencola Sullivan, was the first black woman to finish among the top five finalists, but the first black contestant to be crowned Miss America occurred in September 1983, thirteen years after Brown's entrance. Williams represented a changing nation and the beauty of black womanhood, but she also called into public discussion the politics of race and racism, disfranchisement, sexuality, beauty, and national identity that were defined by white standards.

Many may not perceive the crowning of Williams as a sign of continued racism, although one could interpret the inclusion of black contestants as finalists as an indicator of a system of power that makes every attempt to contain race on its own terms of tolerance.[26] This containment of blackness exists and is governed by a set of safe principles that reflect a discourse of whiteness that works to authenticate the identity, respectability, sexuality, morality, grace, and femininity of white women. The pageant's acceptance and public construction of Williams as America's queen reiterated, momentarily, its own discourse of power: to prove, despite a racist history, that the pageant was raceless in its representation of all American women. The black body became a sign of racial harmony by standing side by side with the historically white model of beauty. Such a representation further denigrated the black body and its cultural politics: Black contestants were given limited exposure in the selection of a national representative[27] at the same time that their bodies, minds, and interactions were judged by white standards.

Without realizing it, Williams's short-term reign as Miss America forced people to critique the semiotics of power, sexuality, and virtue that qualitatively define beauty in a white patriarchal America, and according to Stephen Haymes in *Race, Culture, and the City: A Pedagogy for Black Urban Struggle*, such semiotics must be challenged if we are to "free the black body and personality from white control and domination."[28] Robin Gregory, Miss Howard University 1968, did just so. Proudly wearing an Afro, she challenged the images of beauty and power on a black college campus and, according to Paula Giddings, a fellow student of Gregory, "Robin talked about the movement. Robin talked about black politics. Robin was not the traditional homecoming queen candidate. She would also go around to the dorms in the evenings, which was something very, very different."[29] She engaged in the creation of black subjectivities by redefining the role and feminine attributes of beautiful black women; she raised hard questions about the nature of society and created self-defining terms. Clearly, "what Robin did was not only in terms of race but also talking about the role of women and what they should be doing and talking about and being taken very, very seriously, not just because of any physical attributes but because of her mind. And this I think was as important as the racial aspect of her campaign."[30]

Gregory, like Williams, represented a challenge to the semiotics of power, sexuality, and virtue, proving, as Holloway tells us, "Blackwomen's [sic] black and female bodies complicate the reductive visual stereotypes of prejudice, challenging its simplemindedness. Blackwomen's [sic] bodies visually assault the systems designed to neatly and easily identify the unempowered."[31] This is why the swimsuit competition of the Miss America Pageant serves as a site of power for white women's bodies, which are seen as docile,[32] and as a site of contestation for black women's bodies, which are culturally marked. Thus it becomes a challenge, while not impossible, for black women to affirm a positive sense of black identity while countering the images and bodily values of whiteness, particularly when many white people view "racism as the prejudiced behaviors of individuals rather than as an institutionalized system of advantage benefiting Whites."[33] Williams, Gregory, and other black women contestants, whether consciously or unconsciously, altered the landscape of America through the presence of their black bodies and identities, their black forms of beauty, and their black voices in the culture of both local and national pageantry. Their presence supported the belief that "Black Is Beautiful."

When Difference Becomes Too Much: Beauty, Sexuality, and the Decrowning of Vanessa Williams

In many ways, Williams entered into and conquered temporary ownership of the space of the Miss America Pageant, a space of estrangement for many black women. Yet her blackness still was contained within the dominant narratives of white America. She would come to represent a respectable woman in a black body who was not affected by the realities of black womanhood.[34] In the 1980s era of Reaganism, these realities, welfare, promiscuity, single-headed households—became a part of every major political platform in America as the nation tried to make sense of the black female body. Insomuch as the Miss America Pageant is political, the pageant too tried to "make sense" of this body by containing it, making it acceptable, safe, and feminine in standards and morals as the white female body. Nevertheless, the black female body has a long history with sexualization that the white female body does not have, and Williams's body was not an exception. In her study Black Looks, bell hooks discusses how the black female body becomes accepted by being sexualized: "Undesirable in the conventional sense, which defines beauty and sexuality as desirable only to the extent that it is idealized and unattainable, the black female body gains attention only when it is synonymous with accessibility, availability, when it is sexually deviant."[35] Williams's beauty, body, and blackness, with some similarities to the features of whiteness, became markers of sexuality both in a nation where she was Miss America and in a culture where she was transformed into a public sex queen for *Penthouse* magazine.

While Williams, during her ten-month reign as America's queen, came to represent, in the words of Miss America 1945 Bess Myerson, "You can't be beautiful and hate," her blackness was quickly reinscribed in social narratives of immorality and erotic desires when *Penthouse* magazine published photographs of her in sexual acts with a white woman (photographs taken three years before her crowning). As a result, Williams was asked by representatives of the pageant to relinquish her crown and her title, and her identity was disassociated from the protection, or safeguard, of white femininity guaranteed by the pageant. One could argue that white femininity and national identity, as articulated by the pageant, came under scrutiny for accepting a black woman as queen. Vanessa Williams became the first black woman to be crowned Miss America, and her crowning threatened traditional feminine aesthetics of American beauty. In other words, to have this beautiful and multitalented black woman erected as the pinnacle presented an abominable threat to the traditions of white (national) beauty; therefore, her validity, beauty, talent, and femininity were negated by her occupying two divergent spaces: virginity (the Miss America Pageant culture) and sexuality (the *Penthouse* photographs).

This act of negation and of occupying two different spaces further proves that as much as the crowning of Williams as the first black Miss America brought increasing publicity to conversations of race and representation, so did her decrowning. In the dominant social narratives of blackness perpetuated by white culture, Williams no longer represented what individual black women can accomplish, acceptance into a domain of whiteness, but rather black women's assumed symbolic linkage to sexuality. The problem here is *how* Williams and other black women attempt to cross "the historically all-white barrier of the Miss America pageant . . . [to] be included within the parameters of white femininity"[36] in ways that further disassociate them from black femininity, radical black subjectivities, and black politics. In other words, black women first must compose their own identities by acknowledging both the limitations imposed on them by controlling images of womanhood and the existing ideology of racial domination and exploitation. As far as black women and the Miss America Pageant are concerned, we need only examine the almost fifty years that black women were prohibited from participation. For black people, the act of becoming requires an understanding of how the body represents an important function in the establishment of black identity in the presence and absence of whiteness. Acts of exoticizing blackness, whether on the stage of the Miss America Pageant, in *Penthouse* magazine, or in dominant social narratives that depict black culture as dangerous and oversexed reinforce a hierarchal relationship between black and white bodies: As a result of the slave era, black women have received various demeaning labels, from mammies and matriarchs to welfare mothers and Jezebels. White women, as referenced in sociologist Patricia Hill Collins's 1991 study, have been encouraged to possess the four cardinal virtues: "piety, purity, submissiveness, and domesticity."[37] Understanding how Williams could in fact occupy two competing spaces, of the virgin queen and the sexualized queen, symbolizes the problematic relationship between black women and white institutional events: how both represent specific values that are multifaceted in the reconciliation of differences between a private identity and a national identity.

The decrowning of Williams, then, should be conceptualized as a moment in American history where dominant social narratives of black women as sexual beings resurfaced only to exist as an act of becoming complicatedly visible in the definition of self. By embracing radical black subjectivities and political and social campaigns for positive black identity making, black women would not have to enter into the mental and physical spaces of becoming like white women contestants in the Miss America Pageant. Black women already would exist as viable contestants with a significant agenda: to alter the Miss America Pageant and in turn alter public perceptions and white ideologies of beauty, femininity, and the national identity of America. This alteration is necessary, but difficult. It requires the recognition, in the words of songstress Aretha Franklin in a 1973 interview with *Essence* magazine, that "[b]eing black means being beautiful. It also means struggles, and it also means pain. And every black woman knows of that struggle, that pain, and she feels it whenever she looks at her man and her sons. Being black also means searching for oneself and one's place among others. There is so much we need to find. Like more purpose in life, and more self-love. That must come first."[38] Self-love for black women, according to black feminist thought, will not result from accepting and adopting standards of western beauty and femininity, as those standards are often catalysts in vying for the Miss America crown. Nevertheless, victimization of black beauty forms will continue.

Black Beauty, Black Feminism, and the Miss America Pageant

In talking about the black female body, it is essential to acknowledge how contemporary feminist activists challenged sexist thinking about appearance, beauty, and image. In *Feminism Is for Everybody,* hooks vividly recalls how women, thirty years ago, reclaimed their bodies by "stripping [them] of unhealthy and uncomfortable, restrictive clothing bras, girdles, corsets, garter belts, etc."[39] This defining moment in how women came to perceive themselves and their bodies represents the Atlantic City protest in which women threw high heels, false eyelashes, wigs, and women's magazines into a large "freedom trash can" on September 7, 1968, the same day as the crowning of Miss America 1969, Judi Ford. This event, under the leadership of a feminist platform, validated the naturalness of women as they rejected standards of *the* beautiful woman perpetuated by white ideologies, including the culture of the Miss America Pageant.

Cornel West, in *Race Matters,* talks about the terroristic way ideologies of white supremacy work to inculcate fear and self-hatred in people's images of themselves. Concerning black bodies and terrorism, West says, "White supremacist ideology is based first and foremost on the degradation of black bodies in order to control them. One of the best ways to instill fear in people is to terrorize them. Yet this fear is best sustained by convincing them that their bodies are ugly, their intellect is inherently underdeveloped, their culture is less civilized, and their future warrants less concern than that of other peoples."[40] In many ways, the history of the Miss America Pageant directly reflects the sentiments of West in its long belief that national identity was gender and race specific: the long-standing Rule 7 of the pageant's bylaws restricted participation of contestants to white women.[41]

As the media gathered in 1968 to photograph Judi Ford, a group of more than one hundred protesting women stood with placards on the Boardwalk of the Convention Hall in Atlantic City to "bestow the title of Miss America on a sheep,"[42] making known their belief of the idiocy of a pageant culture that parades, exploits, and denaturalizes the female body all while denying race. Insofar as black feminist resistance is concerned, this moment heightened the preexisting experiences of black women regarding beauty standards. Patricia Collins highlights how the ideal of feminine beauty has denigrated black women's encounters with their own beauty: "African-American women experience the pain of never being able to live up to externally defined standards of beauty, standards applied to us by white men, white women, black men, and, most painfully, one another."[43] Collins, as well as Toni Morrison, West, and hooks, encourages black people to decolonize their minds by critiquing white "normalcy:"

> Externally defined standards of beauty long applied to African-American women
> claim that no matter how intelligent, educated, or "beautiful" a Black woman may
> be, those Black women whose features and skin color are most African must "git
> back." Blue-eyed, blond, thin white women could not be considered beautiful

without the Other—Black women with classical African features of dark skin, broad noses, full lips, and kinky hair. Race, gender, and sexuality converge on this issue of evaluating beauty. Judging white women by their physical appearance and attractiveness to men objectifies them. But their white skin and straight hair privilege them in a system in which part of the basic definition of whiteness is its superiority to blackness.[44]

It is not hard to include in Collins's discussion the ramifications and consequences of using white beauty standards to judge black contestants in the Miss America Pageant. On one level, we are faced with confronting white access to black bodies and the demystification of how degrading names (Jezebels, mammies, welfare queens) and demoralizing acts (rape, slavery, Jim Crow) have been scripted and rehearsed on black bodies for decades. On another level, we must understand that the stage of the Miss America Pageant is not a space where black women can engage in acts of individual and collective self-healing or cultural affirmation, for the pageant has never been and probably will never become, to use hooks's terminology, a *homeplace,* a place of safety.[45] For black women, it has always been, to use Mary Louise Pratt's phrase, a *contact zone,* a space of asymmetrical power relations.[46]

The feminist movement has played a crucial part in promoting a vision of social change that challenges race and racism in addition to issues of class, sex, age and gender in a patriarchal society. If black women continue to compete in pageants in general, and the Miss America Pageant in particular, then the presence of a black feminist agenda that calls into question the inequities and positive strides of the past, the social and political reforms for women's rights of the present, and the anticipated struggles with sexualization, degradation, and exclusion is needed. Black beauty is positively affected by the productive work of black feminism, the establishment of black subjectivities, the promotion of black politics, and the constructive strategies used to unite black with beauty and beauty with culture. National pageants, with the underpinning of racism, can never affect or support such relationships.

Conclusion

Black women make and remake themselves everyday. From Harriet Tubman's Underground Railroad system, Sojourner Truth's "Ain't I A Woman?" speech, Bessie Smith's "Backwater Blues," Madame C. J. Walker's hair care products, June Jordan's *On Call* (1985), Angela Davis's *Women, Culture, and Politics* (1989), Robin Gregory's crowning as Miss Howard University 1968, Vanessa Williams's selection as Miss America 1984, and onward, black women have questioned and pushed the parameters that traditionally have defined nationalism and power against stereotypes buttressing ideologies of domination and privilege. For over fifty years, black women could not turn to the Miss America Pageant to validate black beauty: in 1921, fifteen-year-old Margaret Gorman became the first Miss America; twenty-four years later, Bess Myerson, concerned with the bigotry of pageant officials questioning her Russian Jewish background, was crowned Miss America 1945; Yolanda Betbeze, Miss America 1951, condemned the pageant for its exclusion of black contestants. With the obvious exclusion of black women, the pageant maintained its principles to value the beauty of white women while devaluing that of black women. The Miss America Pageant serves as but one example of how white ideologies work to displace and degrade black culture, values, and bodies.

To overcome the detrimental effects of black people internalizing the negative images of blackness perpetuated by a nonblack culture, black people must embrace the fundamental essence of our natural beauty. For many ·of us, our physical attributes resonate with the pain of colonization and the denial of public images of black beauty, yet our physical attributes should more strongly resonate with public movements promoting "Black Power," "Black Is Beautiful," "Say It Loud: I'm Black and I'm Proud," "Soul Sisters and Soul Brothers," "Young, Gifted, and Black," "Black Subjectivities," "Black Pedagogies," and "A Body of Black Political Thought."

Additionally, we must privately and publicly accept our physical attributes in establishing terms of love and endearment. Songstress Nina Simone and musician Weldon Irvine in 1969 wrote the lyrics to the song, "To Be Young, Gifted, and Black" to pay tribute to the life and work of playwright Lorraine Hansberry and to express pride in the accomplishments of black people. The song speaks to the perpetual search for truth and beauty as inscribed in Blackness, a search that is often hindered by a most haunting history with hate, oppression, violence, and images of brutal ugliness. Nevertheless, the ending of the song is predicated upon one significant, albeit multi-layered belief—to be Black, to be young, to be talented within a historical tradition that has sought to imprison the very essence of Black struggle, liberation, intelligences, and freedom is a social and political location worth fighting for and existing within. The song resonates in the urgency of self-love that propels Black people to establish specific terms of self-definition in fighting against colonizing misrepresentations of the Black body politic.

Much like Simone's and Irvine's lyrics, contemporary Songstress India.Arie [sic] in her 2001 song, "Video," highlights how she has learned to accept and love herself as a queen without altering her body image (her lips, her feet, her thighs, nor her eyes). She makes a declaration of difference that disassociates herself from the traditionally sought after video girl, beauty queen, and supermodel, proving that beauty should not be manufactured, sanctioned, and based on homogeneous standards. Beauty, for India.Arie, is not ascertained by the accumulation of wealth, materiality, or physicality, but by an unconditional commitment to self-affirmation manifested within a commitment to communal love. Other Black artists (i.e., TLC in their song "Unpretty;" Amel Larrieux in her song "I N I;" and Lauryn Hill in her powerful declaration to men and women about the politics of sex, love, and money in "Doo Wop, That Thing"), committed to publicly displaying an agenda of differences (i.e., physically, socially, and even linguistically), share India.Arie's statement of beauty and love. Their musical works are evidence of their efforts to promote both communal and individual standards of beauty that oppose traditional social narratives of the whiteness and richness of true beauty. The commentaries on beauty within these songs are quite clear: the perpetuation of acceptable standards of beauty, constructed around other people's value systems, has long been historicized in larger issues of a rhetoric of rights rooted in power movements, civil revolutions, the under-representation of Black people in national decision making processes, class divisions, racial segregation, and the fight for quality community and educational resources. These songs encourage people, with a particular focus on Black women, to reject Western society's judgment of pretty and unpretty by doing the following: embracing internal beauty; engaging in consciousness-raising efforts; challenging sexist ideologies of the Black female body; interrogating the perverted classist and racist politics of beauty, meaning making, identity formation, and thus power; and educating ourselves, our families, our communities, and our children to fully embrace the beauty of the image that stares at them as they stare in the mirror.

In other words, the work of consciously liberated people is to analyze the very barriers to justice and freedom, the very dynamics of wealth and poverty, the very forces of racism and classism, as we tread our way into a nation of heterogeneity in promoting a declaration of differences in politics, in communities of privilege, in national pageants of beauty. Scholar Cornel West, in talking about liberation, redemption, healing, civil responsibility, and race, says it best:

> In these downbeat times, we need as much hope and courage as we do vision and analysis; we must accent the best of each other even as we point out the vicious effects of our racial divide and the pernicious consequences of our maldistribution of wealth and power. We simply cannot enter the twenty-first century at each other's throats, even as we acknowledge the weighty forces of racism, patriarchy, economic inequality, homophobia, and ecological abuse on our necks. We are at a crucial crossroad in the history of this nation—and we either hang together by combating these forces that divide and degrade us or we hang separately. Do we have the intelligence, humor, imagination, courage, tolerance, love, respect, and will to meet the challenge? Time will tell. None of us alone can save the nation or world. But each of us can make a positive difference if we commit ourselves to do so.[47]

The multiple public declarations of inequality and racism, pain and struggle, love and beauty, along with the will to eradicate the injustices that separate us, can forge an alteration to occur within particular events, communities, and institutions that work to re-define the national identity that is America.

In reference to the Miss America Pageant, many obstacles exist in the asserting of such declarations in the face of the pageant's racist structure, even after the crowning of Vanessa Williams (1984), Suzette Charles (1984), Debbye Turner (1990), Marjorie Vincent (1991), Kimberly Aiken (1994), Erika Harold (2003), and Ericka Dunlap (2004). While the argument can be made that the crowning of these Black beauty queens represents a new national pageant focused on the inclusion of Black women,[48] one can continue to argue that the presence of Black women has represented a political shift in our national agenda: no longer can America, at least on a public stage, idealize Whiteness without somehow including the marked Other with which this idealization occurs. No longer should America publicly display acts of racism, but America does; understanding the racist politics of this nation should bring into question the how's and the why's of what it really means when a Black woman is crowned Miss America.

I want to see black women being crowned Miss America who have not altered their natural beauty for the sake of acceptance: black women with natural hair, little to no makeup, a politically charged black agenda grounded in black feminist thought and community building. This is not to say that I seek a black Miss America who disregards the national climate that is America; nevertheless, I seek a black Miss America who loves herself and her body so much that she can choose to refrain from participating in the beauty culture/beauty standards of white supremacy and still assert the ideals of being "Young, Gifted, and Black." She can wear her beauty without her beauty wearing her.

Notes

1. J. Miller, *Beauty* (San Francisco: Chronicle Books, 1997).
2. For research on beauty pageants, see Candace Savage, *Beauty Queens: A Playful History* (New York: Abbeville Press, 1998); and Sarah Banet-Weiser, *The Most Beautiful Girl in the World: Beauty, Pageants and National Identity* (Berkeley: University of Berkeley Press, 1999); on beauty, see Rita Freedman, *Beauty Bound* (Lexington, MA: D.C. Heath and Company, 1986); and bell hooks, *Outlaw Culture: Resisting Representations* (New York: Routledge, 1994); on race theory, see Cornel West, *Race Matters* (New York: Vintage, 1993); hooks, *Outlaw Culture;* and Stephen Haymes, *Race, Culture, and the City: A Pedagogy for Black Urban Struggle* (New York: State University of New York Press, 1995); and on feminist critique, see Patricia Hill Collins, *Black Feminist Thought: Knowledge, Consciousness, and the Politics of Empowerment* (New York: Routledge, 1991); Karla Holloway, *Codes of Conduct: Race, Ethics, and the Color of Our Character*

(New Brunswick, NJ: Rutgers University Press, 1995); b. hooks, *Yearning: Race, Gender and Cultural Politics* (Cambridge, MA: South End Press, 1990); b. hooks, *Feminism Is for Everybody* (Cambridge, MA: South End Press, 2000); and b. hooks, *Feminist Theory: From Margin to Center* (Cambridge, MA: South End Press, 2000).

3. Haymes, *Race, Culture, and the City,* 27.
4. Freedman, *Beauty Bound,* 26.
5. Ibid., 26.
6. hooks, *Outlaw Culture,* 173.
7. "In 1968 feminists targeted the Miss America Pageant for protests. They staged a theatrical demonstration outside of the Atlantic City Convention Center on the day of the pageant. The protest was one of the first media events to bring national attention to the emerging Women's Liberation Movement. Over the next decade, the women's movement would rival the civil rights movement in the success it would achieve in a short period of time" (www.pbs.org/wgbh/amex/mis-samerica/peopleevents/e_feminists).
8. Savage, *Beauty Queens,* 104.
9. hooks, *Outlaw Culture,* 77.
10. Ibid., 104.
11. hooks, *Outlaw Culture,* 174.
12. Quoted in Savage, *Beauty Queens,* 105.
13. Holloway, *Codes of Conduct,* 61.
14. Ibid., 66.
15. Banet-Weiser, *The Most Beautiful Girl in the World,* 58.
16. Freedman, *Beauty Bound,* 42.
17. Banet-Weiser, *The Most Beautiful Girl in the World,* 63.
18. Carmichael's argument is an important one; however, it is complicated in that he views the role of women as *prone.*
19. S. Carmichael and C. Hamilton, *Black Power: The Politics of Liberation in America* (New York: Vintage, 1967), 34–35.
20. Cornel West. *Prophesy Deliverance! An Afro-American Revolutionary Christianity* (Philadelphia: Westminster Press 1982), 28.
21. Banet-Weiser, *The Most Beautiful Girl in the World,* 9.
22. Ibid., 9
23. S. Carmichael, and C. Hamilton, *Black Power;* bell hooks, *Sisters of the Yam: Black Women and Self-Recovery* (Boston: South End Press, 1993); hooks, *Outlaw Culture:*); bell hooks, *Killing Rage, Ending Racism* (New York: Henry Holt & Company, 1995); bell hooks and Cornel West, *Breaking Bread: Insurgent Black Intellectual Life* (Boston: South End Press, 1991); Haymes, *Race, Culture, and the City;* Holloway, *Codes of Conduct.*
24. Banet-Weiser, *The Most Beautiful Girl in the World,* 125.
25. Ibid., 126.
26. Ibid., 128.
27. Carmichael and Hamilton, *Black Power;* West, *Race Matters;* Haymes, *Race, Culture, and the City;* Iris Young, *Justice and the Politics of Difference* (Princeton N.J: Princeton University Press, 1990).
28. Haymes, *Race, Culture, and the City,* 61.

29. C. Carson, D. Garrow, G. Gill, V. Harding, and D. Hine, *The Eyes on the Prize Civil Rights Reader* (New York: Penguin, 1991), 460.

30. Ibid., 461.

31. Holloway, *Codes of Conduct*, 34.

32. M. Foucault, *Discipline and Punish: The Birth of the Prison* (New York: Random House, 1977); M. Foucault, *The History of Sexuality*, R. Hurley (New York: Pantheon, 1978).

33. Beverly Daniel Tatum, *Why Are All the Black Kids Sitting Together in the Cafeteria? And Other Conversations About Race* (New York: Basic Books, 1997), 46.

34. Collins, *Black Feminist Thought: Knowledge*); W. Lubiano, "Black Ladies, Welfare Queens, and State Minstrels," *Race-ing Justice, En-Gendering Power: Essays on Anita Hill, Clarence Thomas, and the Construction of Social Reality*, Toni Morrison, ed. (New York: Pantheon Books, 1992); Toni Morrison, *Playing in the Dark: Whiteness and the Literary Imagination* (New York: Vintage, 1992).

35. b. hooks, *Black Looks: Race and Representation.* (Boston: South End Press, 1990), 65–66.

36. Banet-Weiser, *The Most Beautiful Girl in the World*, 143.

37. Collins, *Black Feminist Thought*, 71.

38. Quoted in D. Nathan, *Young, Gifted and Black: Aretha Franklin, 1972 & 1993* Record Jacket (Los Angeles: Atlantic, 1993).

39. hooks, *Feminism Is for Everybody*, 31.

40. West, *Race Matters*, 122–123.

41. Banet-Weiser, *The Most Beautiful Girl in the World*; Savage, *Beauty Queens*.

42. Savage, *Beauty Queens*, 2.

43. Collins, *Black Feminist Though*, 79–80.

44. Ibid., 79.

45. hooks, *Yearning*.

46. Mary Louise Pratt, "Arts of the Contact Zone," *Professions* (New York: The Modern Language Association, 1991), 33–40.

47. The Nina Simone Web, www.boscarol.com/nina/html/where/tobeyoung-gifted.html.

48. West, *Race Matters*, 159.

49. Cohen, C., R. Wilk, and B. Stoeltje, *Beauty Queens on the Global Stage: Gender, Contests, and Powe,* (New York: Routledge, 1996).

5

Princess Literature and the Miss America Pageant

Iset Anuakan

Popular public events like the Miss America Pageant, which place women's value at their purpose, are important bellwethers for how American society evaluates femininity, race, and class. The pageant, a colossal yearly media event, is conditioned by antiquated ideals as a consequence of its alignment with fairy tale mythologies. Children's fables like "Cinderella," "Rapunzel," and "Snow-White" published and popularized since the nineteenth century, continue to exert influence over women's identity. The thematic structures in this body of literature, where the heroine is described as a princess, draw conclusions among femininity, beauty, race, and success, creating a perceptible formula—the measure of ideal womanhood. In a corresponding manner, the pageant places similar limits on possible outcomes for women. Those who vie for the title of Miss America follow a list of criteria—the rules that determine which among them will reign for the year. Princess literature supplies cues and examples for women to follow, without entertaining the idea that diverse strategies and women of unique backgrounds have a multitude of routes to choose from in order to reach their goals.

Women's appearance is the continual subject of weights and measures. The standard ideals lean toward narrow definitions, conventional guidelines that feminist writings have protested against since the 1950s. Betty Friedan's *The Feminine Mystique* and Simone de Beauvoir's *The Second Sex* voiced objections to sex-role stereotypes and media images that placed burdens on women's self-esteem. African American writer Gwendolyn Brooks won the Pulitzer Prize for *Maud Martha,* the 1953 novel that valued the life of an ordinary-looking black girl. Her success was followed by Toni Morrison's critique of the shadow of white beauty in *The Bluest Eye.* Even as women of varying shapes, hues, and incomes assert their worth, rarely do models of beauty represent nature's many sides.[1]

Ironically, some of the seventy-five winners of the Miss America Pageant share the view that they did not fit the conventional mold of gender and beauty when they won. Phyllis George (1971) described her awkwardness walking down the ramp. "I started walking and the crown fell on the floor. Stones went everywhere, the banner fell off my shoulders, my hair was sticking up; I looked like a ragamuffin." Mary Ann Mobley (1959) described her hometown image as "little, short, squat Mary Ann." Suzette Charles (1984) was "one of the shortest [Miss Americas] at 5'3"." Judith Ford (1969) was a tomboy. Pageant officials told her "'You have three strikes against you: You're too young, too blonde, and too athletic. Miss America is not supposed to sweat.'"[2]

Although many of these winners did not initially see themselves as examples of model beauty, they ascended to supermodel status once they earned the title of Miss America. The crown created opportunities for them to hopscotch onto stage, screen, and magazine covers. What is troubling is that commercial media—from film to television to print—rarely represents these women as less than perfect, as human beings with foibles and flaws. Instead, their faces and bodies are presented to the public with sex appeal and provide limited versions of body types, hairstyles, and racial differences. Often, their unique strengths, talents, and personal triumphs are hidden from the cameras.

These images contribute to teenagers' impressions of success in society. According to psychologist Melissa Milkie, young black and white girls admit they do not feel equipped with the ideal qualities of beauty and womanhood featured in glamour magazines. Many teens feel that magazines emphasize a narrow range of attributes, one that mythologizes female beauty. One girl described the models as "so beautiful" and having "really great bodies. . . . Perfect hair, the perfect boyfriend, the perfect life," as indicative of what every girl wants. Teen girls realize the images are unrealistic, a consequence of using enhanced photography to attract readers. They are aware that fashion publications embellish the lifestyles of wealthy celebrities, but many tend to evaluate themselves, physically and emotionally, according to the mediums. These mythologies demonstrate a strong correspondence to images in princess literature.[3]

Portraits of women in fairy tales similarly affect women of varying backgrounds well into adulthood. Respondents to a survey by researcher Kay Stone on children's tales like "Cinderella" reveal that women harbor resentment toward their emphasis on beauty. Many felt unable to fit into princess mythology, or that fairy tales do not nurture their individual personalities. These images continue to have long-lasting effects on women's psyche because the princess ideal is an inescapable social force. Kay Stone examined the long-term impact that children's tales can have on young minds in general. These stories are "usually read early in life when a child is struggling to find a place in the world and a sexual identity." The author interviewed women about their feelings toward the tales; many discussed their resentment of the emphasis on beauty. Stone says: "For males, fairy tales apparently cease to function at an early age, but for many females these stories continue to function on some level well past childhood. . . . Girls and women who have felt that in some way they cannot or will not fit themselves into an image that does not suit their individual characters and needs, still cannot free themselves fully from the fairy tale princess."[4]

The polarized dimensions of small sizes and large shapes are only parts of the equation stipulated as desirable traits in women. Women of color are less frequently invited to see themselves, their distinctive hair types, skin tones, or figures, in a positive light. All too often, racism has impeded on the measure and rules of beauty. Standard folktales that circulate in western American culture do not feature Black women as primary characters; when dark figures appear, their images often manifest as foreboding background characters. Marginalization in fairy tales is compounded for Black women when the haunting, horrific images within them possess dark skin, dark hair, and curly hair types resembling kinky hair. Unrealistic, homogenous renderings of "positive" females limit our ability to imagine women of all ages, backgrounds, and physical variations. This narrow lens minimizes our appreciation for female differences.[5]

Black women who find themselves trying to measure up to a "perfect beauty" patterned after European ideals that Anglo American women confess is unachievable would be even more inclined to doubt their natural appearance, place in the world, and self-esteem. The absence of Black female figures in popular European tales is not only culturally consistent, it underscores the generic role of women in these writings. Folklorist Kathryn Morgan recalls her confrontation with this form of embedded cultural racism: "In school we were learning about 'Little Black Sambo,' and our textbooks were chockfull of disparaging things about blacks and their African background. . . . As our teachers were all white, we learned no black history in school. . . . This was the world of books and movies—a world of Goldilocks and Shirley Temple curls."[6]

The Anglicized version of beauty is a measurable trait, outlined in fiction that is traditionally served up to children as bedtime stories of magical places where endings are happily resolved. Children's folktales are didactic presentations; they establish worldviews that encourage young people to embrace specific solutions to problems, both structurally and implicitly. The dream world of children's drama becomes the basis for psychological instruction. Approaches to the structural analysis of folk literature bear this out in three areas. First, some effort has been made to identify the psychology of color and *dark feminine* aspects in princess literature, even when black women are absent from folktales like Cinderella as explicit characters. An examination of African American women in American folktales also provides comparative frameworks to popular European folklore. These works are, for the most part, blatantly hostile toward women who do not embody a passive, blond, childlike image. Second, the linear outline of folktales verifies the limited possibilities open to women, which echoes the script for pageant contests. Third, deeper values of the folktale become apparent using anthropologist Claude Levi-Strauss's structural analysis of oppositional traits. Symbolic oppositions (i.e., good/bad, beautiful/ugly, cold/hot, dry/wet) establish nuanced, paradigmatic significance in folktales. In the story "Cinderella," the Ash Girl, character action, linear structure, and cultural oppositions provide a basis for generating theories on race, class, and gender.[7]

Cinderella is a motherless child. In the children's parable, she is the slave to her father's newly adopted family, but is rescued by her godmother—another maternal substitute. The godmother, magically aided by an entourage of mice and birds (popularized in the Disney version), insures her attendance at the ball with a wave of wand. Her clothes and hair are made over glamorously. The Ash Girl meets the prince, who deems her his favorite among all the other women. She flees the ball before midnight—before her ball gown and chariot revert to rags and pumpkin—leaving only a glass slipper behind. The prince searches the village to find her, testing each woman with the slipper. Upon finding Cinderella, matching the shoe to her foot, he makes her his princess.[8]

It is the tale of a girl who rises from poverty and social obscurity, who meets and marries a successful, handsome man with social status. The crown redeems Cinderella from working-class status, aided by characters outside her family structure. The fairy godmother in the story befriends the young girl and provides her with the means to change and conceal her identity. She is the agent that transforms Cinderella overnight, not unlike coaching support hired to make women more attractive, graceful, talented competitors in beauty pageants.

The film *Miss Congeniality* (2001) illustrates the linkages between the fairy godmother and the agent who works magic when Sandra Bullock, an undercover cop, hires a beauty consultant to achieve the impossible. In twenty-four hours, Bullock undergoes a strenuous makeover, transforming her from a guffawing, unkempt police detective, into a curvy, glamorous Miss New Jersey. But in real life, beauty coaches can be a hindrance. Debra Sue Maffett, Miss America 1983, felt coaching critiques crippled her confidence. They harped on pursuing perfection and caused her to realize that women can groom themselves "to the point where it becomes a barrier."[9]

Together, Cinderella and the godmother are the heroines of the story and serve as vivid contrasts to other female contenders in both looks and action. The rival older sisters provide oppositions to her good nature. Alternately, the stepmother and stepsisters behave badly toward the young Ash Girl. In the 1950s Walt Disney version, they are grotesque. Their feet are too big, they have crass mannerisms, their voices are shrill, and they mistreat their younger sibling. The ball is their last desperate chance to snag the prince. The sisters are stereotypes of women on the clock, running out of time before they become barren old maids.

The myth teaches boys and girls gender identity. Cinderella is also subject to time constraints, to meet a curfew that safeguards her place in life. She must conceal her beauty secrets, for these too are destined to change with time. Men in princess literature seldom undergo such restrictions. Instead, the folktale does not instruct children to berate men who grow old yet remain bachelors, unattached to the responsibilities of a wife and children. Their physiology does not prevent them from reproducing by a certain age; consequently, men in our culture are able to elude negative stereotypes.

Instead, the prince serves as judge in selecting a wife, the widely sought after office carrying both wealth and status. After eyeing one among the throng of would-be hopefuls, he conducts a slipper-test to be certain he has chosen correctly. The prince in the Miss America Pageant is ostensibly an anonymous figure. A court of judges assumes his place as the legitimate ruling body. But on careful examination, the unnamed suitor appears in the backdrop as the male announcer—a young, attractive Bert Parks, then Ron Ely, later Gary Collins. Popular TV star Tony Danza, the male announcer for the September 2001 pageant, introduced the prospective winner to the court, acting as an observer during the evening gown and swimsuit rounds. Wayne Brady, the first African American host, conducted the "slipper-test" in the 2002 pageant. After interviewing finalists on lofty questions, he serenaded the winner as she received the crown. The princess-elect clutched her roses and scepter, symbols of her rule over love and domain.[10]

Some of the most popular folktales in the western repertoire duplicate and perpetuate classical definition of European ideals on color and beauty. Retold constantly, folktales reinforced cultural "norms" in premodern cultures much as advertising and broadcast media do now. More than two hundred folktales were collected by Wilheim and Jacob Grimm, two brothers who traveled throughout the German countryside, listening to stories told by housewives. The brothers Grimm transcribed these folktales and published *Kinder-und Hausmärchen* in

1812. Passed around orally for generations, the märchen convey familiar ideas from Anglo folk tradition. Although the origins of several folktales are unclear, they diffused around the world and circulated through the West. Celebrated as children's stories, many of these folktales spotlight feminine beauty as central themes of moral drama and youthful dilemma. Even though many lack direct references to race, their villains are painted as dark, haunting figures, manifesting as foreboding background images. A variety of folktales in the Grimm Brothers' collection (erroneously called fairy tales) depict heroines resembling chalk-white, golden-haired, angelic young girls. They model gender roles in which female characters are passive princesses waiting to be rescued, cared for and protected by men.[11]

Beauty pageants are one of the human forums in which girls become true-to-life princesses. The narratives in twenty-first-century pageants, where a winner is crowned, follow a similar pattern as that in many folktales. It is a rite of passage where a young girl becomes a woman. Even the appraisal by advocates of female competitions that these events serve to provide scholarships conforms to the stories in which a girl rises out from under obscurity. The aspects of female competitions that provide opportunities to advance economically are consistent with centuries of mythmaking in princess literature.

As an aesthetic event, the pageant wields the power to reconfigure outworn attitudes on race, gender, and beauty for women. Historically, its winners have waged these battles on their own, at individual levels. Bess Myerson, the first Jewish woman to win the pageant in 1945, was assaulted with bigoted attitudes, including managers who urged her to change her name. Myerson refused to placate prejudiced attitudes. Vanessa Williams, the first black woman to win the Miss America title, had armed guards outside of her motel room due to death threats. Victory for an African American woman came at a high price due to media attention that debated whether she was black enough to be considered a racial first and played a part in her resignation after ten months. Arguably, Williams's nude photos were not far removed from the parade of nearly naked women on the pageant ramp. The implication, however, was that the photos were out of keeping with the sacred symbols of supposed innocence of the pageant. Williams's skin color further magnified this sacred measure.[12]

Between 1921, when the Miss America Pageant began, and the late 1960s, the pageant was a Jim Crow affair. Winners conformed to a similar set of norms established in princess literature. In addition to scholarships and thousands of dollars, they won a rhinestone tiara and a royal scepter as they vied for the opportunity to represent America's ideals of grace and beauty. Pageant contestants were always white, often blond, slim, and youthful.[13]

Similarly, an overt feature in the Grimm stories is the depiction of women with long blond tresses, described as "fairest in the land" and therefore the most beautiful. Some scholars argue the term "fair" originated as a euphemism for equality. "Fairness" in Greek implied a balance of power relations rather than beauty, which was a metaphor for a character trait indicating spiritual worth. It frequently was used to describe orators, the men who invoked principles of justice and democracy. Beauty was a by-product of soulful experiences, the insignia of gifted speechmakers who were known for wearing extravagant dress, odorous perfumes, and expending a great deal of effort on their body and hair. Philostratus, a scribe in fifth-century Athens, reported that one orator, Alexander of Seleucia, possessed an intoxicating beauty like a "divine epiphany." His appearance enthralled his audiences, "by the splendor of his large eyes, the lush locks of his beard, the perfect line of his nose, his white teeth, and long slender fingers," even before he opened his mouth to speak. The assumptions that beauty's transcendent nature could be detected on the body evolved as a mechanism of public presentation; beauty was condensed into a fixed attribute, associated with elite, celebrity speech, and public elegance.[14]

Classical definitions of fairness and beauty were compressed centuries later into print culture. The Grimm tales synthesized these aesthetic ideals such that they became characterized by lack of color and were associated most often with women. The Miss America theme song still contains lines identifying the winner as the fairest of all and as "your ideal." Because the pageant is women's space, it reinforces our ideas of femininity. It is also cultural space, entertainment, fashion exhibition, and theater, where each phase of presentation is judged. Evaluations of what women think, wear, and look like in swimsuits and evening gowns—what talents they possess and how congenial they are in competitive circumstances—might be stimulated by the rainbow of cultures that exist in the United States. Increasing the access of black, brown, red, and yellow women onto the pageant stage would test the myths of femininity and fairness.

Lessons in the Grimm stories implicitly define color and race as much as gender. From "The Golden Key," "The Golden Goose," and "The Golden Bird," to "Snow-White," "The White Bride and the Black Bride," and "The Golden Children," these sagas celebrate whiteness and make the underworld synonymous with darkness. Women in them are cursed into turning "black as coal and ugly" or blessed into becoming "beautiful and pure as the sun." In a sequel to the well-known "Snow-White," the tale of Snow-White and Rose-Red, whiteness is privileged in its comparison of two sisters—one blonde, the other dark-haired with rosy cheeks: "Snow-White (was) more quiet and gentle than Rose-Red. Rose-Red liked better to run about in the meadows and fields seeking flowers and catching butterflies; but Snow-White sat at home with her mother, and helped her with housework, or read to her when there was nothing to do." The tale is resolved by Snow-White's marriage to the Prince and

Rose-Red's union with his brother. Descriptions of color designate Snow-White as the central figure and Rose-Red as tangential. Their names are guides for personalities and good-naturedness. A hierarchy of success is established by each sister's triumphant marital and material status; the blond wins the prince, the brunette wins his less affluent brother. Like other celebrated stories in the European tradition, black women's images were absent—until Brandy and Whitney Huston's 1997 TV remake of *Cinderella*, appearing a little more than a decade after the first black Miss America was chosen.[15]

Another very explicit illustration on the value of whiteness and long blond hair is "Rapunzel." The maiden in the tower's golden braids mediate relationships between her and others. The story begins with a couple who bargain away their firstborn child to a sorceress as payment for lettuce they stole from her. The witch hides the child, Rapunzel, in a tower, maintaining daily visits by climbing up Rapunzel's braids like a ladder. When she reaches puberty, a handsome prince discovers her. Described as "the most beautiful child under the sun," with hair that was "long and radiant, as fine as spun gold," she is a visual contrast to her captor, the stepmother whose dark hair stands on end.[16]

The literature projects more than simple lessons on honesty or lost love. References in these stories to rare metals lend themselves to theories on class and capitalism; gold and silver, as descriptives of hair color, historicize the western world's attraction to wealth. In "Rapunzel," braids symbolize the "binding" of her hair with subtextual economic messages. Gold is the metaphor of adoration used to describe her appearance. Commercial exchange, the motivation for centuries of European expansion, underlies this symbolic construction and contextualizes Rapunzel's braids as an object of trade used to bargain for freedom. Dark hair like that of Rose-Red's, conversely, represents seductive qualities in folk literature, while red complexions and tresses project fiery emotionalism. The shades of color operate on the spectrum of worth, blond to black, correlating sexuality with cultural values.[17]

Analytic psychologists are inclined to render the feminine aspects of blondeness and beauty as measures of women's thought processes. "Rapunzel" represents valuable yet involuntary ideas where golden hair acts as a halo, an allusion to enlightenment. The maiden's hair is a metaphor for reflections of the unconscious, and Rapunzel inadvertently acts as a conjurer, using her hair to do the bidding of her unconscious thoughts. Rapunzel's golden plaits give agency to her ideas. The braids cause upliftment exhibited by the menacing witch and the rescuing prince who climb the woven ladder twenty ells (seventy-five feet) into her tower. The maiden's actions are flooded with subconscious power, implying that Rapunzel manipulated the man with her hair.[18]

A cultural critique of the feminine in folktales merits discussion of the "dark feminine" in them as well. The power of the sorceress is juxtaposed to the passive maiden. Her desires are not unconsciously driven, but are assertive; she is often formidable in controlling her circumstances. African American folktales consistently inscribe the dark woman as a healer or miracle worker. But in princess lore, the dark feminine is neither a magician nor seductive. Instead, darkness underscores the contest between good and evil, serving as a contrast to the passive princess, not only in deeds and dress, but more often in age and name. In western folktales, archetypes of the dark feminine are old hags, wicked witches, and evil stepmothers. The German märchen is blatantly hostile toward these outcasts, described as ugly, decrepit, and undesirable.[19]

The historical significance of these romantic ideas, embraced through the English Renaissance and modern ages, is the existence of real "dark" figures, their sociocultural status in western society, and the stereotyping of their images as villains. Some experts on the children's märchen suggest a detached reading of the tales, as comical and devoid of serious realism. But any dismissal of a connection between the depiction of human evil in tales and their resemblance to real people ignores the dynamics of how truth and myth are constructed. Reliance on hags and witches as conduits of wicked events has led to serial portraits of the female personality in which age, style of dress, dark skin color, and physical handicaps are maligned. As characters in children's fiction, they most often exhibit dangerous attitudes and intentions toward innocent youth. These notions of evil generate overt stereotypes that mock female difference. They are contrasts to established archetypes of beauty in which whiteness, youth, and demureness are the preferred heroines of the imagination.[20]

Princess literature uses myth and magic to codify values about women and their success. These mythological assumptions are revived in public cultural events like beauty pageants. The western canon of children's literature teaches patterns of social climbing to young girls. Typically, it instructs them on routes of escape from social constriction: from controlling parents, jealous siblings, and lower-class status. In this culture, it seems that women are asked to draw on their unique female powers to confront problems and issues differently than men.

In February 2002, the Bush administration proposed that women who receive welfare seek another way out of poverty. If these women would just find husbands, the president suggested with his $19 billion welfare package, they could climb out of economic obscurity. "Stable families should be the central goal of American welfare policy," the president said. "Building and preserving families are not always possible—I recognize that—but they should always be our goal." Oklahoma City announced a similar initiative in April. Federal and state-sponsored initiatives promoting marriage claim to confront two social issues: poverty rates and single parenting. Yet a marriage policy for men at the poverty level seems antithetical. Government intervention is, not surprisingly, on par with age-old wisdom taught to young women around the world. Fifty-one percent of the public polled agreed with this policy, even though it casts a blind eye to gendered notions of family. It ignores how women are socialized to be caretakers in marriage, jobs for which they are not likely to receive a salary.[21]

As economic solutions go, finding a husband is an option that girls learn at an early age. It is part of the global tradition that mothers teach their daughters and sons in folk literature. The suggestion that women can solve their problems by catching a suitor draws on feminine power of seduction. That myth—that women have the power to control their circumstances with their feminine wiles instead of with brains, talent, and persistence—plays at the current juncture of pageant aims. Advertising that the Miss America Pageant is "The World's Leading Scholarship Provider" is linguistic window dressing. Many of the winners apply part of their $200,000 winnings toward college education, but their interests in professional careers tend toward exclusive areas of entertainment, not academic ones. Winners attend schools for acting or journalism, then go on to model for tabloids, host talk shows, anchor news programs, or take to the stage as dancers and actresses. The title is perhaps their greatest asset in building professional lives in front of audiences and cameras, and it does allow them to champion social and political causes in a brighter spotlight. Surely the pageant purse could finance a scholar's education as winners opt for career directions that favor justice in the global marketplace. It is the legacy in which the pageant has evolved.

The civil rights era generated new scripts for what it means to be female and successful, for what it means to be American Indian, African American, Latina, Asian American, ethnic and empowered. But the scripts of poverty have not shifted significantly and may indicate why the parables continue to be so powerful. Women who are poor are vulnerable to social judgment. Women who are poor are subject to pronouncements from male authorities who recommend solutions that read like a fairy tale. And women of color are more likely to endure moral tirades from patriarchal conservatives.

In the post–civil rights era—fifty years after "Black Is Beautiful" became a slogan, and the feminist and womanist liberation struggles—there is evidence that the ideals outlined in princess literature survive. And there is evidence that these ideals negatively impact the self-esteem of black women and women of color. Certainly the princess of folktales is an absurd standard for women of every race. But as more brown-skinned and black-skinned women enter the pageant's enchanted forest where they are judged on looks, there is evidence that the pressure to conform to the old standards of beauty prevail. African

American women who were marginalized by the American standard of beauty during the course of the twentieth century hosted their own beauty pageants. They sponsored debutante balls and cotillions, and groomed their daughters for school proms, rites of passage for young girls treading the color line into adulthood. By 1984, black women had broken through one of the most powerful mythical barriers in American society.

Vanessa Williams was simultaneously congratulated and punished for breaking the mold of the blond, white princess, penalized for choices she had made with her own body. Williams's reign challenged the values in princess mythology, the meaning of having our own BAP (black American princess). As a result, the number of titles for African Americans has risen to seven, all within a twenty-year span. Ericka Dunlap, winner of the 2004 pageant, is noted for her sense of humor and independent stance on diversity. In one crowning photo, Dunlap wears a yellow flower in her hair, reminiscent of Billie Holiday, with two fists raised in victory. The image generates new meanings of African American women's leadership in revising the standards of princess ideology.[22]

The meanings of the gown, the crown, and the swimsuit were challenged with the 1984 Williams title. The bathing suit prerequisite, in particular, loomed as incongruent in an arena that prides itself on cultivating proper social graces, although the women do not have to demonstrate swimming capabilities. A controversy ensued over *Penthouse* magazine's publication of previously taken nude photographs. Pictured with another female, the photos for which she was chided were not sexually explicit. Yet Williams's poses arched the back of American prudery and homophobia, but not its tolerance of widespread pornography. It forced women to consider whether the mythology shapes us or we shape the mythology.

Clearly, those who enter the pageant are less inclined to be judgmental. One state representative in the 2001 contest remarked, "I don't care if these are Hooters girls, these are the cream of the crop." The association between pageant contestants and busty waitresses is a reasonable one. Shortly after MTV aired its program on pageant runners, A&E broadcast a biography of Hugh Hefner. The emphasis on women's bodies in each program was similar. Researchers have drawn connections among pageant runners, models, and Hefner's playgirls, specifically that their body measurements in ratios from waist to hip are nearly identical. Fashion icons like Twiggy and Kate Moss popularized extreme measurements for nude models and Miss America contestants between 1960 and 1990. During that period, averages for waist-to-hip ratios of women in *Playboy* and the pageant kept pace, and they had all grown an average of two inches taller.[23]

Contemporary values of contestants also reshape pageant interests as evidenced by recent controversial platforms espoused by title holders such as

Kate Shindle, Miss America 1998, who, as an advocate for AIDS education and prevention, supported distribution of condoms in the public schools and needle exchange programs. Reassessing its aesthetic goals will prevent the pageant from serving as just another museum fixture in American culture, one continuing to house remnants of nineteenth-century art without dedicating space to new creative presentations. It is a question for future winners to address, whether the symbolic trophies—the crown, the gown, and the swimsuit—need to be refreshed with more relevant accoutrements.

Whether the icons of princess literature will relinquish their hold over young women's ideals is a question for parents to consider. "Cinderella," read across the globe, is more than an insinuation of its entertainment value. As a saga of women's ascension into the upper echelons, "Cinderella" is a formula for success. Her beauty is a caveat. As medical technologies make it easier to alter body images, the prospects for achieving ideal looks becomes feasible. This is truer for women who have economic resources. Healthcare workers could become the new magicians of external beauty. But they cannot mediate the problem of racial bias.

Since Vanessa Williams's ascendancy into an acting and singing career, other black females have entered and won pageants for cash and prizes. Kimberly Aiken, Miss America 1994, credits her entrance and subsequent win to Williams. "It was a huge motivation," Aiken said. Before being eliminated in the 2001 competition, Miss Kentucky, another African American contestant, exclaimed, "This is the dream." She was inspired not only by previous Black winners, but by the prospect of winning a title that every little girl is taught to covet. Miss America is the rapture of princess ideology.[24]

Notes

1. Betty Friedan, *The Feminine Mystique* (New York: W.W Norton, 1963); Simone de Beauvoir, *The Second Sex* Trans. H. M. Parshley) 1952; reprinted (New York: Vintage, 1989); Gwendolyn Brooks, *Maud Martha* (New York: Harper, 1953); Toni Morrison, *The Bluest Eye* (New York: Holt, Rinehart and Winston, 1970).
2. *People,* October 16, 2000: 138–175.
3. Melissa Milkie, "Social Comparisons, Reflected Appraisals, and Mass Media: The Impact of Pervasive Beauty Images on Black and White Girls' Self-Concepts," *Social Psychology Quarterly* 62, no. 2 (1999): 190–210.
4. Kay Stone, "Things Walt Disney Never Told Us," in *Women's Folklore Women's Culture,* ed. June Jordan, A. Rosan, and Susan Kalick, American Folklore Society 8 (Philadelphia: University of Pennsylvania Press, 1985): 130–142; Janet Malone, "The Self-Esteem of Women," *Human Development* 17, no. 2 (Summer 1996): 6; Kaz Cooke, *Real Gorgeous: The Truth about the Body and Beauty* (New York: Sagebrush Educational Resources, 1996).
5. Stone, "Things Walt Disney Never Told Us."
6. Kathryn Morgan, *Children of Strangers: The Stories of a Black Family* (Philadelphia: Temple University Press, 1980), xvi-xvii.

7. Raymond Firth, *Symbols, Public and Private* (Ithaca: Cornell University Press, 1983), 74; Marie Louise Von Franz, *The Feminine in Fairy Tales* (Dallas: 1972); Rosemary Minard, ed., *Womenfolk and Fairy Tales* (Boston: Houghton Mifflin, 1975); Sibylle Birkhauser-Oeri, "The Imprisoning Sorceress" in Marie-Louise Von Franz, eds., *The Mother: Archetypal Image in Fairy Tales* (Toronto: Inner City 1988), 15–21; Janice Lynn Stockard, *The Role of American Black Women in Folktales: An Interdisciplinary Study of Identification and Interpretation,* Ph.D. diss., Tulane University, 1979; Vladimir Propp, *Morphology of the Folktale,* trans. Laurence Scott (Austin: University of Texas Press, 1968; Alan Dundes *Cinderella: A Casebook* (Madison: University of Wisconsin Press, 1982), 25.

8. Versions of Cinderella have been discovered across the globe. See Dundes, *Cinderella;* also Jan Harold Brunvand, *The Study of American Folklore: An Introduction* (New York: Norton, 1986) on Kaarle Krohn, the Finnish folklorist who traced the presence of this kind of literature in different regions throughout the world and found it on nearly every continent.

9. *People,* 16 October 2000: 172.

10. Elwood Watson and Darcy Martin, "The Miss America Pageant: Pluralism, Femininity, and Cinderella All in One," Journal of Popular Culture 34, no. 1 (Summer 2000): 112.

11. *The Complete Fairy Tales of the Brothers Grimm,* trans. Jack Zipes (New York: 1988). One of the earliest literary accounts of Cinderella was found in ninth-century China. America's popularized version was created by Walt Disney and circulated in mass-market publications. These scripts revised the character into a narrow, passive, unactualized figure. See Jan Yolen, "America's Cinderella," in Dundes, ed., *Cinderella,* 295.

12. *People,* 16 October 2000: 136–138; Williams resigned when *Penthouse* magazine unearthed and published a series of nude photos.

13. On the history of African American women in beauty pageants, see R. Iset Anuakan, "We Real Cool: Beauty, Image, and Style in African American History," Ph.D. diss., Berkeley: University of California, 2002; also Shane White and Graham White, *Stylin': African American Expressive Culture From its Beginnings to the Zoot Suit* (New York: 1998).

14. Elaine Scarry, *On Beauty and Being Just* (Princeton, NJ: Princeton University Press 2001), 54–58; Efrat Tseëlon, *The Masque of Femininity: The Presentation of Woman in Everyday Life* (London: Sage, 1995); Paul Zanker, *The Mask of Socrates: The Image of the Intellectual in Antiquity,* trans. Alan Shapiro (Berkeley: University of California Press, 1995), 14.

15. Titles in *The Complete Fairy Tales of the Brothers Grimm.* Quote from "The White Bride and the Black Bride," 479; Excerpt from "Snow-White and Rose-Red," in Bryna and Louis Utermeyer, eds., *Old Friends and Lasting Favorites: The Golden Treasury of Children's Literature,* vol. 4 (New York: Golden, 1962): 86.

16. Utermeyer, *Old Friends and Lasting Favorites,* 86–99.

17. Firth, *Symbols, Public and Private,* 290.

18. Sibylle Birkhauser-Oeri, "The Imprisoning Sorceress," in *The Mother,* ed., Von Franz, 200.

19. Von Franz, *The Feminine in Fairy Tales;* Minard, *Womenfolk and Fairy Tales;* Stockard, "Role of American Black Women in Folktales," 20.

20. Max Luthi, *Once Upon a Time, On the Nature of Fairy Tales* (Bloomington: Indiana University Press, 1976); Barbara Walker, ed., *The Woman's Encyclopedia of Myths and Secrets* (New York: Harper & Row, 1983), 366. In folklore, the ideas of myth are considered to be the truth. The criteria folklorists use to characterize stories as true or not true are based on the figures rather than the events in the stories. For example, fables and trickster tales are not considered true because they contain animal characters (with anthropomorphic qualities). Myths are stories of the distant past in which human beings have magical powers, and are considered true. The latter are less apt to be disproved than the former.

21. CNN.com, "Bush Welfare Plan Promotes Marriage, Work," *Inside Politics,* 27 February 2002.

22. "Whatever Happened to the Black Miss Americas?" *Ebony* 57 (March 2002): 105; "50 Years of Black Beauty Queens," *Ebony* 51 (19 November 1995): 206; "Beauty, Another Black Miss America," Africana Gateway to the Black World, www.africana.com (26 September 2003).

23. MTV, interviews with Contestants in the Miss America Pageant (January 2002); A&E, "The Life of Hugh Hefner," *Biography* (February 2002); Nancy Etcoff, *Survival of the Prettiest: The Science of Beauty* (New York: Anchor 1999), 192–201.

24. *People,* 16 October 2000: 179; MTV, interviews with contestants.

6

Wiregrass Country Pageant Competitions, or What's Beauty Got to Do with It?

Jerrilyn McGregory

Someday I'll be Miss America
and that will be the happiest day of my life.

A historic region of the South, Wiregrass Country defies geopolitical boundaries. Covering a tri-state area, it begins above Savannah, sweeping across the rolling meadows of the Georgia coastal plain of a vast portion of southwest Georgia before fanning over into the southeastern corner of Alabama and dipping down into the northwest panhandle of Florida. Wiregrass, *Aristida stricta*, refers to a flora that depends on a fire ecosystem to germinate. Because of Smokey the Bear and other fire prevention campaigns, in our minds, fire is equated solely with destruction and devastation. Yet because of restrictions on burning, wiregrass no longer thrives as it once did. The so-called experts least understood the role of fire in the regeneration of the region's pine forest. The Wiregrass ecosystem created a unique set of circumstances, which contributed to the cultivation of a certain way of life. Those with any knowledge of the cultural area characterize it as being historically underpopulated, economically poor, and predominantly white.

Because of its supposedly poorer soil quality and the threat of malaria, the rustic frontier and not the aristocratic plantation typified the region's developmental history. Enslaved Africans were not widely owned in this part of the South. Instead, yeomen farmers populated Wiregrass Country and owned the largest farms. After emancipation, African Americans migrated into the region because of the prospects of becoming landowners themselves, since land was relatively cheap. As points of commonality, many within the Wiregrass region concede to being communal-minded, frugal, and hardworking people.

Locally and globally, small pageants are the sites where young women perform femininity according to a designated script. On one hand, pageantry speaks to the systemic nature of women's oppression; and on the other, it multivocally addresses the symbolism that accompanies wish fulfillment. How might one interpret the social construct involving young girls competing to become Miss Sweet Gum and Turpentine, Miss Peanut, or Miss Swine Time? Seemingly, every rural community in Wiregrass Country celebrates a local festival with a theme to feature an item of regional pride and, sometimes, esoteric interests such as peanut festivals, Gnat Day, and Possum and Mayhaw festivals. The crowning of the festival queen is the highlight of most. Contestants often use them to hone their skills to compete in a regional Miss America Organization (MAO) feeder pageant. In Wiregrass Country, recently, this level of contests includes Miss Tattnall County, Miss Thomasville, Miss Valdosta, Miss Georgia Southern (all of Georgia); Miss Panama City (Florida); Miss Greater Dothan, Miss Southeast Alabama and Miss Troy State (all of Alabama).

In Wiregrass Country, beauty pageants are the cornerstone of most community-based festivals. Festival parades do not come close to the level of the televised variety. However, they do engage the same social functions as ways of creating and celebrating community. Viewing these processions often requires less than a half hour of one's time Like the circus parades of the past and barnstorming baseball league parades, these processions operate as preliminaries to the main festival event. In most instances, without beauty queens, there would be no parade or festival. Since the parades themselves do not fulfill great expectations in the classic sense, with marching bands and an avalanche of floats, they instead offer motorcades teeming with beaming "beauties." These queens act as pied pipers or lures, leading the masses to the festival grounds. In the name of civic duty, these contestants present a self for public scrutiny. Entry into a pageant requires a monetary commitment from local sponsors with the possibility of the contestant winning an additional scholarship or prize.

For instance, in Wiregrass Georgia, Claxton's Rattlesnake Roundup promotes itself as "the beauty with the beasts" contest. Commencing in 1968, this festival owes its genesis to an actual snakebite fatality in the community. The queens were added as an afterthought the next festival year. The festival offers the odd dual spectacle of a beauty contest and an unpredictable and dramatic display of snake handling. The festival simultaneously conjoins a rattlesnake contest, with prizes for the most snakes captured and the biggest snake, and coronation of the round-up queen. In the context of this event, a biblical reference is unavoidable: Beauty contestants signify Eve tempted by a serpent and become themselves emblematic of masculine entrapment. Rattlesnake round-ups are relatively commonplace events within this region as well as elsewhere.[1]

As a by-product of western patriarchal society, female beauty is a normalizing standard, signifying, not merely beauty, but wholesomeness. Beauty, as reified through pageantry, is overdetermined by its construction of femininity in relation to the societal markers of modesty, domesticity, and delicacy. Beauty pageants prop up the old cult of true womanhood without significantly rewriting the script. The cult of true womanhood refers to a nineteenth-century culturally sanctioned belief in a feminine ideal. Foremost, it decreed the necessity of chastity, piety, and submissiveness as norms for women. In addition, the physical appearance and behavior of most contestants are aesthetically situated within certain "normative" standards. In actuality, the dynamic being judged pertains to the acquisition of a certain cultural literacy; that is, the contestant's ability to read and write herself in the language of society's cultural reproduction of its dualistic thinking regarding idealized beauty and femininity. The role of contestants, the role of the judges, the role of the sponsors, all coexist with set objectives and rewards.

For instance, the judges exemplify outside readers of a foregrounded text. Organizers tend to recruit outsiders. Folklorist Robert Lavenda writes: "Because they are from the outside, however, they are not aware of the local context within which the pageant unfolds—the status of the candidates' families, for example. In this contextual vacuum, they can judge only what they see."[2] Nonetheless, the judges certainly attend with their own idealized script of what will constitute competency in this performance. Of course, the outcome is left to the judge's own subjectivity. In a personal interview with a judge, as her criteria, she insisted that contestants, indeed, be physically beautiful. If young women enter a public ritual called a beauty pageant; then, in this judge's estimation, they should fulfill the western aesthetic of beauty. This judge perceived herself as a subversive force within the competition arena. She refused to be hoodwinked by the reinscribing of pageants as scholarship programs or defusing them with platforms and interview sessions. Despite her well-known stance, she regularly judges pageants. Her criteria, apparently, is not regarded as problematic by organizers.[3]

Feminist scholar Susan Brownmiller defines femininity "as a romantic sentiment, a nostalgic tradition of imposed limitations."[4] To succeed, contestants must suppress anything outside of these limitations, especially any markers of social class. By role playing, savvy contestants create an optimal experience for self by experimenting with otherness. When local Wiregrass contestants announce that they entered "for the fun of it," they do not necessarily delude themselves. Wiregrass pageants only require that a contender be ambulatory (no physically challenged need apply yet). They operate as mannequins modeling daytime apparel and evening gowns. Most pageants do not require personal interviews, platforms, or knowledge of current events. Yet, like early folk dramas, Wiregrass beauty pageants are parodic. Similar to voguing, where African American and Latino gay men perform a stylized mix of gymnastic dancing and modeling poses culled from the high-fashion photo pages of *Vogue* magazine to cross boundaries, pageant participants, too, parody a social reality to which many do not belong or necessarily aspire. Let us say, in the spirit of carnival, as part of the public display, they play at being what they are not.[5] As part of their transgression, beauty contestants play into gender or play out race or play around with social class. As literary critic Mikhail Bakhtin inscribed for carnivalesque festivals: "One of the indispensable elements of the folk festival was travesty, that is, the renewal of clothes and of the social image. Another essential element was a reversal of the hierarchic levels."[6] By playing into gender, a contestant participates in her own construction as a hyperfeminine creation.

Adding to this discussion, folklorist Beverly Stoeltje says: "Focusing on women's appearance and placing women in a competitive display event that licenses the public gaze on them, beauty contests utilize the principle of competition to determine the 'best,' the woman who comes closest to the ideal image of a woman in a given context."[7] However, as relates to cultural diversity issues, few researchers question the pluralistic conservatism that often requires the erasure of one's personal and ethnic identity to fit into even this level of pageantry. In *Beauty Queens on the Global Stage,* however, several articles attest to "how local knowledge and practices intersect with and diverge from Western ones."[8]

Wiregrass Country does not have a monopoly on pageants with a distinctive regional or ethnic flavor. In the United States, the Creek Nation in Oklahoma has its Muskogee Princess and Zeta Phi Beta, Inc., a black sorority, has its Miss Zeta, and so on. For American Indians, the competition often includes poise, personality, talent, an essay, interview, and traditional dress, the latter incorporating a localized aesthetic. For African Americans, traditionally, contestants competed on the basis of relatively impersonal ticket sells. Symbolically, someone from a low-income background with a sizable support network could defeat someone from the upper middle class. Outside local boundaries, success shifts, as communications scholar Sarah Banet-Weiser writes: "The charge for those African Americans who are represented in beauty pageants is to deny that racism exist simply by virtue of their representation in mainstream culture, while simultaneously constructing this representation in accordance with feminine disciplinary practices that translate into a white body."[9]

The Miss America Pageant system now has a multiethnic participant base, but it still retains an assimilationist, melting pot mode, rather than a truly multicultural one. The participation of ethnic contestants speaks to heterogeneity; however, the prologue demands homogeneity, one of the most important tasks of such formal structures. The inclusion of women of color evokes a false universality. The participation of minorities does not automatically empower, nor does it offer a diversity of cultural voices. Instead, these contestants must play out whiteness by conforming to the cultural literacy paradigm of that pageantry that demands. Many who discuss the diversity in beauty contests tend to center the "beauty myth." For instance, cultural anthropologist Penny Van Esterik says: "Thai women's groups also objected to beauty contests because they created a situation where a North American criterion of beauty—straight nose, large eyes—is encouraged, leading to a greater homogenization of standards for evaluating women's physical appearance."[10] Indeed, this criterion is an issue; however, Van Esterik critiques the Miss America Organization's implicit demand that contestants erase multiple layers of their "social reality."[11]

Pageantry unquestionably has a stronger hold in the South than in other regions. In fact, one of its historians has noted, "Atlantic City is south of the Mason-Dixon Line, and every day of the Pageant it drifts farther into Dixie. The modern Southern belle has, of course long been the Pageant Ideal, so that—even in those years when a Southerner does not win—the likely winner is still probably patterned after that type."[12] Yet a transformation of codes currently is in effect. Once locked into a historicism evoked by the "lost cause" sentiment, Wiregrass pageants currently abrogate this code. Although the southern belle rarely existed in the historic Wiregrass, the New South manufactured its share after the fact. Today, in regional pageants, those who don hooped skirts and debutante gowns rarely win in competition. Researchers such as Stoeltje privilege gender: "Certainly the more formal the dress is, the more it distinguishes the female from the male, calling attention to the subordination of women, especially in the formal gown which limits movement."[13] Yet any real breach usually involves culture or social class. As it might relate to pageantry, just recall the stir Venus and Serena Williams typically bring to the tennis world as their attire defies that sport's venerated traditions. Such fashion gaffes are not likely to be rewarded in the context of beauty pageants.

Pageantry functions more like a royal coronation than a southern debutante ball. Author Frank Deford interjects that "Since [the] U.S. has no royal family, Miss America serves as its homegrown Princess. She represents a fairy tale come true—a Cinderella found in the ranks of the commoner."[14] As fairy tale princesses, the script now engages a bowdlerized version of folktales. Adapted to the bourgeois value system, the classic fairy tale as recorded by the Grimms and others were sanitized to protect young children from vulgarities, rough language, and blasphemies, but not the cruelties. Psychologist Rita Freedman writes: "We are all fed a gourmet diet of Cinderella sagas and Miss America pageants, in which passivity is richly rewarded and beauty transformation buy security and love."[15] Stoeltje rightfully assesses beauty contests as a form of symbolic inversion: "Queens, like kings, are associated with monarchies, the opposite of democracies, so their appearance in modern societies constitutes a form of symbolic inversion."[16] The coronation mystique, no doubt, has trickled down to influence pageantry on all levels today.

In 1938, Miss America contests adopted the talent competition as a requirement. The MAO then intimidated state pageants to count talent double relative to other criteria. The talent competition promotes a unitary and elitist view of culture. State and local pageants resent it because they recognize, too, that the requirement is exclusionary and serves only to enhance the nationally televised pageant, weeding out many local hopefuls. According to feminist Jane Kneller, "Taste and femininity contribute to culture only when they exhibit discipline and restraint."[17] The pageant values talents that only people of a certain socioeconomic class can afford to cultivate. In past eras, "archery, with balloons as targets; reciting the Lord's Prayer in Indian sign language; and fly-casting qualified."[18] Most Wiregrass pageants (with the exception of feeder pageants to the MAO) do not privilege talent, exhibiting the tensions between elite and popular culture. The disparity between the talent component of the Miss American Pageant, where talent counts twice as much as the other categories, and other pageants is well known within this system.

In another regard, although there is no criterion upholding virginity, the edict that women be never married and without children at least symbolizes chastity. Because most judges hail from outside a community, the danger of selecting the "biggest whore" in town constitutes a critical deception. The societal expectation is that the one labeled, "whore" will be unable to negotiate boundaries signaling respectability properly. However, systemic "failures" transmit an inured message. To attain one's goal only to face public ostracism sours the experience and acts to censor sexuality. Vanessa Williams's scandalized short reign as Miss America reinforced this concern.[19] The overall effect results in a maintenance of a strategy directed toward impressionable young women, propping up the cult of true womanhood.

Furthermore, locally, to legitimize pageants, swimsuit competitions have fallen from grace, sometimes replaced by a platform.[20] The platform is purported to allow contestants to champion social causes; however, highly politicized issues such as Amnesty International or abortion rights rarely emerge. Rather, the platforms promote noble, safe social causes such as literacy and the prevention of teen pregnancy. For instance, I judged a local pageant in which the following platforms held sway: "a no-nonsense approach to HIV/AIDS education"; "I am H.E.A.L.E.D. (Helping Encourage Adoptions Legally, Easily and Debt-Free)"; "Saying Yes to Life," a positive approach to saying no to drugs; "Building Dreamers," cultivating children with set goals; and "Mentoring with Music." Such platforms echo those in which the first lady now directs a national platform to establish a separate identity from the president. For example, Laura Bush's national first lady platform battles illiteracy. Contestant choices, too, tend toward direct social policies central to the family, community, and domesticity.

To rationalize their willingness to fashion themselves into passive objects of beauty, contestants cite poise, discipline, and confidence as the intangible gains. These qualities are privileged in our society, and practice makes perfect. Until the introduction of question-and-answer sessions or interviews into pageantry, graceful body movement was the main dynamic requirement. According to Susan Brownmiller, in *Femininity,* "grace may be defined as an aesthetic value that we place on fluid, coordinated motion."[21] Walking and pivoting is to pageantry what the skyhook and slamdunking is to basketball. To move with grace is to walk in beauty. As Freedman notes, "Their special beauty is not innate but an acquired disguise. To act out a myth is to impersonate a caricature."[22] In Wiregrass Country, they walk; but rarely do they talk.

Once again, the exception is those few pageants that lead to appearances in state competitions and ultimately Miss America. The presence of young, successful men as judges, pageant directors, and producers cannot be ignored. On the panel on which I served, the two male judges worked for a brokerage firm and a management consultant firm. They also served major roles throughout the state of Florida's pageant system. One was appointed head judge. Prior to the evening's contest, we scored contestants in a formal interview constituting 30 percent of the outcome. These men possessed large binders containing literally hundreds of interview questions. One question asked: "How do you define traditional family?" Only the African American contestant, a student at the University of Florida, spoke with conviction about a personalized platform dealing with sexual harassment. She did not win.

We have thus far examined young women's participation in pageantry; however, most pageants in Wiregrass Country also incorporate young girls and, to a lesser extent, boys. Today's contestants first enter as candidates at high school football homecoming queen contests, competing to be Junior Miss, Little Miss, and Wee Miss, or Diaper Princess. In competition, judges select a winner on the basis of a Sunday dress criteria alone. Although few pageants require any viable talent, the children's parents often enroll potential participants in dance or gymnastic schools to gain competence in performance. Many teenagers are pageant veterans by their senior year in high school. Those who enter at tender ages, as part of their enculturation, are being socialized into the world of pageantry. According to play theory, play prepares the child for adulthood.

Although pageantry is problematic enough for women who must mask any sense of self derived from race, class, feminism, or sexual orientation, for children, who have not fully formed a sense of self, it is even more problematic. According to Freedman: "Children also learn that power and happiness do not come to women through active pursuit and assertive engagement with life, but rather through obedience, servitude, patience, and, ultimately, through the magic of cosmetic make-over."[23] This chapter does not engage the issue of pedophilia. Nonetheless, one must be concerned about the sexualizing of little girls in pageantry.[24] Brownmiller graphically notes this process: "Color her eyes, color her lips, color her cheeks, color her fingertips and toenails."[25] A little girl pretending with makeup may seem relatively harmless; however, as institutionalized through pageantry, one senses a more overt training in submission to patriarchal power. In many regards, play can show children how to disrupt established forms and effect social change. Transgressive play can be used to reveal unjust practices in such a way as to suggest specific cures.

On another level, the "pageant mom" obtains legendary proportion. Without revision, motherhood customarily becomes problematized as a text. Mothers often are villainized as the culprits who produce eating disorders, homosexual children, and aggressive pageant queens. Like the stage mom, the pageant mom is stereotyped as a scourge, living out her own ambitions through her daughter. One pageant winner informed me that her mother vicariously reinvented herself through her daughter's victories. Another pageant queen described how she and her pageant mom operated as a team. At pageants, her mother lurked in bushes to photograph highlights and also used surveillance schemes to gain insider information. Moreover, personal experience narratives are riddled with lore about the deadbeat pageant mom who literally burns her daughter out. Then there is the legend of the maniacal pageant mom who, according to some, murdered her boss to obtain money for her daughter's wardrobe. There are endless stories of divorces fueled by such pageant fanaticisms. Ironically, Brownmiller, too, says: "Aggressive nurturance looms as yet another unfeminine fault, or perhaps as a contradiction in terms."[26] Motherhood and ambition are interpreted as negative forces.

Although containing parodic elements, the intent of contestants does not appear to be to disrupt. Instead, their intent is to achieve some gain—whether self-valuation, monetary, or just a moment of fame. The impetus to gain something, however, also implies a lack. What women, locally and globally, often lack is visibility. Pageantry, along with sports and scholastics, offers a degree of redress. To aspire through pageantry, though, requires that one play into the very system that oppresses with patriarchal tools that excessively universalize a set beauty standard as well as establishing certain norms. As a result, to be deemed the winner, contestants must suppress any cultural markers signifying a particular race, social class, or sexual orientation. What appears on the surface to be multicultural, in reality, just reinforces the status quo.

Notes

I base this chapter on Wiregrass fieldwork in which I engaged in participation observation, conducted interviews, and served as judge for the now-defunct Miss West Florida Scholarship Pageant. In 1994, I documented a children's performance at Glennville, Georgia's Sweet Onion Festival, which featured these lyrics.

1. Beverly Stoeltje interrogates a Texas variant of the same public display. She writes, "Whether one associates snakes with serpents of the Garden of Eden, bearing knowledge and connoting evil, or with the phallic symbolism so pervasive in popular culture, or with the murky unconscious, snakes reverberate with symbolic messages suggesting the power and danger of sexuality." Stoeltje, "The Snake Charmer Queen: Ritual Competition, and Signification in American Festival in *Beauty Queens on the Global Stage*, ed. C. Cohen, R. Wilk, and B. Stoeltje (New York: Routledge, 1996), 20. Her assessment ultimately empowers women beauty contestants, but she overlooks the cultural imperialism these pageants reinforce. Also, structurally, the Texas round-up does not contain the same structural units as those in Wiregrass Country. Opp, Alabama along with Fitzgerald and Whigham, Georgia are the sites of other rattlesnake round-ups in this region.

2. Robert Lavenda, "Minnesota Queen Pageants: Play, Fun and Dead Seriousness in a Festive Mode," *Journal of American Folklore* 101 (1988): 171.

3. Sarah Banet-Weiser, too, in *The Most Beautiful Girl in the World: Beauty Pageants and National Identity* (Berkeley: University of California Press, 1999), notes the dialectical relationship between calling such contests "beauty pageants" or "scholarship pageants," 69–71.

4. Susan Brownmiller, *Femininity* (New York: Linden Press/Simon & Schuster, 1984), 14.

5. A seminal definition of play derives from Huizinga, who says "play is a voluntary activity executed within certain fixed limits of time and place, according to rules freely accepted but absolutely binding, having its aim in itself and accompanied by a feeling of tension, joy, and the consciousness that it is 'different' from 'ordinary life,'" 47.

6. Mikhail Bakhtin, *Rabelais and His World*. Trans. Helene Iswolsky. (Bloomington: Indiana University Press, 1984), 81.

7. Stoeltje, "Snake Charmer Queen," 18.

8. Cohen and Wilk, "Introduction," *Beauty Queens*, 10.

9. Banet-Weiser, *The Most Beautiful Girl,* 137.

10. Penny Van Esterik, "The Politics of Beauty in Thailand," in *Beauty Queens on the Global Stage,* 204.

11. Satya Mohanty, "The Epistemic Status of Cultural Identity: On Beloved and the Postcolonial
    Condition." *Cultural Critique* (Spring 1993): 41–78.

12. Frank Deford, *There She Is: The Life and Times of Miss America* (1971; reprint New York:
    Penguin Books, 1978), 220.

13. Stoeltje, "Snake Charmer Queen," 230.

14. Deford, *There She Is,* 221.

15. Rita Freedman, *Beauty Bound.* (Lexington, MA: D. C. Heath and Company, 1986), 70.

16. Stoeltje, "Snake Charmer Queen," 15.

17. Jane Kneller, "Discipline and Silence: Women and Imagination in Kant's Theory of Taste," in *Aesthetics and Feminist Perspective,* ed. Hilde Hein and Carolyn Korsmeyer (Bloomington, IN: Indiana University Press, 1993), 182.

18. Quote is by Nancie Martin in *Miss America Through the Looking Glass: The Story behind the Scenes* (New York: Messner, 1985), 27. Stoeltje footnotes that "Since 1990 a talent component has been added to the contest, challenging the contestants to invest more time and preparation in the event," Stoeltje, "Snake Charmer Queen," 29. With Texas, as the site for the pageants Stoeltje studied, given its diverse population and border location, one could extrapolate that talent becomes a guise to delimit participation, not merely based on race but social class, especially if its contestants tend to have MAP aspirations.

19. See chapter 3 for a more detailed interpretive analysis.

20. With the exception of local MAO feeder pageants, in which contestants must compete in bathing suits, most other Wiregrass pageants eschew having their young neighbors parade before judges in swimwear.

21. Brownmiller, *Femininity,* 178.

22. Freedman, *Beauty Bound,* 47.

23. Ibid., 157.

24. Remember Jon-Benet Ramsey's unsolved murder, which was the first introduction of this level of pageantry to the nation.

25. Brownmiller, *Femininity,* 228

26. Ibid.

Part III

Personal Reflections

I Was Miss Meridian 1985

SORORPHOBIA, KITSCH, AND LOCAL PAGEANTRY

Donelle R. Ruwe

I am a scholar of British Romanticism, an award-winning poet, an English professor, and Miss Meridian 1985. My older sister, whom I defeated for the Miss Meridian crown, won Miss Boise that same year, and we competed against each other for Miss Idaho. We did not win, though this time around my sister placed higher than I and was awarded second runner-up. My younger sister was in pageants too. She became Miss Meridian after me and, several years later, won the Miss Idaho crown and went on to the 1990 Miss America Pageant in Atlantic City. My sisters and I swapped performance outfits, shoes, rhinestone jewelry, and swimsuits. We sewed on sequins and glued glitter for each other; we critiqued each other's speeches and runway walks; we ran mock interviews. We had a wonderful time traveling around the state, competing in local pageants, and racking up college scholarships and clothing allowances. My older sister and I had no romantic illusions about becoming national winners, so when we finished college, debt-free, we contacted up-and-coming pageanteers and sold our sequined wardrobes for a nice profit.[1]

My understandings of the body, gender performance, and sisterhood were shaped in surprisingly positive, perhaps even feminist ways by my experiences in the local and state levels of the Miss America Pageant system. Although I do not insist that the American beauty pageant is a cultural and aesthetic gem that must be preserved at all costs, I do insist that we who are feminists and scholars challenge the blanket assumption that the effects of the beauty pageant system are only destructive and antiprogressive. I ask two fundamental questions in this chapter: Can the lived experience of the pageant, as distinct from the imaginary ideal promoted by the pageant, be empowering to the individual women who participate? I suggest yes and, in the first section of my chapter, offer my own lived experience as an anecdotal example. Through personal recollection, I show how pageants construct gender by identifying specific repetitions of acts and regulatory practices found at the local levels of the Miss America system: These formally (and informally) regulated acts include everything from the Miss America runway walk and wave to the memorization of perky, programmed interview answers. I then suggest how specific material practices can produce unpredictable effects that run counter to the dominant, misogynistic discourse of the pageant. My second question arises from the first. Although I understand why mainstream feminism is uninterested in acknowledging that the lived experience of the pageant can produce positive effects, why have feminist scholars not even examined the actual material practice of local and regional pageants? I offer several explanations for this lack of analysis in my conclusion: sororophobia and kitsch attribution.

I begin with an essential point—Miss America does not exist. She is an imaginary construct as the Miss America theme song itself shamelessly reveals, "There she is, your ideal." As an ideal representation of a particular kind of 1950s' femininity, "Miss America" the image is well worth protesting. The beauty pageant, as an instrument reinforcing hegemonic ideals of gender, is useful for feminists in part because its degrading idealizations of femininity are obvious rather than implied and are played out in a national arena. In other words, the pageant is more than just another social practice that constitutes and validates the power relations between men and women: The obviousness of this specific social practice exposes these power relations and thereby opens up the system to challenges. Thus, the 1968 "No More Miss America" protest-in which bras, wigs, and curlers were thrown into a huge "freedom trash can"—was effective in allowing feminists to manifest their beliefs, with great clarity and before a national audience, for the Miss America Pageant was then and is now an instantly identifiable distillation of the patriarchal ideal of femininity opposed by feminists.[2] The 1968 protest was so successful, it became *the* touchstone moment of 1960s radical feminism in the public's eyes, and feminists were ever after labeled, inaccurately, as bra burners. As a widely recognized construction of a particular ideal of femininity, then, Miss America always has been of practical use to feminists.

But there is a significant gap between the imaginary and troubling ideal and the lived experience of a quarter of a million real women who perform the Miss

America version of femininity in thousands of local and state pageants. As feminist scholar Susan Bordo notes, although our cultural work as feminists can and should expose the oppressiveness of social institutions such as the Miss America Pageant system, the pleasures of participation, of decorating and shaping the body, can have subversive potential. Although social control constrains the body, creative and resistant responses continually disrupt that control. Imaginary, hegemonic ideals (such as Miss America) are fairly stable, but actual subjects (the pageant participants) are active, fragmented, and unpredictable. Actual subjects often "confound dominant discourse." For example, a woman may believe in a damaging ideal, such as that only thin women are attractive. However, in the process of dieting and exercising, a woman actually might improve her physical health and energy level and thereby also gain self-esteem and greater independence.[3] In other words, although a system is oppressive, the individual effects of the oppressive system on the oppressed are idiosyncratic and unpredictable.

In making my argument, I am attempting to shift our discussion about the pageant system from an earlier mode of feminist discourse, which attacks patriarchal systems for objectifying and denigrating women as the second sex (a mode sometimes derogatorily called "victim feminism"), to a different mode, which attempts to locate women's individual agency within patriarchal systems. By applying this second feminist mode to the beauty pageant system, I am able to ask not only why women voluntarily participate in something as degrading as a beauty pageant, but whether it is possible that an individual agent, such as myself, might participate in a such a system and receive unexpectedly positive consequences.

The Material Practice of the Local Pageant

Each staging of a beauty pageant, in contrast to the imaginary ideal of Miss America, is a material practice, a system of repeated performances of specific bodies that are in the ongoing process of becoming gendered. Individual participants are learning, practicing, and thereby internalizing the pageant's version of womanhood. Today the material practice of pageantry appears within multiple disciplines, modes, and moments of American society: the Miss Rodeo America pageant, the Mrs. America pageant, the Mr. Universe bodybuilding contest, high school cheerleading contests, and even television shows like *Who Wants to Marry a Millionaire?* These pageants and pageant variations are each precisely the sorts of stylized repetitions of acts that constitute gender.[4] In this version of gender creation, what must be examined is not the idealized image but the repetitions of acts, the reiteration of norms through various regulatory practices that materialize sex/gender.

The actual practice of the thousands of local and regional pageants that take place across America has little in common with the nationally televised Miss America finals. The preliminary rounds of the national pageant have been on-going for several nights before the final, televised event. These preliminary rounds are judged by trained and experienced pageant judges, unlike the celebrity judges who appear in the televised final. Only those contestants who have already honed their "Miss America" pageant act and image through years of regional and state competition make it to the top ten. The extremely stylized performances—the walk, hand wave, smile, hairdo, tone of voice—are all prac-ticed behaviors, learned through years laboring in the ranks of state, regional, and local levels of the pageant.

All pageants sponsored by the nonprofit Miss America Association must fol-low the national pageant board's rules and guidelines. In the years when I was competing, 1984 to 1986, the winners were selected based on the following weighted criteria: 15 percent swimsuit, 15 percent evening gown, 30 percent in-terview, and 40 percent talent. Each competition area was strictly regulated. The talent performance could last no more than two minutes, and no clothing could be removed or the contestant would be disqualified. The swimsuit had to be a plain-colored one-piece with no cut-out sections, and each contestant wore pumps, not sandals, with the swimsuit.[5] The interview with the judges lasted thirty minutes. I signed a contract each time I entered a pageant: I testified that I was not and had not been married; that I had had no children and was not pregnant; and that I was between the ages of seventeen and twenty-six. Contes-tants could compete in more than one pageant as long as they did not hold a current title. As soon as someone won a "crown" (in my case, Miss Meridian 1985), she then moved on to the state level and represented her local pageant at the state competition (Miss Idaho). Once the state competition was over, and one had relinquished her crown to the next local winner, she could start again at the local levels and try to make her way up to the state level once more. In the Miss America system, contestants pay no fees to enter pageants; and the pageant is required to offer scholarship money to the winner and/or the runners-up. The Miss USA franchise, by contrast, did require an entrance fee. In the mid-1980s, each pageant competitor in the Miss Idaho-USA pageant had to have a sponsor, who paid over $300 to the pageant.

In the 1980s, the Miss America Pageant system was the largest distributor of scholarships for women in the United States. The scholarships were not large, particularly at the local level, but they were numerous. I won six differ-ent scholarships through the Miss America system, although all combined they totaled less than $1,300.[6] Clearly, my incentive to enter local pageants was not monetary but something else. For me, frankly, it was about wearing glamorous clothes and feeling beautiful. I was not a beautiful child. I wore braces, orthodontic headgear, and glasses in grade school and junior high. In high school, I wore a back brace to correct a curvature of the spine. I was a good student and an active musician, but I stayed away from public competitions and avoided thinking about my body whenever possible. I never competed for cheerleader, class officer, or prom queen, and I would never have thought to compete in a pageant if my sisters and I had not been solicited by pageant organizers. I knew that I was a talented pianist; I did not realize that I was a potential "beauty queen" until I became one. Participating in a pageant changes a woman's relationship to her body. For me, ironically, the change was positive.

I competed in five pageants: one local, three at-large, and one state.[7] I attended multiple others, frequently as a guest, emcee, or performer. I even worked behind the scenes: for example, I conducted mock interviews for contestants. To provide a clearer sense of the material practices of local pageants, I will focus on three of the pageants in which I competed: Miss Meridian 1984 and two at-large pageants, Miss Idaho National Guard and Miss Eastern Idaho.

The Miss Meridian pageant was a carefully orchestrated affair. The pageant staff and co-chairs included a local medical doctor, the branch president of a local bank, and a funeral home director. In addition to the regular staff, each contestant was assigned a volunteer assistant who worked backstage on the day of competition, helping contestants to change costumes quickly and fix their hair. Despite only nine young women having entered the contest, the organizers took their mission seriously: The first orientation meeting for the pageant was held on June 19, and between the orientation session and the pageant on August 9, they sponsored fourteen seminars, gatherings, and practice sessions. These included a judging seminar, "What Are the Judges Looking For?"; three modeling and poise workshops; clothing consultations; hair and makeup seminars; mock interviews; talent workshops; luncheons at a senior citizen's home and at the Chamber of Commerce; an interview on the local CBS affiliate station; a field trip to observe the neighboring Miss Washington County Pageant; rehearsals; and a swimming party. These seminars and workshops, essentially a variation on a finishing school for young ladies, were free to the contestants. One of the prizes that I received as Miss Meridian was a gift certificate to attend a course at the Blanche B. Evans's School of Modeling. I attended the course and spent two hours each Saturday for six weeks learning how to walk down a runway in high heels and to make runway turns. The course did, in fact, help me to walk more gracefully.

Over a thousand individuals, more women than men, attended the Miss Meridian pageant, which was held in the middle school auditorium, an astonishing number for, in the early 1980s, Meridian's population was approximately seven thousand people.[8] The actual stage performances of the competitors varied much more in quality than the presentations at the national, televised competition. The most common talent was singing a current pop ballad or Broadway number. I saw other young women perform ballet, drill team routines, banjo (my older sister's talent), fiddle (my younger sister's talent), koto (a Japanese zitherlike instrument), baton twirling, and saxophone. In the swimsuit competition, the young women were of dramatically varying sizes and body types; none of us was even close to the ideal figures presented at the national competition. For the evening gown presentation, some contestants wore prom dresses or bridesmaid's gowns. The more experienced, polished contestants in my era wore flat-sequined sheaths, an evening gown style that had just replaced the long, chiffon dress. Most contestants ordered gowns from bridal catalogs, although I did know a few women who had gone to dress shops in Salt Lake City that catered to pageant competitors. My sisters and I got our dresses secondhand or on sale and then doctored them with glitter or sequinned patterns that we purchased from ballet and dance supply shops. We videotaped the national competition and studied how these winners set up their performances, outfits, hair, and makeup. We learned certain "tricks," such as smearing Vaseline over our teeth so that they would look shiny onstage, and our lips would not stick after smiling nonstop for twenty minutes. We learned that we could duct-tape the outsides of our breasts together for the swimsuit competition (to provide the same sort of lift and illusion of fullness offered by a Wonderbra).

After I won the Miss Meridian competition, I received a "Judges Critique," a typed, one-page document containing an in-depth critique of my effectiveness in the interview, evening gown, talent, and swimsuit competitions. For example, the judges had specific suggestions for improving my physical appearance: I needed a more graceful walk; I needed to "tone thighs and firm legs with exercise"; I needed a new hairstyle and flair with makeup and clothes. The commentary I received about my performance in the interview is particularly revealing of the pageant's gender expectations. Although the interview portion should not be evaluated on appearance but rather on intelligence, the judges' comments included: "Be aware of posture during interview, especially not to relax legs into an unsightly position. Need to have more eye contact with judges, eyes have a tendency to wander at times. Needs to be more knowledgeable about our State and current events in general. Needs to have *warmer feeling* toward person she is communicating with at the time. Be observant in conversation, be interested in other person and project a *warmer feeling*" [emphasis added]. The judges' comments were explicitly gendered, for example, in their expectation that I project emotional warmth in my interview and maintain a controlled, ladylike posture at all times. The critique told me that I should behave in a less self-assured way: "It's good to be self-assured; however, a sprinkling of humility would be most becoming." One judge suggested that the "problem" was that I overenunciated my words and that they sounded, therefore, clipped and brusque. I now attribute these comments to the pageant system's expectation that women be warm and good-natured, but not be intellectual, challenging, argumentative, aggressive, or professional. In fact, comments such as these confirm our worst expectations of the pageant and its promotion of a submissive, decorous femininity.

In addition to this local pageant, I also entered several at-large pageants. Unlike local pageants, at-large pageants accept contestants from larger regions and can be handled in a much more pro-forma manner. The contestants in these pageants often were experienced competitors who had been finalists in local pageants or who had previously won their area's local pageant, and so were ineligible to compete for a local title again, but who wanted another chance to compete at the state level.[9] Idaho had two at-large pageants: Miss Idaho National Guard (contestants had to be Idahoans) and Miss Eastern Idaho (contestants had to come from eastern Idaho). The Miss Idaho National Guard pageant was held in the officer's club of the National Guard Base in Mountain Home, Idaho. The contest took one day. The judge's interview happened in the morning; the contestants ran through their numbers and practiced where to stand for the swimsuit and evening gown judging in the afternoon; and the contest happened at night. The stage was tiny, and the sixty or so family members and friends who attended sat in folding chairs. It was a no-nonsense show for both the organizers and the competition. It was my first pageant. I was first runner-up and won a Seiko watch. Only the winner received scholarship money.

The other at-large pageant that I entered was Miss Eastern Idaho. This pageant's character was shaped by the politics of eastern Idaho, and the organizers actually engaged in some questionable practices. Eastern Idaho is rural, primarily agricultural, and, in terms of religion, approximately 98 percent Latter Day Saints (Mormons).[10] In the Miss Eastern Idaho pageant in which I competed, my older sister and I were "ringers," non-Mormons who came from Idaho's only populous area, the Boise valley. The Mormon organizers of this pageant broke with the official Miss America rules. They elected to have the swimsuit portion of the contest the night before the actual contest and in the home of one of the contest organizers. I have no doubt that the organizers provided a private swimsuit showing in order to protect the modesty of the young, unmarried female contestants (sleeveless blouses are against Mormon teachings) and that they felt morally justified in doing so. Whatever their motivations, it was inappropriate. In the national arena the following year, the conservative gender politics of the Miss America pageant and of the Mormon religion came together. The same year that I won Miss Meridian, Sharlene Wells, a Mormon and Miss Utah, was crowned Miss America 1985. Her conservative, morally upright attitude appealed to the pageant community, which was still reeling from the scandals following the publication of the erotic photographs of Vanessa Williams, the previous year's Miss America. My local Meridian pageant was also closely aligned with the Mormon faith: The first Miss Meridian was a young Mormon woman who had graduated in my high school class. In Meridian's third pageant, when I was the reigning queen, she was invited back by the pageant's Mormon director to act as the emcee. He and she performed an original running skit throughout the evening's show in which he acted the part of the "pageant angel," who was overseeing the young women competing for the crown, while she relived the highlights of her year and sang Andrew Lloyd Webber's "Memories." Figures of angels are profoundly important to the Mormon faith, for it was founded by Joseph Smith after he was led by the Angel Moroni, a resurrected ancient prophet and warrior, to the place where golden tablets containing new versions of scripture were buried in a hillside in New York state.

Because local pageants such as these are organized by nonprofessionals to meet the demands of the audience, the community, the organizers, and the contestants, they reveal the ways in which performances of gender, even within a standardized system such as the Miss America Pageant, are always contextualized, local, and in excess of the system. Indeed, my most profound memories of my years of participating in the pageants are about two things: my changing feelings about my physical body, and my realizations of how the ideals of the Mormon faith became imbricated within a supposedly neutral, national system. I saw how the pageant producer never even questioned the suitability of developing a pageant script in which an angel was overseeing the selection of the winner. I saw how the swimsuit competition was kept off-stage in eastern Idaho. The paternalism of Mormon elders, particularly in predominantly Mormon communities, can be almost palpable. It is an intensely patriarchal faith, from its early roots in polygamy to its contemporary focus on the importance of women bearing multiple children (childbearing can be a woman's entry into heaven) and the importance of women's submission to the authority of men and the church's (male) elders.

The Pageant as American Kitsch

Although documents like as my "Judges Critique" could provide rich fodder for scholarly analysis, feminist scholars have not yet addressed the material practices of the pageant. Historically, feminism has desired to see women as sisters united against patriarchal oppression. Feminists often elide the differences between women by seeing all women as "others" within patriarchal systems and by emphasizing a utopian sisterhood rather than female competitiveness. On one hand, patriarchy has a similar desire—that women behave noncompetitively—

but on the other hand, patriarchy fears that women, in behaving non-competitively, might even unite.[11] Both these desires for and fears of female solidarity are satisfied by the beauty pageant.

The feminist literary critic Helena Michie has named patriarchy's fear of women as sisterhood "sororophobia." The pageant is a sororophobic display in that it stages comforting, if contradictory, responses to patriarchy's fears of female unity and female aggressiveness.[12] First, the pageant provides images of women who behave with a socially acceptable congeniality, as when they hug their competitors on stage or vote for a "Miss Congeniality." Second, the pageant is an overt display of women's disunity, a comforting or even titillating exhibition of women competing against women for the pleasure of men.[13] Interestingly, the Miss Congeniality award is not a standard part of the Miss America beauty pageant system, and individual pageants can choose or not choose to present this award. That the popular imagination has fixated on this side element of the pageant—as demonstrated by the popularity of the recent Sandra Bullock blockbuster *Miss Congeniality*—suggests society's deep investment in watching women simultaneously compete and display friendship. Bullock's character is a masculinized woman in a violent profession (the opening scenes even present her physically fighting with her male partner). Once she goes undercover and enters the pageant, she begins to take on the trappings of femininity and to develop friendships with women. Ultimately, Bullock's character abandons competition with her male partner in exchange for affectionate kinship with women (even receiving the pageant's "Miss Congeniality" award) and a simultaneous active competition with women (the women pageanteers and the corrupt, controlling woman who runs the national pageant).

The complex academic and societal responses to women's unity and women's competitiveness explain only a small part of feminism's disapproval of the pageant and society's fascination with it. An additional explanation for feminism's reluctance to analyze the material practice of the local pageant is found when we consider the aesthetic value of the pageant itself. I link the beauty pageant—its displays of music, dance, and theater, the tawdry display of beauty, and commodified presentation of the female body—to kitsch. I suggest that academia's distaste for analyzing the pageant can be linked to a profound fear of being associated with kitsch. This fear is expressed not only by feminists and academia at large, but even by the pageant participants themselves. The kitschy iconography of Miss America is familiar to all Americans: her sash, rhinestone crown, the big glowing (lipstick-ringed) smile, the runway walk and wave, the bouquet of roses. The image is repeated year after year in the national pageant and repeated in the state, regional, and local pageants, and, indeed, even in my local pageant.[14] The images of the pageant are one level of kitsch, and the actual performances of the contestants are yet another level of kitsch. The two-minute melodramatic renditions of classical music, jazz ballads, or dance are the very image of high art being rendered in a popular context, with no redeeming sense of irony.[15]

I do not challenge the kitschiness of the pageant itself or of particular pageanteers' performances. What I do suggest is that feminism and academia at large have not given the pageant's material practice adequate consideration because of a fear of being contaminated by kitsch. The contemporary queer theorist Eve Kosofsky Sedgwick has identified and explored this fear of kitsch contamination, which she terms "kitsch attribution." Sedgwick shifts analysis away from the typical focus on kitsch as a thematic or subject matter (calendar shots of kittens playing with red yarn balls, for example, or melodramatic renditions of Broadway songs). Instead, she defines kitsch as a structure of human response and relation, typically one involving author or audience relations of spectacle. Something kitschy is something audiences might identify as insincere or manipulative. Kitsch is not a quality that inheres in objects, it is something grafted onto the object through the audience's response. Thus, when spectators or critics call something kitschy, they are attempting to distance themselves from the contagion of being identified with something kitschy. To ask if something *is* kitsch means that it *becomes* kitsch and, as if it were a contagion, must always be held at arm's distance-a process of kitsch attribution that always proclaims: "I am not one of those people taken in by this tacky thing." The use of the epithet "kitschy" claims to exempt knowing critics from the contagion of the kitsch object by demonstrating, on one hand, that they are not taken in by kitsch and by positing, on the other hand, the existence of a true kitsch consumer. The true kitsch consumer is imagined to be completely naive and uncritical and, thus, to be completely vulnerable to manipulation by the kitsch object and kitsch creator.[16] For the intellectual, the feminist, or the cultural critic (and I include myself in all of these categories), the pleasure of watching or participating in a pageant becomes a kind of voyeurism, a guilty pleasure that must be hidden and denied.

The narratives of prior Miss Americas and other beauty pageant participants provide rich examples of kitsch attribution. Over and over again, these narratives show beauty queens defensively explaining that, although they participated in pageants, they were never taken in by them. Bess Myerson, the first and so far only Jewish Miss America, explains that she would never have entered the pageant if it had been up to her and that it was all her mother's fault, her mother made her do it. Her mother entered her without her knowledge, and then her mother forced her hand by contacting her employers directly to arrange for Myerson to take time off work to participate. The author of Myerson's personal narrative, Susan Dworkin, indicates repeatedly that Myerson had no choice, that others made her do it. As Miss America, Myerson traveled the country on behalf of the pageant and then for the Anti-Defamation League of B'nai B'rith. Her visibility led to a spot as a panelist on popular television shows. She then became commissioner of consumer affairs in New York City, promoting far-reaching consumer protection legislation and earning a *Life* magazine cover for her efforts. She eventually served as Mayor Ed Koch's commissioner of cultural affairs. Although Myerson's political and professional success is directly connected to her celebrity as Miss America, she speaks of the title as an embarrassment that the public (as if it were a deluded kitsch consumer) will not let her live down.[17] Sharlene Wells also distanced herself from Miss America, claiming that she competed only for the scholarship opportunities, that "she would never [have taken] part in 'one of those contests'" if not for the scholarships.[18] The intensity of Wells's scorn—"those contests"—is not surprising given that she, as the then-current Miss America, needed to work especially hard to distance herself from the kitsch contagion of the pageant.

Even Anastasia Makeeva, Miss Akademia 2001, who won a pageant in Russia endorsed by the Ministries of Education and Culture, denied her engagement in the pageant. She was a voice student who entered the contest, she explains, by sheer happenstance. She stumbled on a poster listing a famous singer as one of the judges. This Russian pageant, which the Ministries of Education and Culture claim will develop "alternative forms of student activity and a civilized attitude toward female beauty," adopts all of the kitschy iconography of the Miss America Pageant: The just-crowned winner carries a full bouquet of flowers, boasts a big, lipstick-ringed smile, and wears a rhinestone crown and a white sash emblazoned with the title "Miss Akademia." Further, in a *Chronicle of Higher Education* article about this pageant, the author's tone exemplifies kitsch attribution. Whether the writer, Bryon MacWilliams, enjoyed the pageant or not, his pleasure is couched in an ironic mode. His feature article focuses on the materialism of the pageant and its sponsors, and he is careful to identify for his scholarly audience all of its tacky moments. His pleasure is not in the show itself, but in identifying the kitschy elements. Even the gentle sarcasm of the article's title depends on audience recognition of the Miss America theme song: "There She Is, Miss Akademia."[19]

I, too, engaged in a variety of kitsch attribution strategies, for I also denied my engagement with beauty pageants. For example, I proudly differentiated between the Miss America *scholarship* pageants that I entered and those other beauty pageants provided by the exploitative Miss USA system. Further, I have carefully omitted this prior experience from all of my job interviews, my curriculum vitae, and my talks with professional acquaintances. When speaking about this chapter to several colleagues, I found myself blushing. The beauty pageant is not an American institution that is much respected or admired by academia. While several Ivy League women have competed in the pageant, only one, Evelyn Ay Sampier, Miss America 1954, has won the crown. Erika Harold, Miss America 2003, will attend Harvard Law School in fall 2004.

Sedgwick describes a counterprocess to kitsch attribution, "camp recognition," that does not ask "What kind of debased creature actually likes this stuff?" but rather, "What if the audience for this is me?" For example, the difference between identifying as kitschy or campy the same Judy Garland rendition of "Somewhere Over the Rainbow" is not in the content (it is the same singer and the same song) but in the composition of the audience (straight or gay). Camp recognition's sensibility always sees that it is dealing in reader relations and projective fantasies. This counterprocess, a type of recognition rather than rejection, is useful in thinking through academia's responses to pageants. Rather than criticize beauty pageants for their flaws, rejecting them as tacky and kitschy, something that feminist's *critique* but do not *do,* I am, in this chapter, attempting to embrace them and all their tackiness.[20] I recognize that what is performed in pageants by the contestants is not naive and uninformed. Rather, it is a self-aware gender performance. It is not a version of gender that I respect, but I can respect the power of such repeated displays of gender. Further, I can recognize that participating in a beauty pageant might even have unpredictable, positive effects on individuals such as me. In retrospect, I can see that the pageant system taught me how to consciously perform an admittedly problematic construction of gender. I also can see that it taught me how to link religious and local politics to specific gender performances, how to be a public speaker, how to frame my speech to persuade others, and how to participate in a process while simultaneously critiquing that process.

Patriarchy requires women to shape and control their bodies, and feminists have tracked the significant material and psychological costs of these demands on women—the violence of liposuction and plastic surgery, anorexia, insecurity, anxiety, lowered self-esteem, the time lost in primping instead of productive labor. Beauty pageants seem particularly perverse in this context: Sponsored by beauty product companies at the national level and men's groups like the Brotherhood of Elks at the local level, the pageant system seems to be an obvious site at which young girls are trained in the pathology of looking pretty and competing against their sisters in order to play patriarchy's game. As feminist scholars, we are appropriately invested in fighting the artificial and exploitative images of femininity promoted by the Miss America pageant: thin, attractive, chaste, body conscious, talented (but not professional), intelligent (but not challenging), and youthful (not mature). But in fighting the imaginary construct that is Miss America, we lose sight of the fact that she exists only at the level of the imaginary. The actual Miss America Pageant system teaches its participants that the Miss America ideal is imaginary; the woman who wins the crown in the nationally televised event does not exist in nature; her looks are not real but manufactured. The ideal is produced and crafted through labor, and the winner understands how to play the system. The winner wears the right costume, makes the right speeches, and puts on the right appearance through various techniques such as Vaseline on the teeth or duct-taped breasts.

However problematic it may be, society does insistently evaluate individuals by their appearances, and so it mattered enormously to me that I could actually succeed in a beauty contest. Our society's regimes of beauty and of the body, its arbitrary and often unhealthy standards of beauty, "describe in precise terms the relationship that an individual will have to her own body."[21] Under these regimes, I was not pleased with my body. Succeeding at a beauty pageant, being formally successful within a patriarchal institution that measures "beauty," changed my relationship to my body. For the first time, I felt that I was attractive. That new confidence in my appearance ironically meant that I felt freer to interact with others in nonphysical ways, to challenge and to be challenged intellectually. Once I no longer bore the burden of being unattractive, I no longer needed to worry about being attractive. Feminist consciousness-raising activities have a similar effect on women's lives in that they help women to recognize and thus to fight the damaging effects of patriarchy. In Idaho in 1985, in a small, predominantly Mormon town, I did not have access to feminist-oriented, alternative discourses of beauty and womanhood. It is ironic but nonetheless true that my success at a beauty pageant helped me to understand beauty as a performance that I could choose or not choose to give.

The image of American femininity promoted by the pageant system is a bankrupt one, and my success within this system does not change that fundamental fact. But at the same time, how and when the body will be understood and lived as gendered cannot be predicted. The positive effects of the pageant on my own physical and intellectual well-being could not have been predicted by feminist scholarship any more than I could have predicted, at an awkward age twelve, that I would some day enter a beauty pageant and win.

Notes

1. I would like to thank Dr. Janice Alberghene from Fitchburg State College, Dr. James Leve from Northern Arizona University, and Diane Long Hoeveler from Marquette University for assisting with this chapter; the junior faculty writing group at Eastern Illinois University; and my sisters Kiley Ruwe Shaw and Kendra Ruwe Clark for allowing me to share our pageant experiences with the readers of this collection.

2. My discussion is drawn from Susan Bordo's particularly rich discussion of the "No More Miss America Protest," the protest that caused feminists to be associated with bra-burning. Bordo reprints the manifesto that was distributed by the protestors, analyzes the gender politics of the protests, and contextualizes the protest within an early and effective phase of feminist protest. Susan Bordo, "Feminism, Foucault, and the Politics of the Body," *Up Against Foucault: Explorations of Some*

Tensions Between Foucault and Feminism, ed. Caroline Ramazano?lu. (London: Routledge, 1993), 193. Elwood Watson and Darcy Martin provide a good overview of the 1960s and 1970s feminist protests of the pageant, which included burning in effigy the 1972 Miss America and a National Organization of Women "Wonder Woman Convention" held in Atlantic City. Elwood Watson and Darcy Martin, "The Miss America Pageant: Pluralism, Femininity, and Cinderella All in One," *Journal of Popular Culture* 34, no.1 (Summer 2000): 110–112. Susan Faludi also discusses the importance of the pageant protests in attracting media attention to the feminist movement. Susan Faludi, *Backlash* (New York: Anchor Book/Doubleday, 1992).

3. To explain her point about the unexpected positive consequences of participation in a usually negative discourse, Bordo describes a woman who believes she is too fat to be attractive to men. Convinced that she is unattractive, she joins a health club and suddenly has more energy and drive at work and becomes more successful. Bordo also acknowledges, however, that contemporary feminists who focus on women's agency must be careful, for in searching for the unexpected positive consequences of women who participate in patriarchal systems, these feminists leave unexamined the damaging patriarchal system itself. Bordo, "Feminism, Foucault, and the Politics of the Body," 193.

4. I am using Judith Butler's definition of gender: "an identity tenuously constituted in time, instituted in an exterior space through a stylized repetition of acts." Her discussion of gender as a stylized repetition of acts is particularly evocative of the stylized and repetitive pageants. Judith Butler, *Gender Trouble: Feminism and the Subversion of Identity* (New York: Routledge, 1990): 140.

5. Since 1995, contestants no longer wear high heels with their swimsuits. In 1997, contestants were allowed to wear two-piece swimsuits.

6. As Miss Meridian, I won a $600 scholarship and an additional $50 certificate for winning the talent portion of the contest. At the state competition, I was semifinalist and received $350; my sister, who placed as second runner-up, received $750.

7. I competed in Miss Meridian, Miss Idaho National Guard (twice), Miss Eastern Idaho, and Miss Idaho. In addition to the five contests that I entered, I attended multiple other local pageants, sometimes to watch my sisters compete, sometimes as an official guest or an emcee, and sometimes as an invited performer who provided "filler" when the contestants were backstage changing costumes.

8. These numbers are somewhat misleading, for although Meridian's population was only 6,658 in 1980, the population of Ada County (where Meridian is located) was approximately 173,125. Boise, the most populous city in Ada County, is only a few miles from Meridian. The gendering of audience, performer, and producer in beauty pageant productions is worth consideration. In my experience, the composition of the audience at local pageants was more female than male, even at pageants such as Miss Idaho National Guard. In the pageants that I entered, the individual responsible for producing/directing the stage show was always a man; the pageant boards and the judges were a mixture of men and women. (The men involved as judges were frequently the husbands of women involved in pageants.) The audience at local pageants was primarily female. The women who enter pageants are competing for women and against women within a profoundly patriarchal system that values

women's physical appearance, decorative social accomplishments, and a sweet and positive demeanor.

9. The region of a local pageant can be anything from a particular city or town to an entire county. Miss Meridian contestants were drawn from the township of Meridian. The Miss Boise pageant drew its contestants from Ada County, which included the town of Meridian as well as Boise. Thus, residents of Meridian could enter both Meridian and Boise's pageants. The state of Idaho had eleven local and two regional pageants in 1985; the winners of each competed directly for Miss Idaho. In more populous states such as California, local pageant winners compete in semi-final regional pageants, and the winners of the regionals go on to the state competition. The state winners, of course, compete in the nationals for the title of Miss America.

10. The various counties and towns of eastern Idaho have a history of church-state tensions, particularly in the separation between public schools and religious practice. For example, graduation ceremonies or the prom might be held in the local Mormon church's gym.

11. My older sister and I were the first sisters to compete against each other at the state competition, a fact that the newspapers made much of in articles; see, Rick Mattoon, "Ruwe Sisters Compete in Pageant," *Valley News,* 12 June 1985: A1.

12. See Helen Michie, *Sororophobia: Differences Among Women in Literature and Culture* (New York: Oxford University Press, 1992).

13. Various movies and other forms of popular entertainment have also focused on the competitive element of the pageant and the ultimate triumph of the individuals who present nonaggressive emotion. See, for example, the film *Beauty,* which presents Minnie Driver as a woman who obsessively and, by the contest's rules, illegally competes with women in pageants until she finally learns that being a good mother and friend is more important.

14. An additional level of critique, which is outside the boundaries of this chapter, would be to identify beauty pageants as ritual reenactments of fertility rites: each year the choice virgins of a given society are paraded before the men, and the queen of the year is selected. The continual repetition of certain images, such as the red cape and the flowers, are classic archetypal images of sexual nubility.

15. Catherine A. Lugg, *Kitsch: From Education to Public Policy* (New York: Falmer, 1999), offers a useful concept of kitsch as a political tool. Kitsch, when used for political purposes, is a type of propaganda that is readily accessible in everyday life: The kitschy object is a symbol or referent that draws on a given history and culture and carries both information and emotional significance. It builds and exploits cultural myths. The 1968 Miss America protest, which used the kitschy iconography of the pageant to communicate a political message, is an excellent example of political kitsch.

16. Eve Kosofsky Sedgwick, *Epistemology of the Closet* (Berkeley: University of California Press, 1990), 155.

17. Susan Dworkin, *Miss America, 1945: Bess Myerson's Own Story* (New York: Newmark Press, 1987).

18. Quoted in Watson and Martin, The Miss America Pageant: Pluralism, Femininity, and Cinderella All in One," 113.

19. Bryon MacWilliams, "There She Is, Miss Akademia," *Chronicle of Higher Education,* 14 September 2001: A64.

20. I am aware that it is problematic to use a kitsch/camp binarism in a context that is outside of queer theory. However, the dynamic of attribution/recognition is usefully framed by Sedgwick and of importance to this discussion. Also of interest is Judith Butler's *Gender Trouble,* which analyzes the drag pageant to demonstrate the instability of gender and sex identity. Drag reveals that the structures of impersonation are one of the key fabricating mechanisms through which the social construction of gender takes place. In other words, men who impersonate women dramatize gender as something we "wear" rather than something to which we are born. Drag pageants subvert the inner/outer psychic space distinction and mock the expressive and essentialist models of gender.

21. Andrea Dworkin, *Woman-Hating* (New York: Dutton, 1974), 113.

8

My Miss Americas

PEDAGOGY AND PAGEANTRY IN THE HEARTLAND

Mark A. Eaton

*L*ittle did I know when I took a teaching position at Oklahoma City University (OCU)—my first job out of graduate school— that the institution had a long-standing tradition of recruiting young pageant winners and grooming them for the Miss America Pageant. Indeed, OCU touts itself as the best school in the country for aspiring Miss Americas, having produced three of them over the years (Jane Jayroe, 1967; Susan Powell, 1981; and Shawntel Smith, 1996) as well as thirty state pageant winners—more than any other college or university in the nation. The commitment to pageantry at OCU is serious business: The university sponsors a Miss Teen OCU pageant every year to help recruit promising teenagers and even provides scholarships to anyone who already has won some type of pageant, whether it is Miss Teen Wyoming or Miss Cherokee Nation. Young women come to OCU from all over the country to develop their talents before competing in the Miss America qualifying pageants in their home states. Why Oklahoma City University? Past success is no doubt the biggest reason, but full scholarships and nationally recognized programs in dance, music, and theater also play a role in recruiting. Focusing on American dance—jazz, modern, tap—and musical theater, both the School of Music and the School of American Dance offer the perfect training ground for young women who want to compete in the Miss America Pageant or, failing that, to pursue careers in the entertainment and tourism industries.[1] The university's legacy of beauty queens is on display in the Hall of Pageants, a portrait gallery in the lobby of the Petree Performing Arts Center featuring portraits of its three Miss Americas along with every student who has ever won a pageant. The number of portraits must be in the hundreds.

When I arrived on campus as a first-year assistant professor, Shawntel Smith, a recent graduate and MBA student, was just finishing her term as Miss America. She was the third Miss America from OCU, the first in fifteen years. Not content to rest on its laurels, however, the university's administration seemed eager to win another crown. The new faculty dinner that I attended featured not one but *three* state pageant winners—Arkansas, Colorado, and Oklahoma— who would compete for the Miss America title in Atlantic City in a matter of weeks. (This was late August.) Each of the contestants gave a short speech and performed her "talent" musical number, followed by an unveiling of her gilt-framed portrait for the Hall of Pageants. Indeed, the whole evening was a sort "mini" pageant, and I confess that I had some misgivings about the institution at which I was beginning my career. I had been living in Boston for several years and suffered initially from a bit of culture shock. Eventually I came to expect this annual display of Miss America contestants. During the four years I taught there, in fact, no fewer than seven students from Oklahoma City University competed in the Miss America Pageant.

Two of these women were actually in my courses—I like to think of them as my Miss Americas—and these are the ones I will focus on in this chapter. I did not know at the time that they eventually would be Miss America Pageant contestants, although I was well aware by then of the school's reputation for producing beauty pageant contestants. Having taught each of them in the same required literature course during two different semesters, I watched with interest as one became Miss Oklahoma in 1999 and the other Miss Minnesota in 2000. They were both excellent students: articulate, diligent, and intelligent. Both young women were tall, slender, and, yes, attractive. They struck me immediately as ambitious women, with a determination to succeed in whatever they put their minds to doing, beginning with getting an A in my course (which they both did). There was one salient difference between them: One was white, the other black. I mention this fact because, in what follows, I want to address the issue of race with respect to the Miss America Pageant since Vanessa Williams's historic win in September 1983. Besides, race also played a role in my assumptions about the two women: Although the white student with blond hair and blue eyes looked very much like an aspiring beauty queen, the black student did not seem like the type. I am not convinced that race alone accounts for my presumption that the black student was not also a Miss America wannabe. For one thing, I simply did not know as much about her extracurricular activities, whereas I did know that my white student had been a contestant in the Miss OCU pageant and had, according to the student news-paper, triumphed in the swimsuit competition (without taking the overall crown). Yet I was somewhat surprised when I found out two semesters later that the black student in my class had been named Miss Oklahoma. Despite the recent naming of several black Miss Americas, and as much as it pains me to admit it, I still apparently associated blond hair and blue eyes with a typical pageant contestant look. Interestingly, the white student also competed for the title of Miss Oklahoma that same year, but when she lost out to the black student in that contest, she went on to win the Miss Minnesota crown the fol-lowing year, thus taking that crucial last step—winning a state crown—toward fulfilling her lifelong dream of becoming Miss America. She was not alone in competing for a state title more than once. Indeed, it is not unusual for young women to compete in several state pageants, even in different states, before fi-nally winning. In one case, as journalist Richard Corliss relates, "a woman who had lost the Miss New Jersey competition four times decamped to Delaware and won the title there"[2]

Having two of my own students compete in the Miss America Pageant brought pageantry home to me in a new way. It was no longer something to watch while channel surfing on an early September evening, or to read about disinterestedly in the newspaper the next morning. My Miss Americas chal-lenged my assumptions about pageant contestants in another way too: Both had performed very well academically; they were friendly and open-minded; they had forceful personalities without being overbearing. Moreover, I was *im-pressed* with both of them. Confirming a trend toward older, more academi-cally accomplished Miss America contestants, the two women I knew had already graduated when they competed in the pageant. At twenty-three they were not the oldest in the competition, yet they were nearing the cutoff age of twenty-four. Both had graduated with honors (cum laude), and one was al-ready pursuing an MBA, while the other planned to do graduate work in music and then pursue a career in vocal performance.

Previously I had been somewhat disdainful of the Miss America Pageant. I felt that it objectified young women, encouraging them to derive their sense of self-worth from physical beauty alone, and that it represented some of the worst aspects of a patriarchal, beauty-obsessed culture. I sometimes watched the pageant on television and, along with many other guilty intellectuals, was always struck by the kitschy quality of the proceedings: Bert Parks's stentorian tones; the heavy hairspray and plastered-on smiles of young women parading in bathing suits and high heels before a panel of judges filled with the likes of Donald Trump, not to mention in front of a massive worldwide television au-dience (probably the same audience that made *Baywatch* for a time the most popular American television show overseas).[3]

Although such criticisms of the Miss America Pageant are legitimate and necessary, my experience teaching two future Miss America contestants made me feel a bit more self-conscious about my condescension. I began to wonder whether feminists, rather than pageant contestants, are the ones who need to rethink their views of gender and femininity for the twenty-first century. At the least, feminists may need to rethink the rather entrenched position that people have come to expect from them nowadays: namely, that women are powerless victims of objectification in a patriarchal society. Feminist scholar Susan Bordo has written eloquently of the need for feminism to move beyond a simplistic oppressor/oppressed model of gender relations, in which patriarchal institutions and practices—indeed all men—are viewed as "possessing and wielding power over women—who are viewed correspondingly as themselves utterly powerless."[4] After my own brush with pageantry in the heartland, I came to feel that feminism has reached an impasse of sorts as a form of cultural criticism, so far removed from the concerns of many women across the country that it has rendered itself virtually irrelevant to them. Feminism's knee-jerk condemnation of pageants and other similar institutions are emblematic of this problem. Feminists might be better served by analyzing these phenomena to see what they tell us about the culture at large. Any successful critique of the Miss America Pageant, it seems to me, must be tempered by an awareness of what the pageant means to the young women who compete, just as any nuanced understanding of female identity must acknowledge and come to terms with the thriving cosmetics, dieting, and fashion industries. Outmoded as such conceptions of beauty and femininity may seem in our postfeminist age, there is just no getting around the fact that the Miss America Pageant exemplifies, after all, our culture's complex, overdetermined relationship to beauty. A sort of "kitsch microcosm of a conflicted country," Richard Corliss remarks, "Miss America is America."[5]

Following the lead of some of the best practitioners of cultural studies, this critique of the Miss America Pageant seeks to analyze the ideologies of beauty, femininity, and identity from the inside, so to speak. This chapter reimagines the standard feminist critique of beauty pageants from the perspective of those who are most invested in them and therefore have the most to gain. Rather than adopt the typically cynical stance of the erstwhile cultural critic, I would like to take seriously for a moment the laudable aspirations and commendable talents of these two women from my classroom. Their talents will no doubt serve them well in the years ahead, even if they were not crowned Miss America. They have already become quite successful professionally, in no small part because of the rigorous training they underwent for the Miss America Pageant. In fact, I want to describe the two women I got to know in my classes as *feminists* in a certain sense. What does it mean to call pageant contestants feminists? It means, first of all, redefining feminism from the standpoint of how young women actually negotiate their identities and gender roles in American society, keeping in mind that most of them do so without much knowledge of or even the slightest exposure to academic feminism. It means, in other words, greatly expanding our notions of what feminism entails, in search of a more pliable feminism that engages a broader range of American women.

The pageant began in 1921 as a bathing beauty contest to help extend the summer holiday season on the Atlantic City boardwalk, notably one year after women won the vote.[6] All of the elements of what Miss America has become were already implicit in that first contest: the curious mixture of innocence and ambition in the young women; the tension between idealizing and objectifying them; the shading of publicity into prurience; the elaborately ritualized aspect of the show coupled with a forced spontaneity when the winner finally is announced.

To understand the fundamentally contradictory nature of the Miss America Pageant, we need briefly to consider its prehistory in the late nineteenth and early twentieth centuries, when technological advances in photography and printing led to the emergence of the connected notions of both imagining and imaging what women are and can be through a proliferation of visual images within mass culture. Cultural historian Martha Banta's massive book *Imaging American Women* exhaustively delineates this prehistory of the Miss America Pageant from the mid- to late nineteenth century, a time when, as she puts it, "the American girl was singled out as the visual and literary form to represent the values of the nation and codify the fears and desires of its citizens."[7] Banta makes clear that the business of imaging American women, which became almost a national obsession by the turn of the twentieth century, was from the outset a thoroughly commercial *and* cultural phenomenon, since these images embodied contradictory values about female identity, gender roles, and sexuality. Paradoxically, images of women in magazines and newspapers allowed them to capitalize on publicity even as these images often relegated them to conventional roles and types.[8] From Charles Dana Gibson's ubiquitous Gibson Girl sketches to Florenz Ziegfeld's popular Broadway revue the Ziegfeld Follies, women's bodies were central to the emerging mass culture of the period, but at the same time, they embodied the culture's schizophrenia about the so-called New Woman, a popular term by the 1920s for newly independent, nontraditional women.[9] The birth of the Miss America Pageant is best understood in the context of a larger national obsession with visual representations of women, even as the country was experiencing seismic shifts in terms of women entering the workforce and gaining greater autonomy both socially and politically.[10]

For the seven teenage girls who came to compete in a "bathing beauty" contest in Atlantic City, however, the feminist movement was undoubtedly of little or no concern, and I suspect that indifference to feminism continues to be the norm for most contestants. Meanwhile the Miss America Pageant always has been, understandably, a favorite target of feminists, who strenuously object to the pageant's blatant objectification of women. One of the first public acts of second-wave feminism was the "No More Miss America" demonstration in 1968, where the apocryphal bra-burning episode allegedly took place.[11] This was a turning point in the feminist movement and in the pageant itself. Starting with its first telecast in 1953, the popularity of the Miss America Pageant had peaked in the early 1960s, capturing an estimated two-thirds of all television sets in America, according to the official Miss America website.[12] After the 1968 demonstration, however, the pageant would have to reinvent itself continually in response to the cultural revolution and the rise of multiculturalism in the 1970s and 1980s. "Miss America has changed with the times," as psychologist Jill Neimark remarks; "she has been black, deaf, and a social activist with platforms ranging from AIDS prevention to children's self-esteem and aging with dignity—although she still struts in a bathing suit."[13] In the face of numerous protests and petitions to eliminate the swimsuit portion of the event, organizers have stuck with it—and not without reason, for surely this is one of the attractions of watching for many of the 20 million or so viewers each year.

Embodying cultural contradictions to this day, the Miss America Pageant remains an important annual television event, not unlike the Super Bowl or the Academy Awards. And despite recent poor television ratings, Miss America is at the center of a massive pageant industry involving, by some estimates, 100,000 women a year. Along with the Miss America feeder pageants in each state, the industry includes Miss USA, Miss Teen America, Miss Black America, Mrs. America, Miss Hemisphere, and Miss Universe pageants. Also, nearly every high school and college conducts a similar pageant for prom queen, homecoming queen, or Miss "Fill-in-the-Blank." Together these pageants constitute an extraordinary institutionalization of gender norms based on "the objectification of young women," as theater historian Jennifer Jones observes, "[and] dependent upon women's participation in a competitive rather than cooperative relationship."[14]

The overvaluing of physical appearance in women should not be underestimated, nor can we afford to dismiss the enormous social and psychological effects of the beauty industry. Whatever gains women may have made in the last half century especially, there remain signs of gender inequality, such as salary differentials in most professions, the proverbial glass ceiling, and the persistent pressure on women (and, increasingly, men) to conform to exacting standards of appearance. "In our own era," Susan Bordo has suggested, "it is difficult to avoid the recognition that the contemporary preoccupation with appearance, which still affects women far more powerfully than men, even in our narcissistic and visually oriented culture, may function as a backlash phenomenon, reasserting existing gender configurations against any attempt to shift or transform power relations."[15] Objectification is not just about images, in this view, but about shaping the realities of women's lives in relation to men and each other: "The notion of women-as-objects suggests the reduction of women to 'mere' bodies, when actually what's going on is often far more disturbing than that, involving the depiction of regressive ideals of feminine behavior and attitude that go much deeper than appearance."[16] Beauty culture reflects what women are supposed to look like, yet this process also works prescriptively to influence how women behave. "Through the exacting and normalizing disciplines of diet, makeup, and dress," Bordo concludes, "[women] are rendered less socially oriented and more centripetally focused on self-modification."[17] The beauty industry preys on women's insecurities about their looks and promotes virtually unattainable ideals of weight and body type. At once capitalizing on and producing such ideals, the beauty industry tends to atomize women as individual consumers. As much as the cosmetics and fashion industries pay homage to feminism and attempt to promulgate new ideas about self-determination and power, these industries still encourage women to pay inordinate amounts of attention, money, and time to their physical appearance. But it would be ludicrous to suggest that women do not play a part in this: "Many, if not most, women also are willing (often, enthusiastic) participants in cultural practices that objectify and sexualize us."[18] Certainly my students had *chosen* to enter the whole world of pageantry, however young they were when they started, and whatever part their parents may have played in pushing them in that direction. By the time I met them as college juniors or seniors, they were not only willing participants but deeply committed to the path they had chosen, making tremendous sacrifices on the road to Miss America.

Although acknowledging the powerful effects of beauty culture generally and of pageantry specifically on young women, I want to insist that women themselves play a crucial role in these institutions; if we fail to account for their participation in such institutions, we risk falling into the reductive feminist binary opposition between oppressor and oppressed. Recent feminist theory has offered several ways of moving beyond that untenable opposition; one of these is Judith Butler's influential view of gender as constituted through performance. "The view that gender is performative," Butler informs us in a new preface to her important book, *Gender Trouble,* "sought to show that what we take to be an internal essence of gender is manufactured through a sustained set of acts, posited through the gendered stylization of the body." "It seems to me," she continues, "that feminism ought to be careful not to idealize certain expressions of gender that, in turn, produce new forms of hierarchy and exclusion."[19] No doubt Butler has in mind here the kinds of gender expressions that she elsewhere calls "heteronormative," but I want to use this warning against her, as it were, by defending the decidedly less radical gender identities represented by pageant contestants as ones that feminism ought not to exclude either. Feminism has, after all, been notoriously intolerant of women whose politics do not conform to its orthodoxy.[20] Another way out of the old binary is suggested by the work of Michel Foucault, whose conception of power as productive rather than merely repressive allows us to view women as active agents in their own identities, even where those identities may seem from one perspective to be oppressive. Again Susan Bordo has been a key figure in offering a more theoretically sophisticated view of how women internalize the very patriarchal structures that demean and oppress. "Where power works 'from below,'" she points out, "prevailing forms of selfhood and subjectivity (gender among them), are maintained, not chiefly through physical restraint and coercion (although social relations may certainly contain such elements), but through individualized self-surveillance and self-correction to norms."[21]

The primary example of such norms is our culture's idealization of thinness, which exerts very real pressure on young women, even on very young, prepubescent girls. Put another way, women assimilate and respond to the idealization of thinness by placing enormous pressure on themselves to be thinner than they probably should be. Through dieting regimens, makeup, and styles of dress, their bodies become more and more "habituated to external regulation, subjection, transformation, 'improvement.'"[22] As Joan Jacobs Brumberg has shown in her book *The Body Project: An Intimate History of American Girls,* "girls today are concerned with the shape and appearance of their bodies as a primary expression of their individual identity. . . . At the end of the twentieth century, the body is regarded as something to be managed and maintained, usually through expenditures on clothes and personal grooming items."[23] Brumberg is speaking here about high school girls, but such bodily concerns clearly extend into college and beyond. On almost any university campus in America, although perhaps to varying degrees, depending on what type of students you consider (e.g., sorority women, cheerleaders, athletes), the female body has become more and more of a "project" to be managed along with other aspects of life.

I certainly overheard a lot of comments about weight among the female students at Oklahoma City University, including a conversation by one of my Miss Americas with a male student about how she had worked out a lot before the Miss OCU contest (the very contest in which she won the swimsuit competition). The university's dance program was so invested in thinness as a prerequisite for dancers that students were told from their first day in the program what weight they were expected to maintain and subjected to frequent, often

unannounced "weigh-ins." If they had gained too much weight, at least according to the razor-thin director (an older woman who had been a dancer herself), they were simply kicked out of the program. Smoking was common
among dance majors trying to keep their weight down. Miss America hopefuls
were not usually dance majors, but the same aesthetic standards applied, and
they too often took extraordinary measures to control their weight. Indeed,
perhaps one of the reasons they felt validated at a place like OCU was that their
peers in the dance program, which made up 30 percent or more of each in-
coming class, were under a similar obligation to be thin. Feminists who teach
at ostensibly more radicalized college campuses would do well to keep in mind
that these seemingly backward attitudes (indeed, actual school policies) are not
uncommon in certain parts of the country and probably not entirely absent
even at campuses like, say, Berkeley. "We cannot evade or deny these attitudes,"
Bordo concurs, "and drown out their reality in a pumped-up rhetoric, an-
nouncing the coming of a new age, 'beyond' feminism."[24] Before academic
feminists celebrate the dawn of a new era in attitudes toward women's bodies,
they should spend a day where female students actually live. Since both contestants I taught were large women, I would guess that weight was a particular
concern for them leading up to the Miss America Pageant as well.

The weight profile of Miss America has steadily decreased over the years, and
more than one contestant has struggled with her weight. Karrie Mitchell, Miss
Colorado 1990, admitted that she "worked out until she shrank from a size
twelve to a size five."[25] A few years later, Miss Universe 1996, Alicia Machado,
actually was ordered to lose twenty-seven pounds or have her crown taken
away.[26] And the number of pageant contestants who have chosen to undergo
cosmetic surgery seems to be rising, reflecting a significant increase in surgical
procedures on women nationally. Cosmetic surgery is now a $1.75 billion-a-year
industry in the United States, with nearly 2 million individuals a year undergo-
ing various procedures.[27]

The Miss America Pageant thus reflects normative expectations about
women's bodies, yet these expectations do not originate out of thin air, nor do
they simply realize typical male fantasies. The prevailing norms of clean-cut
appearance and fit body type that govern the selection of Miss America are systemic; that is, they cut across a number of ideological fault lines and inform
the aesthetic preferences of women and men alike. Critics have too often assumed that women simply can dismiss or ignore these norms.[28] But in the real
worlds of undergraduate life and most certainly of pageants, beauty reigns.
Feminist scholar Susan Brownmiller has argued that femininity in the United
States largely conforms to an aesthetic of limitation: "Appearance, not accomplishment, is the feminine demonstration of desirability and worth."[29] Insofar
as feminism has fought against the overvaluation of appearance by promoting

alternative qualities such as inner strength, intellectual prowess, and professional accomplishment, it has done us a great service. But insofar as feminism has discounted the power of aesthetic standards of beauty, or blamed them on patriarchal institutions, or dismissed those women who adhere to them as a means of self-definition and advancement, it has failed adequately to address the widespread internalization of such standards, to the point that many women more or less embrace them. "A backlash against women's advancement does not originate in a smoke-filled room," writes Naomi Wolf in *The Beauty Myth*, "it is often unconscious and reflexive, like racism . . . a generalized atmosphere in which men's fears and women's guilt are addressed and elaborated through the culture's images of women, and its messages to women about the relationship between their value and their bodies."[30] Although I am uncomfortable with the unspecified agency implied by her use of the term "backlash," I think Wolf nicely captures the systemic nature of our culture's attitudes toward beauty.

Only in the last twenty-plus years has the Miss America Pageant come to terms with its legacy as what Gerald Early scathingly calls "a national white doll contest."[31] As if signaling that the 1980s would finally see the Miss America Pageant respond to the gains of the civil rights movement of the 1960s and the rise of multiculturalism in the 1970s, the start of the decade saw Lencola Sullivan, Miss Arkansas 1980, become the first African American to finish in the top five (fourth runner-up), winning the swimsuit competition outright. Three years later, Vanessa Williams became the first black Miss America. Another black woman, Suzette Charles, was named first runner-up. Charles became the second black Miss America by default when Williams relinquished her crown after some compromising photographs of her were published in *Penthouse* magazine (to this writer's mind, an unconscionable decision by the unrepentant publisher Bob Guccione). Subsequently, five other black women have been named Miss America: Debbye Turner, Miss America 1990; Marjorie Vincent, Miss America 1991, Kimberly Aiken, Miss America 1994; Erika Harold, Miss America 2003; and Ericka Dunlap, Miss America 2004. "With minority contestants becoming commonplace and frequent winners," write Elwood Watson and Darcy Martin, "the pageant seemingly has moved beyond issues of race."[32]

Or has it? The pageant certainly has gone beyond an all-white contestant base, but the preferred body type for these women—whether white, black, or Pacific Islander—is still fairly homogenous and still predominantly Euro-American in terms of their facial features and physical traits. This is still true of the beauty and fashion industries as well; the most successful minority models are usually the ones who conform to the expected "look" of white models. The cultural norm for female beauty is one of the areas that is far from color blind, despite periodic assurances to the contrary by fashion magazines. *Essence* mag-

azine, for one, "has consciously and strenuously tried to promote diverse images of black strength, beauty, and self-acceptance. . . . The magazine's advertisers, however, continually play upon and perpetuate consumers' feelings of
inadequacy and insecurity over the racial characteristics of their bodies."[33] A
1989 poll of *Essence* readers revealed that "68 percent of those who responded
wear their hair straightened chemically or by hot comb."[34] Although blacks
comprise only about 6 percent of all cosmetic surgeries in the United States,
their share of these types of procedures rose 2 percentage points between 1994
and 1997. By far the most common procedure performed on African Americans is rhinoplasty, which specifically treats patients' complaints of "flared nos-
trils" or a "low, wide nasal bridge."[35] Michael Jackson's multiple rhinoplasty
procedures have obviously been quite dramatic, but many blacks, including
adolescent girls, have used this procedure to thin their noses. One prominent
New York surgeon notes that the twenty-one-year-old black aspiring model is
among the most common patient profiles for those requesting rhinoplasty in
his office, suggesting that the expected look for models includes thinner,
smaller noses.[36] There are a few notable exceptions to the rule—e.g., models
who have been somewhat successful despite anomalous facial features—but the
exceptions prove the rule. Representations of the female body in U.S. culture
most assuredly homogenize, smoothing out racial and ethnic differences in
favor of a generic, all-purpose "model" look, irrespective of race or national origin. "White models may collagen their lips," Bordo suggests, "but black models are usually light-skinned and Anglo-featured."[37]

The belated, yet important, coronation of seven black Miss Americas in the
last two decades infuses the pageant with a racial politics to go along with its
complex sexual ones. Everything changed when Vanessa Williams was selected
Miss America, and today, the pageant shows signs of becoming deliberately
more inclusive. Williams is arguably the most recognized former Miss America
ever, in no small part because of the scandal that led to her giving up the crown
with seven weeks left in her reign.[38] Even at the time of her win, though, a few
dissenting black organizations protested that Vanessa Williams was not "in
essence" black because of her white skin and so-called white features, a protest
that possibly influenced the judges' selection of a much darker black woman,
Marjorie Vincent, as Miss America in September 1990.[39] "As with the selection
of Williams," Early has suggested, "the contest gained a veneer of postmodernist
social and political relevance not only by selecting a black again but by having
an Asian, a kidney donor, and a hearing-impaired woman among the top ten finalists. This all smacks of affirmative action or the let's-play-fair-with-the-un-
derrepresented doctrine."[40] Alas, this did not seem to help my African American
student in 1999, but it may well have worked against my white student in 2000,
when Angela Perez Baraquio, Miss Hawaii and Miss America 2001, became the

first woman of Pacific Asian descent to become Miss America. I do not want to hazard a guess why my Miss Americas failed to win, although I have my own suspicions about the increasing importance of racial politics in who gets to be Miss America each year. One disgruntled white contestant, Lisa Bittinger, Miss West Virginia 1989, lodged a post-ad-hoc complaint, condemning the pageant for engaging in decisions that, according to Gerald Early, "smacked of politics."[41]

For their part, intellectuals have taken it on themselves to look down on beauty queens, as if their very participation in a pageant precludes them from having legitimate, career-oriented goals. Richard Wilk, a professor of anthropology at Indiana University, declares that beauty pageants "are always about fundamental contradictions in the culture," but then he cannot help but scoff: "How else could you get millions of people to watch a bunch of relatively untalented women in bathing suits?"[42] Critic Richard Corliss echoes the sentiment: "To have a 'talent' is not always to be talented." And Early agrees: Miss America is "not a revelation of talent but a reaffirmation of bourgeois social conditioning."[43] Although it is true that music and dance numbers are disproportionately represented in the contestants' "talent" choices, the pageant definitely has become more talent-driven and service-oriented in recent years. In contrast to the early days of mostly teenage girls, young women who compete for Miss America today are likely to be both older and more accomplished. In 1995, four contestants stated that they wanted to pursue a career in law, four in medicine. The students I knew who competed in 1999 and 2000, respectively, had both graduated and were either in graduate school or planning to apply. Nonetheless, Corliss makes a point of criticizing the essentially conservative leanings of the pageant: "The Miss America pageant sells an image of young womanhood that is retro and modern, hopelessly uncool—and for all that, we love it."[44] Although he objects to the "cheap earnestness" and "dreamy ideological gauze" of the pageant, Early admits that in "a perverse way, I like the show."[45] He also picks up on a commercial element that Corliss only hints at with the word sell. "Despite its attempt in recent years to modernize its frighteningly antique quality of 'women on parade,'" Early writes, the Miss America Pageant remains 'a kind of maddeningly barbarous example of the persistent, hard, crass urge to sell."[46]

With mixed fascination and disgust, these two cultural critics—one white, one black—weigh in on what they see as the full implications of the Miss America Pageant. The source of their ambivalence is no doubt an embarrassingly retrograde sexual politics, but, for Early, it also has to do with a history of racial exclusion that cannot be redressed no matter how many Vanessa Williamses there are in the future. In this regard, his essay seeks to understand the amazing allure of the pageant to his wife, who grew up watching it at a time when the probability of a black woman being in the competition, much less winning it, was virtually nil. "For my wife," he writes, "the years of watching the Miss America contest were nothing more . . . than an expression of anger made all the worse by the very unconscious or semiconscious nature of it."[47] "It" being, of course, the racist presumption of Miss America's white face. Refusing to watch the show, she knows, would do nothing to alter the racialization of beauty that belied its apparent meritocracy—anyone can win—for "she is not naive enough to think that a simple refusal would be an act of empowerment."[48] Still, the most penetrating, scathing indictment of the Miss America Pageant comes near the end of Early's essay, where he comments on what the shiny veneer of pageantry means, as well as what it may be covering up:

> The Miss America contest has reached a new height of hysteria in both the stridency and compulsion of the competition. . . . Once again, with the Miss America contest we have America's vehement preoccupation with innocence, with its inability to deal with the darkness of youth, the darkness of its own uselessly expressed ambition, the dark complexity of its own simplistic morality of sunshine and success, the darkness, righteous rage, and bitter depth of its own daughters. Once again, when the new Miss America, victorious and smiling, walks down the runway, we know that runway, that victory march, to be the American catwalk of supreme bourgeois self-consciousness and supreme illusion.[49]

The passage is notable for its rhetorical flourishes and for its attempt to get beneath the surface of what the Miss America Pageant reveals about our country and ourselves, but I am not at all certain it would seem as compelling to my students as it does to me, especially to those students who were in a position to experience the Miss America Pageant firsthand rather than from the comfy remove of the critic's chair. And this points to a paradox about cultural criticism in general, namely that it becomes less authoritative the farther removed it is from the thing critiqued. Critical distance is a misnomer in one sense, for it implies that greater objectivity is gained from distancing oneself from the object of critique, whereas I believe that a deeper engagement with the thing allows for a more intimate knowledge of it. Corliss similarly—and tellingly—reserves his most catchy prose less for the purpose of *analysis* than for turning up his nose at the pageant: "Yet for all the perkiness and primping, the look is small town, polyester. This is Sears, not Saks. The women would be prettier with smarter clothes and hipper hairdos. A few display true glamour and grace, but in general this is a triumph of starch over sizzle. The earnestness with which the women sell themselves would make them comfy at a Mary Kay convention. They radiate not fantastic beauty but fanatical effort. For some, striving to be universally liked can trigger the scent of desperation."[50] There is a kernel of truth in his critique: The Miss America Pageant does have a kind of tackiness that is difficult to ignore, and its recent attempts at political correctness are at best ironic, given the fundamentally conservative, even sexist roots of the pageant. Yet there is something almost disingenuous about journalists assigned to cover the pageant who feel compelled to make snide, superior remarks about the show or, worse, about the women themselves, while simultaneously partaking in the guilty pleasure afforded by the scene. Indeed, this has become the signature stance of cultural critics, assuming a kind of critical distance from mass culture that may well be illusory at a time when image and spectacle are part of the very air we all breathe. Without acknowledging one's own enmeshment in and fascination with popular culture, cultural criticism runs the risk of rendering its insights questionable if not irrelevant to real people's concerns and interests.

Coming down from the rarefied air inhabited by these provocative cultural critics, I would like to end my chapter closer to the ground and see if I cannot try to discern what motivated my Miss Americas to want to be Miss America in the first place. At OCU, as earlier mentioned, anyone who had been crowned Miss Anything at a local or state-level pageant was given a scholarship to attend. I learned this when one of my first-year composition students wrote a personal essay on her experience as Miss Teen Wyoming, noting that the title also gave her an opportunity to attend a private university instead of going to a much less expensive state university. Although she had no intention of going further, most of the so-called teen queens understood that their scholarships were intended to allow them time to prepare for a state title while also earning college credit. Thus they came to sing and study while strategizing their next move: to be Miss OCU, maybe, and eventually Miss Oklahoma or whatever state they came from. This was the path taken by both my students during their four years at the school. It would be wrong to say that they put pageantry above their studies, although certainly they were focused on that goal, even as they were also very disciplined academically. What is remarkable to me about their efforts, in retrospect, was how confident they were about their chances to win the title, no matter how much of a long shot it seemed to me at the time or how many roadblocks they encountered along the way. One of them especially was just extraordinarily upbeat. I suspect that whatever they may have gotten out of their experiences as state pageant winners, there must be some lingering disappointment at not reaching that ultimate goal, which proved elusive for both of my Miss Americas. Such disappointment would be exacerbated, I assume, by the single-minded pursuit of one goal for all those years, anticipating victory through the sheer force of positive thinking. I can only hope that the inevitable sense of failure when another girl was named Miss America that night is finally outweighed by a sense of pride for having been there at all.

My brush with potential Miss America fame was admittedly brief and framed by a pedagogical context. I taught those students in a relatively large (thirty-five students) general education course (Western Literature to the Renaissance). I do not claim to know either of them well, and I do not know what was going through their minds at the pageant. In fact, they competed in the Miss America Pageant *after* they were in my courses, as I said, and I did not know at the time—could not have known—that they eventually would make it. But I do know this: My Miss Americas were among the best students in those two classes. They made me watch the Miss America Pageant not only with greater personal interest, since someone I knew was a contestant, but with a new pair of eyes.

Although my uninformed view of the Miss America Pageant was not completely altered by my experiences in Oklahoma, my initially low opinion of the contestants themselves changed dramatically. I gained newfound respect for these young women as individuals, charting their course through life with much determination and resolve. Unlike some of their peers, my students were focused on their goals, unwilling to let anything stop them. They were, moreover, intelligent and curious, eager to learn. No doubt their eagerness can be attributed in part to an instrumental, therapeutic conception of self-improvement: They were ready to do whatever it took to enhance their overall "package" for the pageant. Yet their willingness to learn was, on the whole, admirable. The two young women in my classes were bright, cheerful, dedicated students who appreciated the opportunities that had been given them. They pursued the dream of becoming the next Miss America with due diligence, forever optimistic. Surely they realize in hindsight that winning is not everything, as the saying goes. I hope they also realize what being in the Miss America Pageant brought with it: an education, a sense of purpose, and a certain poise that others lack. "The conflict of the importance of inner beauty versus physical beauty as exemplified by the Miss America Pageant remains unresolved," write cultural studies scholars Elwood Watson and Darcy Martin. "Inclusion of the Miss America platform and promotion of the pageant as the largest provider of scholarships to women reflects society's struggle to remove physical beauty as a measure of a woman's worth."[51] The two women were being socialized to overvalue beauty, to be sure, but they definitely did not value beauty over brains. The maturity and self-assurance they gained from their experiences are no small things when it came to entering a workplace that was just on the verge of a major economic recession.

We are left, then, with a conundrum familiar to us cultural critics, the conundrum of wanting to disparage the institutions and practices of American mass culture while at the same time being drawn to them, perhaps even being impressed with their complexity. "There she is, Miss America" rings in our ears, and it keeps ringing long after we hit the remote control and turn the TV off. She may, however, continue to hover in our mind's eye, and if our interest is piqued enough to ignore the din of disapproval ringing in our ears, we may just learn a thing or two about what drives Americans who love this stuff. Indeed, if we can acknowledge the genuine allure of that which we love to hate, we may learn something about ourselves as well.

Notes

1. The most successful recent graduate is Kristin Chenowith, winner of a Tony Award for her performance in the Broadway musical *Charlie Brown* and star of the musical *Wicked*.
2. Richard Corliss, "Dream Girls," *Time,* 18 September 1995: 102–105, Academic Search Elite, 3 June 2002, http://resources.apu.edu.
3. For a lively discussion of kitsch and "the trashing of taste in America," see James B. Twitchell, *Carnival Culture: The Trashing of Taste in America* (New York: Columbia University Press, 1992).
4. Susan Bordo, *Twilight Zones: The Hidden Life of Cultural Images from Plato to O.J.* (Berkeley: University of California Press, 1997), 23.
5. Corliss, "Dream Girls."
6. Ironically, the Miss America Pageant borrowed certain conventions from the suffrage movement, as Jennifer Jones has pointed out: "The Miss America pageant adopted and adapted the suffragette pageant by opening with the traditional processional parade of states, moving on through several musical numbers, and finally a series of tableaux in which the women were viewed in gowns and bathing suits. . . . The banners worn by all beauty contestants, bearing the names of their states or cites, are eerily reminiscent of suffragette banners first worn at rallies for women's rights." Jones, "The Beauty Queen as Deified Sacrificial Victim," *Theatre History Studies* 18 (June 1998): 102.
7. Martha Banta, *Imaging American Women: Idea and Ideals in Cultural History* (New York: Columbia University Press, 1987), 2.
8. Ibid., 7
9. On the Gibson Girl and the Ziegfeld Follies, respectively, see ibid. and Linda Mizejewski, *Ziegfeld Girl: Image and Icon in Culture and Cinema* (Durham, NC: Duke University Press, 1999).
10. See Kathy Peiss, *Cheap Amusements: Working Women and Leisure in Turn-of-the-Century New York* (Philadelphia: Temple University Press, 1985), for a discussion of how working women at the turn of twentieth the century enjoyed unprecedented freedom of movement and economic independence.
11. "In fact, no bras *were* burned at the demonstration," Susan Bordo claims, "although there was a huge 'Freedom Trash Can' into which were thrown bras, along with girdles, curlers, false eyelashes, wigs." Bordo, *Unbearable Weight: Feminism, Western Culture, and the Body* (Berkeley: University of California Press, 1993, 1995), 19. For other accounts of this incident, see Susan Brownmiller, *Femininity* (New York: Fawcett, 1984), 45–46; and Elwood Watson and Darcy Martin, "The Miss America Pageant: Pluralism, Femininity, and Cinderella All in One," *Journal of Popular Culture* 34, no. 1 (Summer 2000): 111.
12. "Television and Miss America: Over Forty Years of History," 15 October 2003, www.missamerica.org/competition/telecast.asp.
13. Jill Neimark, "Why We Need Miss America," *Psychology Today* (September/October 1998): 42.
14. Jones, "Beauty Queen as Deified Sacrificial Victim," 99.
15. Bordo, *Unbearable Weight,* 166.
16. Bordo, *Twilight Zones,* 124.

17. Bordo, *Unbearable Weight,* 166.

18. Ibid., 28.

19. Judith Butler, *Gender Trouble: Feminism and the Subversion of Identity* (New York: Routledge, 1999), xv, viii.

20. "Academic feminists have yet to adequately address the issue implicitly raised by millions of women," Stange writes, "how to reach politically conservative yet 'liberated' women, many of whom testify, 'I'm not a feminist, but . . .' Some of those women may be feminists without knowing it, although putting it that way implies a certain condescension. Others are openly hostile to feminism." Mary Zeiss Stange, "The Political Intolerance of Academic Feminism," *Chronicle of Higher Education,* 21 June 2002, B16.

21. Bordo, *Unbearable Weight,* 27.

22. Ibid., 166.

23. Joan Jacobs Brumberg, *The Body Project: An Intimate History of American Girls* (New York: Vintage Books, 1998), xxi.

24. Bordo, *Twilight Zones,* 133.

25. Niemark, "Why We Need Miss America," 72.

26. Bordo, *Twilight Zones,* 22.

27. See Bordo, *Unbearable Weight,* 25. See also Sander L. Gilman, *Making the Body Beautiful: A Cultural History of Aesthetic Surgery* (Princeton, NJ: Princeton University Press, 1999), 6. The surge in aesthetic surgeries in recent decades is one indication of the pressure on women to adapt themselves to certain physical ideals. Breast augmentation jumped from 39,247 in 1994 to 87,704 in 1996, while the number of women removing their implants dropped from 37,853 to 3,013 (240). Similarly, in 1995, there were some 63,000 face-lifts performed and a startling 208,000 botox and collagen procedures (316).

28. Few cultural critics are as self-conscious about their own susceptibility to standards of beauty that they deplore as Bordo seems to be. "I do not feel at all superior," she tells us, "to the woman who has a face-lift in order to feel young and attractive for just a little while longer before she becomes culturally invisible; believe me, I understand where she's coming from. . . . But because I experience myself as so completely 'inside' the dilemma of finding my way in this culture, I think of my criticisms—of cosmetic surgery, for example—less as a judgment of others than as an argument with myself, a way to shore up my own consciousness and resolve, which is continually being worn down." Bordo, *Twilight Zones,* 15–16.

29. Brownmiller, *Femininity,* 50.

30. Naomi Wolf, *The Beauty Myth* (New York: Anchor Books, 1992), 3.

31. Gerald Early, "Watching the Miss America Pageant," *The Best American Essays of the Century,* ed. Joyce Carol Oates (New York: Vintage, 2000), 533.

32. Watson and Martin, "The Miss America Pageant," 123.

33. Gilman, *Making the Body Beautiful,* 263.

34. Ibid., 254.

35. Ibid., 117.

36. Ibid., 115.

37. Bordo, *Twilight Zones,* 25.

38. Gerald Early provocatively suggests that the pageant's "preoccupation with the terminology of aristocracy mirrors the public's need for such a person as the American princess." See "Watching the Miss America Pageant," 545.

39. Niemark, "Why We Need Miss America," 43.
40. Early, "Watching the Miss America Pageant," 543.
41. Ibid.
42. Quoted in Niemark, "Why We Need Miss America," 42.
43. Early, "Watching the Miss America Pageant," 542.
44. Corliss, "Dream Girls," 102–105.
45. Early, "Watching the Miss America Pageant," 533.
46. Ibid., 532.
47. Ibid., 536.
48. Ibid.
49. Ibid., 544, 546.
50. Corliss, "Dream Girls," 102–105.
51. Watson and Martin, "The Miss America Pageant," 123.

9

Waiting for Miss America*

Gerald Early

"I'm as good as any woman in your town."

—Bessie Smith's "Young Woman's Blues"

I remember well sitting in a barbershop in the not so once-upon-a-time-long-ago past right after the yearly telecast of the Miss America contest. Most of the patrons, who were black and male, decided that they would not let so insignificant a matter as not having watched the program prevent them from discussing it endlessly. In fact, not having seen the show or having any real idea of what the Miss America contest was about seemed to have fueled their imaginations and loosened their tongues in such a way that, in retrospect, any knowledge of the true proceedings of beauty contests may have been found inhibitive. Most of the men spoke of "white bitches parading their asses across the stage" with much the same expression of mixed desire, wonder, and rage that often characterized the way I heard a good many black men talk about white women in my childhood. As the talk eventually died down, one of the patrons, a black man with a derby and a gold tooth and who looked for all the world like a cross between Lester Young and Stymie from the

*Reprinted with permission from *The Antioch Review,* 42, no. 3 (Summer 1984).

"Our Gang" comedies, said with a great deal of finality: "You know, there are three things in life you can bet your house on: Death, taxes, and that Miss America will always be white." Now that we have a Miss America who is black or who, at least, can pass for a fairly pronounced quadroon, I supposed that the chiliastic inevitability of taxes and death might be called into question.

I use the word "quadroon" because it seems so accurate in a quaint sort of way. When I finally became aware of the fact that our new Miss America is black (something that I was not aware of instantly, even though I watched the pageant on television), I immediately thought of the character Eliza from Harriet Beecher Stowe's famed 1852 novel, *Uncle Tom's Cabin.* Our new Miss America has elevated the image of the tragic mulatto woman from the status of being a quaint romantic figure in some of America's most aesthetically marginal litera-ture to being a national icon. I thought of Eliza not only because she was very light but also because she was the essence of cultured black womanhood. Her hands, according to the witnesses in the novel, never betrayed her as a slave be-cause she never, unlike, say, Uncle Tom's dark-skinned wife, Aunt Chloe, per-formed any hard work. She was shaped in the image of her mistress, Mrs. Shelby, and, like her mistress, possessed little that would have enabled her to es-cape pious mediocrity. She had simply a desperate love for her son and her hus-band and a desperate wish to be good despite the odds against it. And I suppose if there has been anything that has characterized the light-skinned black woman as cultured mulatto, it has been that air of desperation that has made her seem so helpless and so determined in the same instant. She showed such incredible strength bottled in a welter of outmoded morality. This desperation is quite im-portant; any black woman who would want to become Miss America or, for that matter, the first black woman to do just about anything in our country (where such "firsts" *signify* so much while they *mean* so little) has to be a bit desperate. Any act of that magnitude is always reminiscent of Eliza, feet bloodied and hair flying, clutching her son tightly as she jumps from floe to floe across the icy Ohio River. When this desperation has combined with bitterness, it has pro-duced the true tragic genius of the mulatto personality (the term mulatto hav-ing come to indicate a psychological mode rather than a racial mixture) exemplified by such women as Dorothy Dandridge, Billie Holliday, and Josephine Baker.

But our new Miss America is as sweet as any of her sisters before her, so she will not, in the end, bring to mind those great images of the mulatto personal-ity like Holiday, Baker, and Dandridge. Her reign will help us forget them; for while our culture can tolerate desperate black women who want success and love, it cannot tolerate bitter black women who have been denied success and love. Our current Miss America will always bring to mind Eliza and she will clutch her crown and roses in much the same way that Stowe's character clutched her son. She will personify the strength, courage, and culture of black middle-class womanhood, and all of its philistine mediocrity as well.

Far from being the far-reaching, revolutionary breakthrough in race relations (a new chink made in the armor of the annealed idea of white superiority) that such black leaders as Benjamin Hooks and Shirley Chisholm seemed to have thought, I believe it to have been a quaint joke in much the same way that the flights of the first black and woman astronauts were. Surely, no one really believes that the choice of a black Miss America is comparable to Jackie Robinson breaking into pro ball. Or perhaps it is. Professional athletics have always been, in some sense, the male equivalent of beauty contests; because they are a male province, they always have been considered to possess deeper cultural significance. But, leaving simplistic feminist thinking aside, I believe our new Miss America is a bit too ambiguous a symbol to be as powerful a jolt to our racial consciousness as the emergence of the professional black ballplayer.

Suffice it to say that a black girl as Miss America is a joke but not an insult. In the first place, it is difficult to be insulted by an act that is so self-consciously well-intentioned. Vanessa Williams, the young student who won the contest, is such a radiantly beautiful woman that only black nationalist types would find her to be absolutely bereft of any redeeming qualities. Our black nationalists, who constitute a more important segment of black public opinion than many white people realize, have already proffered their opinion that the selection of a black woman as Miss America is a completely negative, conspiratorial attempt on the part of white America further to degrade black people. One might almost wish this were true. What makes race relations in America such a strange and dangerous affair is that white America—at least, the white power elite— never acts in concert about anything. It would be nearly reassuring to be black if only one could always suspect whites collectively of acting from the most malicious, wicked designs.

I heard several black men on a local black radio call-in program complain rather vociferously the Monday following the Miss America Pageant. One caller, who writes for the local black newspaper, thought Ms. Williams to be "politically unaware" because she refused to be a spokesperson for her race, and he considered her "a liability to the black community." Another caller voiced the opinion that the selection of Williams as Miss America was further proof that white America wished to denigrate black men by promoting black women. It is with a great degree of dire anticipation that I await the response from these quarters once it becomes generally known that Ms. Williams has a white boyfriend. She will no longer be simply "politically unaware" or "an insulting hindrance to the ascendancy of black men"; she will be a traitor, "sleeping with the white boy just like the slave women used to do on the plantation." One might almost think Michele Wallace's contention in her sloppy little book, *Black*

Macho and the Myth of the Superwoman, to be essentially correct: the final racial confrontation will not be between blacks and whites but between black men and black women. One hopes that the neurotic concern over miscegenation that seems to bedevil blacks as well as whites will not ultimately display itself in a game of murderous name-calling.

Most black women I know were overjoyed about a black woman becoming Miss America; it was, to their way of thinking, long overdue recognition of the beauty and the femininity of black women. "It might show black men that we're as good as white women," one black woman told me and, despite the humor that surrounded the statement, it seemed to be, underneath, a deeply distressing appeal. Perhaps—and if this is true, then racial psychopathology is more heart-breaking than anyone remotely believed possible—black women needed some giant manufactured event of American popular culture to make them feel as-sured that they were and are, indeed, as good as white women. Winning the Miss America contest has become, for at least some black women, American popular culture's fade-out kiss of benevolence.

At a time when the very purpose and motivation of the Miss America contest is being called into question, and rightly so, by feminists of every stripe, and the entire cultural sub-genre called the beauty contest is being seen as, at best, irrel-evant to modern women and, at worst, an insult to them, one might find the Miss America title to be a very dubious or ambiguous honor. Furthermore, Vanessa Williams was chosen largely because her good looks are quite similar to those of any white contestant. It will take no imaginative leap on the part of most whites to find her to be a beautiful girl. She does not look like the little black girl of the inner-city projects who reeks of cheap perfume and cigarette smoke and who sports a greasy, home-made curly perm and who has a baby at the age of fifteen for lack of anything better to do. (Whose little girl is she? One wonders.) Vanessa Williams will not even in a distant way remind anyone of *that* hard reality and, in truth, she is not supposed to. Her beauty, if anything, is a much more intense escapism than that of her white counterpart. In effect, her selection becomes a kind of tribute to the ethnocentric "universality" of the white beauty standards of the contest; in short, her looks allow her "to pass" aes-thetically. It is an oddly bestowed kiss that white popular culture has planted on black women; it is just the short of kiss that makes the benevolence of white folk seem so hugely menacing. As a friend of mine said, "When white folk get in trouble with their symbols, they throw 'em on black folk to redeem." To be sure, it is for such reasons that the selection of a black woman as Miss America is much more ambiguous and less effective as a symbol of American racial fusion than the breaking of the color barrier in professional sports. So, with angry black nationalists on the one side, with uneasy white and black feminists on the other, with many adoring young black women asking, "How do you do your hair?," and with many adoring older black women saying, "Child, you sing just like so-and-so at my church. Lord, you got a voice," Vanessa Williams is not expected to have an easy time of it.

I would like to think it was an act of God that I should choose to watch (for the first time) the Miss America Pageant the very year that a black woman won the crown. I had never watched the pageant before, partly, I suppose, because as a male I have never found beauty contests to be interesting and partly because as a black I have always thought them to be chilling in an alienating sort of way (I have always found very beautiful white women to be oddly frightening, as if within their beauty resonated an achingly inhuman purity; they have always been in my imagination, to borrow from Toni Morrison's *Tarbaby,* the snow queens of this life) and partly because, in the instance of the Miss America Pageant, the contest took place in Atlantic City and as a native of Philadelphia I have always found this shabby playground of the eastern seaboard to detract from whatever glamour the contest might have possessed. I remember as a kid buying boxes of St. James's salt water taffy, the only souvenir that one could ever really *want* from this resort, and wondering if Atlantic City had ever been the happy place that was pictured on the cover of the boxes. I certainly cannot recall it being so when I was a child, particularly since one had to ride through wretched Camden, New Jersey, to get there and then walk through the endless blocks of despair that made up the black neighborhood in this little town in order to get to "chickenbone" beach—where all the black folk were to be found. I doubt if the casinos have, in any ways improved the place. I understand that the Miss America contest was instituted in 1921 as an attempt by local businessmen to extend the resort season beyond the Labor Day holiday. It was certainly sleazy enough in those early years; no pretense was made that it was anything more than a flesh show: no talent show, no scholarships to the winner and runners-up. It was simply a parade of white "goddesses" who were being exploited in the worst sort of way, a "clean" peep show that was dedicated to making money, endorsing white supremacy, and denigrating women in one fell cultural swoop. It is no wonder, considering what the contest stood for, that women's clubs were, in part, instrumental in shutting Miss America down from 1928 through 1932. It is also no wonder, considering what the contest stood for, that it was recommenced for good in 1935.

I watched the Miss America Pageant this year largely because the subject of beauty contests was on the mind of everyone who lives in St. Louis. The city fathers (and its few mothers, too) decided that St. Louis should play host to the 1983 Miss Universe pageant in an effort to improve the image of St. Louis and to promote tourism. How much playing host for that beauty contest helped this city remains to be seen. The immediate returns show that St. Louis, a city that can ill afford such losses, will have to have a tremendous boost in tourism next summer to recoup its expenses. What I find most striking is the lack of imagination, the sheer lack of inventiveness on the part of local politicians: to think that a beauty contest, itself a confession of a dreadful social tactlessness, would resuscitate a city where poverty and crime are the unredemptive admissions of failures so vast that instead of being frightened *of* the poor, one is frightened *for* them. I have read in the papers that our fair city may next bid for the Miss USA contest which, for the last few years, has been held in Biloxi, Mississippi. If the Biloxi Chamber of Commerce is to be believed, this contest has increased tourism so much that literally countless thousands of Americans now include Biloxi in their summer vacation plans. I have no idea what staging the Miss Universe pageant has done for this city's image, but I believe the gang rape of a teenage girl in broad daylight before a score of witnesses in one of our public parks made a deeper impression on the national mind than the wire-service photo of smiling women in hair curlers visiting the Arch (St. Louis's version of a national treasure) a week before they were to be judged in the pageant.

I had no idea while I watched the telecast that our new Miss America, then Miss New York, was black. I was watching the show on a snowy black and white television and the girls seemed to be either olive or alabaster. I had, rather uncharitably, assumed all the contestants were white. Actually, I was more curious about the fate of Miss Missouri who was, like Miss New York, one of the finalists. She was a blonde girl with a somewhat longish chin named Barbara Webster.

It was a very long program, but surprisingly, not a boring one. I can say this quite seriously even after having watched the talent portion of the program and after having discovered that those young women had precious little of *that*. They made up in earnestness what they lacked in natural gifts, and since they are supposed to symbolize the girl next door or the boss's daughter (the girl every man wants to marry but no one is supposed—pardon the vulgarity, but it is really quite appropriate here—to screw) it is all right if they seem, well, amateurish, like products of a finishing school. The girls fairly dripped sincerity. As a consequence, one cheered them all and felt embarrassed by their shortcomings; they all seemed to be somebody's kid sister or somebody's older sister doing a parody of an audition. Miss Ohio did a song-and-dance number that was as devoid of skill as, say, a first grader's attempt to write a novel; she tried to do some Fred Astaire-sorts of things with her hat, but simply gave the overwhelming impression that she would have been less confounded had she simply left it on her head. I think it was Miss Alabama who played a Gershwin medley on the piano. It is very difficult to convince anyone that you are a serious musician when you have to grin all the time (consider Louis Armstrong, one of the greatest musicians America has ever produced) and your smiles are not in response to the pleasure you derive from your playing but from an unwritten rule that any contestant in the Miss America Pageant must never appear serious for fear that someone might interpret pensiveness as a sullen demeanor. Miss Alabama, we learned, had something like fifteen years of piano lessons and played Gershwin very much like someone who had had fifteen years of piano lessons and never learned to play the instrument. Miss Missouri wound up looking even more ridiculous than Miss Alabama: she played a hoedown number on the violin; she played well, but a toothy grin and a tasseled jumpsuit made her appearance seem so incongruous with the music she was playing that it bordered on being avant-garde. She needed only the Art Ensemble of Chicago playing behind her with tribal face paint and laboratory robes to complete the lunacy of it all. Another young woman, I don't remember which state she represented, did a dance number to the theme song from *Flashdance* that very closely resembled a routine in an aerobics class. This exercise, which is the most apt word for the performance, did not end so much as it petered out. And, of course, there were singers. In fact, most of the talent consisted of singing that sounded very much like bad versions of Barbra Streisand: no subtlety, no artful working of the lyrics or melody, just belting out from the gut with arms flung wide and face contorted with melodramatic emotion. The two numbers I remember most clearly are the medley of "Dixie" and the "Battle Hymn of the Republic" sung by a young woman who represented one of the Southern states, and "Happy Days Are Here Again" sung by Miss New York. The medley seemed to me to be as silly as someone singing a combined version of "The Star Spangled Banner" and "Amazing Grace"; someone might as well do such a medley in a future Miss America contest and neatly tie together all the ideological aspects of being American. To be American has come to mean, in popular culture, not so much being alienated from our history, but insisting that our history is contained in a series of high-sounding slogans and mawkish songs—indeed, that our history resembles nothing so much as the message and the jingle of a television commercial. I suppose that Miss New York was the best singer, surely she was the most professionally fervent. The song she chose was interesting; it reminded me of the little shows put on by the children that were featured on the "Our Gang/Little Rascals" comedy shorts. Not only did the song remind me of those "Our Gang" segments because they are both products of the depression and because they are homely and mediocre, but also because they were both designed to make people forget a harder reality, a more painful reality. The Miss America contest has given us a long line of charming Shirley Temples for a number of years, and now that a black woman has been selected we might assume that she, too, can be Shirley Temple. Or, perhaps, we might assume that it is getting a bit more difficult for the Miss America contest to protect us from our own reality.

"Rich relations give crusts of bread and such."

—Billie Holiday's "God Bless the Child"

For the benefit of whose who never knew
I'm a Miss America! How do you do!
I won a prize in '44 and of course all this is through with;
And I have a great big silver loving cup that I don't know what to do with.
I'm Miss America . . . so what!
They had me posing like I wouldn't
And they photographed me where they shouldn't
But it's nice to be Miss America, it makes like so trés gai,
Now if I could only find a way to eat three times a day.

—sung by Miss Venus Ramey, Miss America of 1944,
in her nightclub act after her inauspicious reign

Dolgin's is the sort of store that reveals just what retailing will be like everywhere in America's future, a future that will show that expansion is reduction, after all; Dolgin's shelves tell the story of the slouch toward a cunning yet bland anonymity that has made the old style of crass salesmanship through the frenzied pitch outmoded. It is stores like Dolgin's that Sears wants to imitate, creating an ambience like an American consumer's fantasyland where customers buy items about which they know very little because through some sort of subliminal hearsay they were informed that the product was good or needful. American retailing nowadays does not seem condensed so much as it seems compressed; every huge retailing outlet must sell everything from blank tape cassettes to baby food, and the workers are no longer interested in selling anything; they simply "ring you out." One is left almost eerily to the mercies of one's own impulses. It was pleasant to think that at one time a store such as Dolgin's thought the customer needed the services of an informed, trained salesperson; but customers no longer have needs that must be accommodated, simply urges that must be appeased. Shopping, to a large extent, is a tawdry sort of therapy; one can push a cart up and down the aisles of any store now, not just supermarkets, and commune with the self while half-believing that America is still a land of plenty. This mass shopping habit, so similar to the vision of retailing in Edward Bellamy's 1888 futuristic novel *Looking Backward,* is simply the intensified loneliness of the herd instinct of popular culture; the alienation we experience these days is not from the strange but from the familiar.

It was at Dolgin's that our new Miss America made her first—and probably only—appearance in St. Louis, giving away autographed snapshots of herself with anyone who cared to be in a picture with her. In fact, the event was advertised as "have your photograph taken with Miss America." I suppose it was fitting that she should be appearing at Dolgin's; she was, in some sense, another product that everyone should certainly be familiar with. There were no introductions made when she appeared before huge crowds waiting to see her and she said little or nothing to the people who came, one by one, to have their picture taken with her. Words were superfluous for someone who seemed to be more of an emanation from the Godhead than a human being. She smiled beautifully and constantly in a way that was completely expressionless. Her smile was not devoid of meaning; it resonated a rather genteel mocking quality that heightened its bored detachment. I especially liked how she stood on the ambiguous edge of being a tragic mulatto and a conjure woman, on the edge of absolute love and absolute power; for, at that moment, sitting in that store, she was the most loved and most suspect woman in America. She was loved as all Miss Americas are loved; she was, after all, no different from her predecessors: a sweet girl with ambition and a more than ardent belief that anyone in America can make it by working hard enough. She was the most suspect woman in America because she is black and, as such, is as inscrutable a symbol of American womanhood as one could hope to find. In other words, some blacks don't trust her motives and some whites don't trust her abilities. Yet she became, for those people in Dolgin's, America's version of a princess without a realm or, to put it more precisely, with a limitless realm since it was the entire fantasy of American popular culture. Doubtless, Dolgin's never had so many black folk pass through its portals or, at least, so many black folk who had absolutely no intention of buying anything. There were young black men with fancy cameras, young black women with little sons and daughters dressed in their Sunday best, older black women who giggled with excitement every time they saw Miss America smile. It was as if they had all come to pay homage to some great person instead of merely having a picture taken with a young woman of twenty who had done nothing more notable than win a contest, which, I suppose, was more an act of chance than anything else. Yet these black people, who had come out in frightful rush-hour traffic in a tremendous autumnal rainstorm, must have felt that it was an act of destiny that this girl was crowned Miss America.

"This is history, man," said one young black man to another. "I would've come through a hurricane to meet *this* Miss America. They sure ain't gonna pick another black woman to be Miss America no time soon."

"That ain't no lie," replied the other. "White folks might be sorry they picked this one before the year is over."

"She sure is pretty," said a grandmotherly looking black woman, "I never thought they'd pick a black girl to be Miss America during my lifetime."

"Hey, white folks gonna think we taking over," said another young black man. "First, we get a black mayor in Chicago, then we get the Martin Luther King holiday, and now we got Miss America. The man who run Dolgin's figure the only time he see this many niggers in his store is if he was giving away watermelons or Cadillacs."

People standing nearby laugh at the last remark.

"That's just it," said a young black woman, "they're not use to *black* people coming out to see Miss America."

And indeed that young woman spoke truer than she knew. In the past, I would imagine that the few black people who bothered to see Miss America when she made a public appearance were motivated only by the most disinterested sort of curiosity, a curiosity approaching the immaculate objectivity of the scientist: for, of course, a white woman as Miss America was merely an object for conversation, not veneration. For the first time, black people can now be motivated to see Miss America for the same reason that whites would crowd stores like Dolgin's to see her in the past: out of admiration, that sort of public love that, in the instance of black Americans, is so dammed up because they have so few public figures that they can love so unconditionally and totally because nothing more is expected of them than that they look beautiful and act in some remotely "cultured," polished way. To be sure, a good many black people will seek excuses to hate our new Miss America, but a much greater number will love her obsessively.

There were many white folk standing and waiting as well, and while some probably came out of curiosity, most seemed to esteem truly and deeply our new Miss America. One blonde woman, looking as though she had just escaped a dull office and a duller job, was positively flushed with the electricity of the moment. A mother had her son rehearse these lines to say to Miss America when he would finally meet her: "I think you're very beautiful and I'm glad you're Miss America." Another woman had her young daughter, perhaps ten or twelve, wearing a blue dress, patent leather pumps, stockings, a tiara, and a banner draped across the shoulder that proclaimed, "Miniature Miss." This youngster, possibly a future Miss America, certainly a future contestant in somebody's beauty contest, was the only person to curtsy before Miss America as if she were meeting the Queen of England. I heard a thirty-ish white man speaking to a young black fellow: "I just had to come and get a picture of Miss America. I think this is wonderful. My wife won't believe that I saw Miss America unless I get a picture. I think this is wonderful. I can't believe it." I think that Miss America must have been gratified and grateful that so many whites were there, not so much because she sought their approval but their acceptance. Their presence might assure that her reign would not be a separate but equal one. The importance of this cannot be overstated, for she has probably unconsciously conceived her symbolic stature as a force to fuse, if only momentarily, our divided culture. Since her black skin, by virtue of the historic burden it carries, brings the element of "social relevance" to the dazzling idiocy of beauty contests, our new Miss America must be aware that she can do more with the title than any white woman ever could, that she can greatly enhance the symbolic yet antique meaning of young womanhood in this culture simply because she is black. She has effectively done two things: she has encouraged blacks to participate in this fairly sterile cultural rite of passage; she has revitalized white interest in the contest by forcing them to see the title in a new and probably more deeply appreciative light. For whites who relish the idea of a black woman as Miss America, she simply serves the artless assumption that America is truly a land without racism, a land of equal opportunity at last. After all, so goes the reasoning from these quarters, twenty-five years ago, if Dolgin's existed in St. Louis, blacks probably could not shop there; they certainly could not work there. Now a young black woman as Miss America is signing autographs in such a store. Racial progress moves apace. Whites who detest the fact that a black woman is Miss America will simply campaign all the harder to make sure that such a lapse does not occur again. For more whites than one might care to imagine, the Miss America crown and the heavyweight title in prizefighting are the flimsy supports for the idea of racial superiority along sexual lines.

The last time a woman who was chosen Miss America was even slightly enmeshed in a similar welter of social and cultural complexities was in 1945 when Bess Myerson, another Miss New York, became the first Jew to win the pageant. Admittedly, only *Life* magazine (of all the publications that ran stories on Myerson during her reign) briefly mentioned her religion; it was never an issue of public discussion because it was never an object of publicity. Yet with the ending of the Second World War—a war fought, in large part, against the absolute nihilism of pathological racism—and with the holocaust and the subject of war trials still fresh on everyone's mind, the selection of a Jew by the Miss America judges strikes one as being, at least, self-consciously but subtly profound or momentous; it was a contrived but important effort to legitimize the contest. Since the 1945 contest was the first in which scholarships were given away, it was essential that the winner also have some real talent. Myerson had already received her B.A. degree in music from Hunter College when she entered the pageant, and during the talent segment she played Gershwin on the flute and Grieg on the piano. There was little doubt that she was not only the most skilled contestant for *that* year, but probably the most gifted entrant in the entire history of the pageant. As the *New York Times* stated in an article printed the day after she won: " . . . the only reason she entered the contest in the first place was because of the lure of a $5,000 scholarship that would enable her to continue for another four years her twelve-year study of music." Myerson was not simply another pretty face; she changed the entire nature of the contest from being a gross flesh show to being, of all things, a scholarship competition. Vanessa Williams is seen by the people who run the

Miss America contest as another possible legitimizing force. The selection of Myerson did not change the fundamental spirit or intention of the contest; nor did her winning enhance the general caliber of the average contestant who came after her. Myerson simply eased the way for the contest to return to its fantasy, pop-culture preoccupations and continue to select gentile mediocrities. Williams will most likely serve the same ends; the judges can, with a cleaner conscience, return to selecting white women almost exclusively. None of this is exactly sinister; it is, in fact, the bald, guileless stupidity and pointlessness of it all that galls one more than anything.

I stood in line for nearly an hour, along with my wife and two small daughters, waiting to be photographed with Miss America. I might not have gone through all of this had my children been boys, but I knew I simply had to have my daughters in a photograph with the first black Miss America. They would, at least, find it amusing to see the picture when they were older and they might even think it to be "significant." The photograph turned out to be less than I hoped for. My four-year-old, who would have infinitely preferred having her photograph taken with Michael Jackson, was a bit confused by it all. My two-year-old was completely terrified of the crowd; she never even faced the camera when the picture was taken. So, the picture shows a smiling, demure, quite lovely Miss America with a blue and black suit, light brown hair, and green eyes as bright and brilliant as slightly moistened, clear glass beads; a young father smiling slightly with his two children on his knees—one faintly nonplused and greatly surprised, the other faintly annoyed and greatly distressed. I suppose I am the most humorous figure in the photograph, looking like nothing so much as candidate for Father of the Year. Miss America probably felt a bit of sympathy for the valiant young father and his uncooperative children—but not half as much as I felt for her, traveling to all the stores like Dolgin's all over the country, signing autographs by the hundreds of thousands, surrounded by more guards than the president, seeing the worst of America as a grotesque phantasmagoria of shopping malls, hotels, and airports. As she sat there in Dolgin's, smiling benignly as each person stepped forward to have his or her picture taken, I could not help but think of her as a courtesan receiving her clients with graceful indifference. All of this was surely immaculate enough; no one was allowed to touch her. But that seems only to have intensified the perversity of the service she was providing; for to maintain the purity of her presence, the public was, in some way, being reminded that it could only defile her, if it had its druthers. And perhaps we would have, since nothing brings out American bloodthirstiness more boldly than the victimization of the innocent.

We are secretly driven slightly mad by the fact that Miss America is sweet and wholesome because it reveals our tremendous preoccupation with our own vehemently stated innocence. Miss America is sweet and wholesome because she symbolizes our deep neurotic obsession with chastity (which is really the only quality that makes a young girly truly sweet and wholesome and *desirable* in our culture). Watching our new Miss America with her beautiful, overly made-up face and perfectly manicured hands, I thought of the direct counterpart of the question that was posed to James Baldwin as he relates his conversion experience in *The Fire Next Time:* Whose little girl are you? And because Vanessa Williams's eyes answered dutifully to each person who came forward and silently posed the question: "Why, yours of course," it occurred to me that the ease with which the answer was given belied the sincerity of the response entirely. The Miss America role is tough work: one must have the beauty and charm of a princess, the elegant fortitude of a courtesan, and the cheap hustle of a tease. She is not America's dream girl, she is America's sick fantasy of girlhood and innocence.

As we were leaving the store with our photographs and our two rather relieved children, my wife turned to me and said, "Wouldn't it be something if one of our girls became Miss America twenty years from now? This photograph would be sought by all the papers: 'New Miss America photographed as child with first black Miss America.'"

"Yes," I said, "that would be something."

Although in one very obvious way it is very wonderful now that black mothers can tell their young daughters, "Yes, my darling, you, too, can become Miss America," one wonders what might be the larger psychic costs demanded by this bit of acculturation. Despite the fact that I do not wish my daughters to grow up desiring to be Miss America, I take a strange pleasure in knowing that the contest can no longer terrorize them; and this pleasure is worth the psychic costs and dislocations, whatever they might be. After all, black folk knew for a long time before Henry James discovered the fact that it is a complex fate to be an American.

Bibliography

Arts & Entertainment. "The Life of Hugh Hefner." *Biography.* February 2002.

Adenkan, Bosede. "Studying History and Miss America." *The Daily Pennsylvanian* 25 January 2002): n.p.

Alexander, Susan, and Alison Greenberg. "You Must Go Home Again: Duty, Love, and Work as Presented in Popular Magazines During World War II." In *Modernism, Gender, and Culture. A Cultural Studies Approach.* Ed. Lisa Rado. New York: Garland Publishing, Inc., 1997,101–110.

Allen, Anne Winsor. "Boys and Girls." *Atlantic Monthly* 125–2 (June 1920): 796.

Allen, Frederick Lewis. *Only Yesterday: An Informal History of the 1920's.* New York: Harper & Row, 1931.

"And Miss Nicest Navel . . ." *Time* (4 August 1997): 17.

Anderson, Benedict Richard O'G. *Imagined Communities: Reflections on the Origin and Spread of Nationalism.* London: Verso, 1983.

Anderson, Karen. *Wartime Women: Sex Roles, Family Relations, and the Status of Women During World War II.* Westport, CT: Greenwood Press, 1981.

Anthony, Susan B. II. *Out of the Kitchen—Into the War: Woman's Role in the Nation's Drama.* New York: Stephen Daye, Inc., 1943.

Anuakan, R. Iset. "We Real Cool: Beauty, Image, and Style in African American History." Ph.D. diss. University of California, Berkeley, 2001.

"Attacks Bathing Review." *New York Times* (11 September 1923): 15.

Baber, Ray E. *Marriage and the Family.* New York: McGraw-Hill Book Company, Inc., 1953.

Bakhtin, Mikhail. *Rabelais and His World.* Trans. Helene Iswolsky. Bloomington: Indiana University Press, 1984.

Banet-Weiser, Sarah. *The Most Beautiful Girl in the World: Beauty Pageants and National Identity.* Berkeley: University of California Press, 1999.

Banner, Lois W. *Women in Modern America: A Brief History.* New York: Harcourt Brace Jovanovich, 1974.

———. *American Beauty.* New York: Alfred A. Knopf, 1983.

Banning, Margaret Culkin. "A Great Club Woman." *Harper's* 149 (November 1924): 744.

Banta, Martha. *Imaging American Women: Idea and Ideals in Cultural History.* New York: Columbia University Press, 1987.

"Bather Goes to Jail; Keeps Her Knees Bare." *New York Times* (5 September 1921): 4.

"Beauties at Atlantic City." *New York Times* (7 September 1921): 13.

"Beauties Dazzle Hulbert." *New York Times* (28 November 1923): 20.

"Beauty Pageants Opposed." *New York Times* (18 September 1927): 27.

"Beauty Show Victor Is Not a Smoker." *New York Times* (11 September 1927): 31.

Beauvoir, Simone de. *The Second Sex.* Trans. H. M. Parshley. 1952. New York: Vintage, 1989.

Benjamin, Louise Paine. "What Is Your Dream Girl Like?" *Ladies' Home Journal* 59 (May 1942): 28–29.

Berlant, Lauren. *The Queen of America Goes to Washington City: Essays on Sex and Citizenship.* Durham, NC: Duke University Press, 1997.

Bias, Mansfield Jr. "You Be the Judge." *Pageantry* (Summer 1995): 10.

Birkhauser-Oeri, Sibylle. "The Imprisoning Sorceress." In *The Mother: Archetypal Image in Fairy Tales.* Ed. Marie-Louise Von Franz. *Studies in Jungian Psychology* 34. Toronto: Inner City, 1988.

"Bishop Condemns Beauty Pageant." *New York Times* (30 November 1927): 10.

Bivans, Ann Marie. *Miss America: In Pursuit of the Crown.* New York: Mastermedia Limited, 1991.

Black, Alexander. "Is the Young Person Coming Back?" *Harper's* 149 (August 1924): 337.

"Black Leaders See a Victory of Hope," *Philadelphia Inquirer* (19 September, 1983): A12.

Bordo, Susan. "Feminism, Foucault, and the Politics of the Body." *Up Against Foucault: Explorations of Some Tensions Between Foucault and Feminism.* Ed. Caroline Ramazanoglu. London: Routledge, 1993, 179–202.

———. *Unbearable Weight: Feminism, Western Culture, and the Body.* Berkeley: University of California Press, 1993, 1995.

———. *Twilight Zones: The Hidden Life of Cultural Images from Plato to O. J.* Berkeley: University of California Press, 1997.

Bourdieu, Pierre. *Masculine Domination.* New York: Cambridge University Press, 2000.

Bragdon, Elizabeth (ed.). *Women Today: Their Conflicts, Their Frustrations, and Their Fulfillments.* Indianapolis: The Bobbs-Merrill Company, 1953.

Breuer, Elizabeth. "What Four Million Women Are Doing." *Harper's* 147 (December 1923): 116.

Breuer, William B. War and American Women: Heroism, Deeds, and Controversy. Westport, CT: Praeger, 1997.

Brooks, Gwendolyn. *Maud Martha: A Novel.* New York: Harper, 1953.

Broughton, Rhoda. "Girls Past and Present." *Ladies' Home Journal* 37 (September 1920): 36.

Brownmiller, Susan. *Femininity.* New York: Fawcett, 1984.

———. *In Our Time: Memoir of a Revolution.* New York: The Dial Press/Random House, Inc., 1999.

Brumberg, Joan Jacobs. *The Body Project: An Intimate History of American Girls.* New York: Random House, 1997.

Brunvand, Jan Harold. *The Study of American Folklore: An Introduction.* New York: Norton, 1986.

Butler, Judith. *Bodies that Matter.* New York: Routledge, 1993.

———. *Gender Trouble: Feminism and the Subversion of Identity.* New York: Routledge, 1999.

Caillois, Roger. *Man, Play and Games.* Trans. Meyer Barash. Urbana: University Press of Illinois, 1961.

Campbell, D'Ann. *Women at War with America: Privates Lives in a Patriotic Era.* Cambridge, MA: Harvard University Press, 1984.

Carmichael, S. and C. Hamilton. *Black Power: The Politics of Liberation in America.* New York: Vintage, 1967.

Carson, C., D. Garrow, G. Gill, V. Harding, and D. Hine. *The Eyes on the Prize Civil Rights Reader.* New York: Penguin, 1991.

Casdorph, Paul D. *Let the Good Times Roll: Life at Home in America during World War II.* New York: Paragon House, 1989.

Cawelti, John G. *Adventure, Mystery, and Romance: Formula Stories as Art and Popular Culture.* Chicago: University of Chicago Press, 1976.

Chafe, William Henry. *The American Woman: Her Changing Social, Economic, and Political Roles, 1920–1970.* New York: Oxford University Press, 1972.

———. The Paradox of Change: American Women in the 20th Century. New York: Oxford University Press, 1991.

CNN.Com. "Bush Welfare Plan Promotes Marriage, Work." *Inside Politics* (27 February 2002).

Cohen, C., R. Wilk, and B. Stoeltje. *Beauty Queens on the Global Stage: Gender, Contests, and Power.* New York: Routledge, 1996.

Collins, Patricia. *Black Feminist Thought: Knowledge, Consciousness, and the Politics of Empowerment.* New York: Routledge, 1991.

The Complete Tales of the Brothers Grimm. Trans. Jack Zipes. New York: Routledge, 1988.

"Congressmen Should Be Literates." *New York Times* (27 August 1921): 8.

Cooke, Kaz. *Real Gorgeous: The Truth about the Body and Beauty.* New York: 1996.

Corliss, Richard. "Dream Girls." *Time* (18 September 1995): 102–105.

Cowan, Ruth Schwartz. "Two Washes in the Morning and a Bridge Party at Night: The American Housewife Between the Wars." *Women's Studies* 3 (1976): 147–172.

Cox, Harvey. "Miss America and the Cult of the Girl." *Christianity and Crisis* 7 (August 1961): 143–146.

Craig, Maxine Leeds. *Ain't I a Beauty Queen? Black Women, Beauty, and the Politics of Race.* New York: Oxford University Press, 2002.

"Criticism Well Deserved." *New York Times* (21 April 1924): 16.

Cunningham, Kamy. "Barbie Doll Culture and the American Waistland." in *Frontier IV.* Ed. Laurel Richardson, Verta Taylor, and Nancy Whittier. New York: McGraw-Hill, Inc., 1997, 122–125.

Cushman, Wilhela. "Now It's Woman's Work." *Ladies' Home Journal* 59 (May 1942): 28–29.

Dabakis, Melissa. "Gendered Labor: Norman Rockwell's Rosie the Riveter and the Discourse of Wartime Womanhood." In *Gender and American History Since 1890.* Ed. Barbara Melosh. London: Routledge, 1993: 182–204.

Davis, A. *Women, Culture and Politics.* New York: Random House, 1989.

Deford, Frank. *There She Is: The Life and Times of Miss America.* New York: Viking Press, 1971.

Delano, Page Dougherty. "Making Up for War: Sexuality and Citizenship in Wartime Culture." *Feminist Studies* 26, 2000: 33–68.

De Lauretis, Teresa. *Technologies of Gender. Essays on Theory, Film, and Fiction.* Bloomington: Indiana University Press, 1987.

Digney, Marita. "No One Wins: The Miss America Pageant and Sports Contests as Failed Initiations." In *The Soul of Popular Culture.* Ed. Mary Lynn Kittelson. Chicago: Open Court, 1998, 263–274.

Dickerson, Vanessa. *Recovering The Black Female Body: Self-Representations by African American Women.* New Brunswick, NJ: Rutgers University Press, 2001.

Djelic, Marie-Laure, and Antti Ainamo. "The Coevolution of New Organizational Forms in the Fashion Industry." *Organization Science: A Journal of the Institute of Management Sciences* 10, no. 5, (September/October 1999): 622.

Du Bois, W. E. B. *The Souls of Black Folk.* Chicago: A. C. McClurg, 1903.

Dundes, Alan (ed.), *Cinderella: A Casebook.* Madison: University of Wisconsin Press, 1982.

———. *Sacred Narrative: Reading in the Theory of Myth.* Berkeley: University of California Press, 1984.

Dworkin, Andrea. *Woman-Hating.* New York: Dutton, 1974.

Dworkin, Susan. *Miss America, 1945: Bess Myerson's Own Story.* New York: Newmark Press, 1987.

Dyer, Richard. *The Matter of Images.* London: Routledge, 1993.

Early, Gerald. "Waiting for Miss America." *The Antioch Review* 42, no. 3 (Summer 1984): 292–293.

"80 Years: American Beauties." *People* (16 October 2000): 132–179.

"88 'Beauties' Arrive." *New York Times* (27 November 1923): 2.

Eley, Geoff, and Ronald Grigor Suny (eds.). *Becoming National: A Reader.* New York: Oxford University Press, 1996.

Erenberg, Lewis A., and Susan E. Hirsch (eds.). *The War in American Culture: Society and Consciousness during World War II.* Chicago: University of Chicago Press, 1996.

Etcoff, Nancy. *Survival of the Prettiest: The Science of Beauty.* New York: Anchor, 1999.

Evans, Sara M. *Born for Liberty. A History of Women in America.* New York: Macmillan, 1989.

Fabry, Joseph. *Swing Shift. Building the Liberty Ships.* San Francisco: Strawberry Hill Press, 1982.

"Fall Carnival Holds Sway." *New York Times* (6 September 1923): 28.

Faludi, Susan. *Backlash.* New York: Anchor Books/Doubleday, 1992.

Field, Elizabeth. "Boom Town Girls." *Independent Woman* 21 (October 1942): 296–298.

Firth, Raymond. *Symbols, Public and Private.* New York: Cornell University Press, 1973.

Florio, Gwenn. "Miss America Contestants Vote 42–50 in Favor of Swimsuit Competition." Knight-Ridder/Tribune News Service (21 August 1995).

Follett, Wilson. "The Soulful Sex." *Atlantic Monthly* 125–2 (June 1920): 736.

Foucault, M. *Discipline and Punish: The Birth of the Prison.* Trans. by A. Sheridan. New York: Pantheon, 1977.

———. *The History of Sexuality.* Trans. by R. Hurley). New York: Pantheon, 1978.

Fox, Richard Wightman, and T. J. Jackson Lears. *The Power of Culture: Critical Essays in American History.* Chicago: University of Chicago Press, 1993.

Fox-Genovese, Elizabeth. "Mixed Messages: Women and the Impact of World War II." *Southern Humanities Review* 27 (Summer 1993): 235–245.

Freedman, Rita. *Beauty Bound.* Lexington, MA: D. C. Heath and Company, 1986.

Friedan, Betty. *The Feminine Mystique.* New York: W. W. Norton, 1963.

Funnell, Charles E. *By the Beautiful Sea: The Rise and High Times of That Great American Resort, Atlantic City.* New York: Alfred A. Knopf, 1975.

Gatens, Moira. "Power, Bodies and Difference." *Feminist Theory and the Body: A Reader.* Ed. Janet Price and Margrit Shildrick. New York: Routledge, 1999: 227–234.

Gere, Anne Ruggles. *Intimate Practices: Literacy and Cultural Work in U.S. Women's Clubs, 1880–1920.* Chicago: University of Illinois Press, 1997.

Giles, Nell. "What About the Women?" *Ladies' Home Journal* 59 (May 1942): 23, 157.

Glassberg, David. *American Historical Pageantry: The Uses of Tradition in the Early Twentieth Century.* Chapel Hill: University of North Carolina Press, 1990.

Gluck, Sherna Berger. *Rosie the Riveter Revisited: Women, the War, and Social Change.* New York: New American Library, 1987.

Goffman, Erving. *Gender Advertisements.* New York: Harper Colophon Books, 1976.

Goldman, William. *Hype and Glory.* New York: Villard Books, 1990.

Gorham, Ethel. *So Your Husband's Gone to War!* Garden City, NY: Doubleday, Doran and Company, 1942.

Gotanda, Neil. "A Critique of 'Our Constitution Is Color-Blind.'" *Stanford Law Review* 44, no. 1 (1991).

Gray, Daphne. *Yes, You Can, Heather! The Story of Heather Whitestone, Miss America 1995.* Grand Rapids, MI: Zondervan Publishing House, 1995.

Harrison, Mrs. Horace L. "Glamour as Usual. A Reply." *New York Times Magazine* (26 April 1942): 33.

Hartmann, Susan M. *The Home Front and Beyond: American Women in the 1940s.* Boston: Twayne Publishers, 1982.

Haskell, Molly. *From Reverence to Rape: The Treatment of Women in the Movies.* New York: Holt, Rinehart and Winston, 1974.

Hawes, Elizabeth. *Why Women Cry, Or Wenches with Wrenches.* Cornwall, NY: Reynal & Hitchcock, 1943.

Haymes, S. *Race, Culture, and the City: A Pedagogy for Black Urban Struggle.* New York: State University of New York Press, 1995.

Hegarty, Marilyn E. "Patriot or Prostitute? Sexual Discourses, Print Media, and American Women during World War II." *Journal of Women's History* 10, no. 2 (Summer 1998): 112–136.

———. "Patriots, Prostitutes, Patriotutes: The Mobilization and Control of Female Sexuality in the United States During World War II." Ph.D. Diss. Ohio State University, 1998.

Helmbreck, Valerie. "Miss America's Changing Face." *Wilmington News Journal* (Wilmington, DE, 18 September 1990).

Hobsbawm, Eric, and Terence Ranger (eds.). *The Invention of Tradition.* New York: Cambridge University Press, 1983.

Holloway, K. *Codes of Conduct: Race, Ethics, and the Color of Our Character.* New Brunswick, NJ: Rutgers University Press, 1995.

"Home City Plans Grand Welcome to Miss America." *Chicago Daily Tribune* (11 September 1927): 8.

Honey, Maureen. "The 'Womanpower' Campaign: Advertising and Recruitment Propaganda during World War II." *Frontiers* 6 (1981): 50–56.

———. *Creating Rosie the Riveter: Class, Gender and Propaganda During World War II.* Amherst: University of Massachusetts Press, 1984.

hooks, b. *Yearning: Race, Gender, and Cultural Politics.* Boston: South End Press, 1990.

———. *Black looks: Race and Representation.* Boston: South End Press, 1992.

———. *Sisters of the Yam: Black Women and Self-Recovery.* Boston: South End Press, 1993.

———. *Outlaw Culture: Resisting Representations.* New York: Routledge, 1994.

———. *Killing Rage, Ending Racism.* New York: Henry Holt & Company, 1995.

———. *Feminism Is for Everybody.* Cambridge, MA: South End Press, 2000.

———. *Feminist Theory: From Margin to Center.* Cambridge, MA: South End Press, 2000.

hooks, b., and Cornel West. *Breaking Bread: Insurgent Black Intellectual Life.* Boston: South End Press, 1991.

Horn, Leonard. "Swimsuits: It's HER Choice, Not Ours, Not Yours." Knight-Ridder/Tribune News Service (9 September 1997).

Huhn, Constance Luft. "War, Women and Lipstick." *Ladies' Home Journal* (August 1943): 73–76.

Hunt, Darnell. *O. J. Simpson Facts and Fictions: News Rituals in the Construction of Reality.* Cambridge: Cambridge University Press, 1999.

Hurst, Fannie. "Glamour as Usual?" *New York Times Magazine,* (29 March 1942): 10–12.

India.Arie. "Video." *Acoustic Soul* [Audio CD]. New York: Motown, 2001.

"Illinois Maid Wins Crown of Miss America." *Chicago Daily Tribune* (10 September 1927): 15.

"Inter-City Beauty Picked." *New York Times* (8 September 1921): 9.

Jewell, K. Sue. *From Mammy to Miss America: Cultural Images & the Shaping of U.S. Social Policy.* New York: Routledge, 1993.

Jones, Jennifer. "The Beauty Queen as Sacrificial Victim." *Theatre History Studies* 18 (June 1998): 88–89.

Jordan, June. *On Call.* Boston: South End Press, 1985.

"Keeps Her Knees Bare in Atlantic City Jail." *New York Times* (5 September 1921): 5.

King, Steve. "Danger! Women at Work." *American Magazine* 134 (September 1942): 40–41.

Kneller, Jane. "Discipline and Silence: Women and Imagination in Kant's Theory of Taste." In *Aesthetics and Feminist Perspective.* Ed. Hilde Hein and Carolyn Korsmeyer. Bloomington, IN: Indiana University Press, 1993.

Larrieux, A. "I N I." *Infinite Possibilities* [Audio CD]. New York: Sony, 2000.

Larsen, Nella. *Quicksand.* New York: Alfred A. Knopf, 1928.

Larson, C. Kay. *'Til I Come Marching Home: A Brief History of American Women in World War II.* Pasadena, MD: The Minerva Center, 1995.

Latham, Angela J. "Packaging Woman: The Concurrent Rise of Beauty Pageants, Public Bathing, and Other Performances of 'Nudity.'" *Journal of Popular Culture* 29, no. 3 (1995): 149–167.

———. *Posing a Threat: Flappers, Chorus Girls and Other Brazen Performers of the 1920's.* Hanover, NH: University Press of New England, 2000.

Lavenda, Robert. "Minnesota Queen Pageants: Play, Fun and Dead Seriousness in a Festive Mode, *Journal of American Folklore* 101 (1988): 168–175.

Levy, Claudia. "Margaret Cahill, First Miss America Dies." *Washington Post* (3 October 1995).

Lingeman, Richard R. *Don't You Know There's a War On? The American Home Front 1941–1945.* New York: G. P. Putnam's Sons, 1970.

Lippert, Barbara. "Cleavages and Causes." *Glamour* (December 1994): 211.

Lipsitz, George. *Time Passages: Collective Memory and American Popular Culture.* Minneapolis: University of Minnesota Press, 1990.

———. *The Possessive Investment in Whiteness: How White People Profit from Identity Politics.* Philadelphia: Temple University Press, 1998.

Litoff, Judith Barrett, and David C. Smith (eds.). *American Women in a World at War: Contemporary Accounts from World War II.* Wilmington, DE: A Scholarly Resources Inc. Imprint, 1997.

Lott, Eric. *Love and Theft: Blackface Minstrelsy and the American Working Class.* New York: Oxford University Press, 1993.

Lowe, Lisa. *Immigrant Acts: An Asian American Cultural Politics.* Durham, NC: Duke University Press, 1996.

Lubiano, W. Black Ladies, Welfare Queens, and State Minstrels: Ideological War by Narrative Means. In *Race-ing Justice, En-gendering Power: Essays on Anita Hill, Clarence Thomas, and the Construction of Social Reality.* Ed. Toni Morrison. New York: Pantheon Books, 1992.

Luce, Clare Boothe. "Victory Is a Woman." *Woman's Home Companion* (November 1943): 34, 121, 122.

Lugg, Catherine A. *Kitsch: From Education to Public Policy.* New York: Falmer Press, 1999.

Lumsden, Linda J. *Rampant Women: Suffragists and the Right of Assembly.* Knoxville: University of Tennessee Press, 1997.

Luthi, Max. *Once Upon a Time: On the Nature of Fairy Tales.* Bloomington: Indiana University Press, 1976.

Lynch, James C. "Trousered Angel." *Saturday Evening Post* (10 April 1943): 23, 84, 87.

MacKaye, Hazel. "Pageants as a Means of Suffrage Propaganda." *Suffragist* 28 (November 1914): 6.

Mackenzie, Jim. "Two Images of Bias." *Oxford Review of Education* 23, no. 4 (December 1997): 487.

MacWilliams, Bryon. "There She Is, Miss Akademia." *Chronicle of Higher Education* 14 (September 2001): A64.

Maddock, R. C., and R. L. Fulton. *Marketing to the Mind.* Westport, CT: Quorum Books, 1996.

Malone, Janet. "The Self-Esteem of Women." *Human Development* 17, no.2 (Summer 1996): 5–7.

Mann, Denise. "Rosie the Riveter—Construction or Reflection?" *Quarterly Review of Film & Video* 11 (1989): 117–120.

Manning, M. M. *Slave in a Box: The Strange Career of Aunt Jemima.* Charlottesville: University of Virginia Press, 1998.

Martin, Edward S. "The Girl That Is to Be." *Harper's* 128 (April 1914): 915.

Martin, Pete. "Right Face." *Saturday Evening Post* (March 1943): 21, 48, 50.

Mattoon, Rick. "Ruwe Sisters Compete in Pageant." *Valley News.* (12 June 1985): A 1.

May, Elaine Tyler. *Pushing the Limits: American Women 1940–1961.* New York: Oxford University Press, 1994.

————. "Rosie the Riveter Gets Married." In *The War in American Culture: Society and Consciousness During World War II.* Ed. Lewis A. Erenberg and Susan E. Hirsch. Chicago: University of Chicago Press, 1996; 128–143.

McGregory, Jerrilyn. *Wiregrass Country.* Jackson: University Press of Mississippi, 1997.

Mercer, Jacque. *How to Win a Beauty Contest.* Phoenix, AZ: Curran Publishing Co., 1960.

Merrill, Francis E. *Social Problems on the Home Front. A Study of War-time Influences.* New York: Harper & Brothers, 1948.

Michie, Helena. *Sororophobia: Differences among Women in Literature and Culture.* New York: Oxford University Press, 1992.

"Midwest Girls in Finals for Miss America." *Chicago Daily Tribune* (9 September 1927): 31.

Milkie, Melissa. "Social Comparisons, Reflected Appraisals, and Mass Media: The Impact of Pervasive Beauty Images on Black and White Girls' Self-Concepts." *Social Psychology Quarterly* 62, no. 2 (1999): 190–210.

Milkman, Ruth. *Gender at Work: The Dynamics of Job Segregation by Sex during World War II.* Urbana: The University of Illinois Press, 1987.

Miller, J. (ed.). *Beauty.* San Francisco: Chronicle Books, 1997.

Millum, Trevor. *Images of Woman. Advertising in Women's Magazines.* Totowa, NJ: Rowman and Littlefield, 1975.

Milsten, David Randolph. *Thomas Gilcrease.* San Antonio, TX: Naylor, 1969.

Minard, Rosemary (ed.). *Womenfolk and Fairy Tales.* Boston: Houghton Mifflin, 1975.

"Miss America." In *American Experience.* Directed by Lisa Ades. Clio Inc. & Orchard Films, 2002.

"Miss America Explains How and Why She Says No to Sex." *People* (26 November 1984): 109–111.

"'Miss California' Wins Beauty Title." *New York Times* (12 September 1925): 6.

"'Miss Philadelphia' Wins Parade Prize." *New York Times* (5 September 1924): 7.

Mizejewski, Linda. *Ziegfeld Girl: Image and Icon in Culture and Cinema.* Durham, NC: Duke University Press, 1999.

Mohanty, Satya. "The Epistemic Status of Cultural Identity: On Beloved and the Postcolonial Condition." *Cultural Critique* (Spring 1993): 41–78.

Moore, Virginia Bennet. "Begrimmed—Bewitching or Both." *Woman's Home Companion* (October 1943): 80–81.

Morgan, Kathryn. *Children of Strangers: The Stories of a Black Family.* Philadelphia: Temple University Press, 1980.

Morrison, Toni. *The Bluest Eye.* New York: Holt, Rinehart and Winston, 1970.

————. "What the Black Woman Thinks about Women's Lib." *New York Times Magazine* (1971).

————. *Jazz.* New York: Alfred A. Knopf, 1992.

————. *Playing in the Dark: Whiteness and the Literary Imagination.* New York: Vintage, 1995.

MTV. "Interviews with Contestants in the Miss America Pageant." (January 2002).

Nathan, D. (1993) (record jacket). Young, Gifted and Black: Aretha Franklin, 1972 & 1993. Los Angeles: Atlantic Records.

Neimark, Jill. "Why Do We Need Miss America?" *Psychology Today* (October 1998): 40–46.

Nelson, C. *Women's Market Handbook.* Detroit, MI: Gale Research, 1994.

Newcomb, Horace, and Paul M. Hirsch. "Television as a Cultural Forum." In *Television: The Critical View,* Ed. Horace Newcomb. 5th Edition. New York: Oxford University Press, 1994.

Newfield, Christopher. "What Was Political Correctness? Race, the Right, and Managerial Democracy in the Humanities. *Critical Inquiry* 19 (Winter 1993): 320.

Nichols, David Perry. "Victory Is Our Business: Theme, Image and Message in Wartime National Advertising 1939–1945." MA Thesis University of Virginia 1993.

"1922 Prize Beauty is Winner Again," *New York Times* (8 September 1923): 8.

Norment, Lynn. "Vanessa Williams Is Black, Brainy and Beautiful." *Ebony* (December 1983): 132–136.

———. "Back to Back Black Miss Americas." *Ebony* (December 1990): 46–49.

Ogden, William Fielding (ed.). *American Society in Wartime.* Chicago: University of Chicago Press, 1943.

Oldfield, Barney. "Miss America and the 301st Bomb Group." *Air Power History* 37, no. 2 (1990): 41–44.

"1,000 Bathing Girls on View in Pageant," *New York Times* (9 September 1921): 15.

Osborne, Angela Saulino. *Miss America: The Dream Lives On.* Dallas: Taylor Publishing Company, 1995.

"Paintless Girl Wins." *New York Times* (29 November 1923): 30.

Pang, Henry. "Miss America: An American Ideal, 1921–1969." *Journal of Popular Culture,* no. 2 (1969): 687–696.

Parker, Dorothy. "Are We Women or Are We Mice?" *Reader's Digest* (July 1943): 71–72.

Paterson, Dorothy. *The Family Woman and the Feminist: A Challenge.* London: William Heinemann, 1945.

Peiss, Kathy. *Cheap Amusements: Working Women and Leisure in Turn-of-the-Century New York.* Philadelphia: Temple University Press, 1985.

———. *Hope in a Jar: The Making of America's Beauty Culture.* New York: Metropolitan Books, Henry Holt and Company, 1998.

Pellow, A. Cleft. "Literary Criticism and Black Imagery." In *Images of Blacks in American Culture.* Ed. J. C. Smith. Westport, CT: Greenwood Press, 1988.

Perlmutter, Dawn. "Miss America: Whose Ideal?" In *Beauty Matters.* Ed. Peg Zeglin Brand. Bloomington: Indiana University Press, 2000, 155–168.

"Philadelphia Girl Gets Beauty Crown." *New York Times* (7 September 1924): 9.

Pickel, Margaret Barnard. "A Warning to the Career Woman." *New York Times Magazine* (16 July 1944): 18–19.

Pratt, Mary Louise. "Arts of the Contact Zone." *Profession 91.* New York: The Modern Language Association, 1991: 33–40.

"Prefers Stove to Husband." *New York Times* (13 September 1926): 10.

"The Pride of the Cities." *New York Times* (9 September 1926): 22.

Probert, Christina. *Swimwear in Vogue since 1910.* New York: Abbeville Press, 1981.

Propp, Vladimir. *Morphology of the Folktale.* Trans. Laurence Scott. University of Texas Press, 1968.

"Prosecutor Saddened by Women on Jury; 'Frightful Evidence Unfit for Their Ears," *New York Times* (5 September 1920): 20.

Quick, Paddy. "Rosie the Riveter: Myths and Realities." *Radical America* 9 (July/August 1975): 115–132.

Renov, Michael. "Advertising/Photojournalism/Cinema: The Shifting Rhetoric of Forties Female Representation." *Quarterly Review of Film & Video* 11 (1989): 1–21.

Riley, Glenda. *Inventing the American Woman: A Perspective in Women's History, 1965 to the Present.* Arlington Heights, VA: Harlan Davidson, 1986.

Riverol, A. R. *Live from Atlantic City: A History of the Miss America Pageant.* Bowling Green, KY: Bowling Green State University Popular Press, 1992.

Robert, John, et al. "Games in Culture," *American Anthropologist* 6 (1959): 597–605.

Roberts, Dorothy. *Killing the Black Body: Race, Reproduction and the Meaning of Liberty.* New York: Vintage, 1997.

Robinson, David. *Hollywood in the Twenties.* New York: A. S. Barnes and Company, 1968.

Roediger, David R. *The Wages of Whiteness: Race and the Making of the American Working Class.* London: Verso, 1992.

Rogin, Michael. *Blackface, White Noise: Jewish Immigrants in the Hollywood Melting Pot.* Berkeley: University of California Press, 1996.

Rosen, Ruth. *The World Split Open.* New York: Viking Penguin, 2000.

Ross, Lillian. "After the Pageant." *The New Yorker* (9 October 2000): 42–47.

R.S.V.P. "Girls." *Atlantic Monthly* 125–2 (April 1920): 490.

Rupp, Leila. *Mobilizing Women for War: German and American Propaganda, 1939–1945.* Princeton, NJ: Princeton University Press, 1978.

Savage, Candace. *Beauty Queens: A Playful History.* New York: Abbeville Press Publishers, 1998.

Russell, Kathy, Midge Wilson, and Ronald Hall. T*he Color Complex: The Politics of Skin Color among African Americans.* New York: Anchor, 1992.

Scarry, Elaine. *On Beauty and Being Just.* Princeton, NJ: Princeton University Press, 2001.

Sedgwick, Eve Kosofsky. *Epistemology of the Closet.* Berkeley: University of California Press, 1990.

"Seeks Beauty Contest Ban." *New York Times* (13 August 1921): 11.

"Seeks Beauty Prize." *Chicago Daily Tribune* (6 September 1923): 4.

"Sex in the Factory." *Time* (14 September 1942): 21.

Shea, Margaret. *The Gals They Left Behind.* New York: Ives Washburn, 1944.

Shephard, Sheri Lynae. "Selling Patriotic Womanhood in a Nation at War: Advertising, Gender and Consumerism in World War II America." MA Thesis Duke University, 1999.

Simon, H. *Sciences of the Artificial,* 3rd ed. Cambridge, MA: MIT Press, 1996.

Simone, N., and I. Weldon. (1969). "To Be Young, Gifted, and Black." Nina Simone Website,5 May 2002. www.boscarol.com/nina/html/where/tobeyounggifted.

Smith, B. *Backwater Blues.* [LP] Columbia 14195-D, 1927.

Sothern, Ann. "What Kind of Woman Will Your Man Come Home To?" *Photoplay* (25 November 1944): 45, 85–86.

Spigel, Lynn. *Make Room for TV: Television and the Family Ideal in Postwar America.* Chicago: University of Chicago Press, 1992.

"Spring and Summer Styles Meet and Blend." *Harper's* 148 (December 1923-May 1924).

Stockard, Janice Lynn. "The Role of American Black Women in Folktales: An Interdisciplinary Study of Identification and Interpretation." Ph.D. Tulane University, 1979. Ann Arbor, MI: University Microfilms, 1980.

Stoeltje, Beverly. "The Snake Charmer Queen: Ritual Competition, and Signification in American Festival." In *Beauty Queens on the Global Stage*. Ed. Colleen Cohen, Richard Wilk, and Beverly Stoeltje, New York: Routledge, 1996.

Stone, Kay. "The Misuses of Enchantment: Controversies on the Significance of Fairy Tales." In *Women's Folklore Women's Culture*. Ed. June Jordan, A. Rosan, and Susan Kalick. American Folklore Society 8. Philadelphia: University of Pennsylvania Press, 1985.

————. "Things Walt Disney Never Told Us." In *Women's Folklore Women's Culture*.

Sutton-Smith, Brian, and John M. Roberts. "The Cross-Cultural and Psychological Study of Games." In *The Cross-Cultural Analysis of Sport and Games*. Ed. Gunther Luschen. Champaign, IN: Stipes, 1970.

Sweeney, Mike. "Patriotism and Profits: A Content Analysis of World War II Magazine Advertising Containing War Themes." Paper presented at the annual meeting for Education in Journalism and Mass Communication, 10–13 August 1994.

Tatum, B. *Why Are All the Black Kids Sitting Together in the Cafeteria? And Other Conversations about Race*. New York: Basic Books, 1997.

Taylor, Susan L. "For Vanessa." *Essence* (October 1984): 79.

"This, Too, Was Once 'Un-American'" *New York Times* (30 November 1923): 14.

Thompson, Morton. *How to Be a Civilian*. Garden City, NY: Doubleday & Company, 1946.

TLC. "Unpretty." *Fanmail* [Audio CD]. Atlanta: La Face Records, 1999.

Truth, S. "Ain't I a Woman." Speech at the Woman's Rights Convention, Akron, Ohio, 1851.

Tseëlon, Efrat. *The Masque of Femininity: The Presentation of Woman in Everyday Life*. London: Sage, 1995.

Tuchman, Gaye, Arlene Kaplan Daniels, and James Benet (eds.). *Hearth and Home: Images of Women in the Mass Media*. New York: Oxford University Press, 1978.

Turner, Victor. *Drama, Fields, and Metaphors: Symbolic Action in Human Society*. Ithaca, NY: Cornell University, 1974.

Tuttle, William M. Jr. "Daddy's Gone to War." *The Second World War in the Lives of America's Children*. New York: Oxford University Press, 1993.

Twitchell, James B. *Carnival Culture: The Trashing of Taste in America*. New York: Columbia University Press, 1992.

"Two More Spurn Beauty Pageant." *New York Times* (10 September 1925): 29.

"Uncorseted, Is Man's Equal," *New York Times* (9 September 1921): 5.

U.S. Bureau of the Census. *Statistical Abstract of the United States: 1996*. 116th ed. Washington, D.C.: 1996.

Utermeyer, Bryna, and Louis, (Eds.). *Old Friends and Lasting Favorites: Golden Treasury of Children's Literature*. Vol. 4. New York: Golden, 1962.

Van Esterik, Penny. "The Politics of Beauty in Thailand." In *Beauty Queens on the Global Stage*. Ed. Colleen Cohen, Richard Wilk, and Beverly Stoeltje, New York: Routledge, 1996.

Von Franz, Marie-Louise. *The Feminine in Fairy Tales*. Dallas: Spring, 1972.

Walker, Barbara (Ed.). *The Woman's Encyclopedia of Myths and Secrets*. New York: Harper & Row, 1983.

Wandersee, Winifred D. *Women's Work and Family Values 1920–1940*. Cambridge, MA: Harvard University Press, 1981.

Watson, Elwood. "Miss America Pageant Evolves with America." *Delaware State News* (16 September 1996).

Watson, Elwood, and Darcy Martin. "The Miss America Pageant: Pluralism, Femininity and Cinderella All in One. *Journal of Popular Culture* 34, no. 1 (Spring 2000): 105–126.

Wauters, Arthur. *Eve in Overalls*. London: Imperial War Museum Department of Printed Books, 2001.

Weatherford, Doris. *American Women and World War II*. New York: Facts On File, 1990.

Wells, Sharlene. "On the Road with Miss America." *Saturday Evening Post* (May/June 1985): 42–45.

West, Cornel. *Prophesy Deliverance! An Afro-American Revolutionary Christianity.* Philadelphia: Westminster Press, 1982.

———. *Race Matters*. New York: Vintage, 1993.

Westbrooke, Robert B. "'I Want a Girl, Just Like the Girl That Married Henry James': American Women and the Problem of Political Obligation in World War II." *American Quarterly* 42, no. 4 (December 1990): 587–614.

"Western Girl Wins Miss America Title." *New York Times* (11 September 1926): 15.

"Whatever Happened to the Black Miss Americas?" *Ebony* 57, no. 5 (March 2002): 108–115.

White, Mimi. "Rehearsing Feminism. Women/History in The Life and Times of Rosie the Riveter and Swing Shift." *Wide Angle: A Film Quarterly of Theory, Criticism* 7, no. 3 (1985): 34–43.

White, Shane, and Graham White. *Stylin': African American Expressive Culture from Its Beginnings to the Zoot Suit*. New York: 1998.

Wiegman, Robyn. *American Anatomies: Theorizing Race and Gender*. Durham, NC: Duke University Press, 1995.

Will, George. "The New Face of America." *Time,* special issue (Fall 1993).

Wilson, Helen Hay. "On the Education of Daughters," *Harper's* 123 (November 1911): 780.

Wilson, Midge, Kathy Russell, and Ronald Hall. *The Color Complex: The Politics of Skin Color Among African Americans*. New York: Anchor, 1992.

Wilson, Sloan. *The Man in the Gray Flannel Suit*. New York: Simon and Schuster, 1955.

Wise, Nancy Baker, and Christy Wise. *A Mouthful of Rivets: Women at Work in World War II*. San Francisco: Jossey-Bass Publishers, 1994.

Wolf, Naomi. *The Beauty Myth*. New York: W. Morrow, 1991; reprinted, New York: Anchor Books, 1992.

Wolfe, Deborah S. "Beauty as a Vocation: Women and Beauty Contests in America." Ph.D. diss. Columbia University, 1994.

"Woman Seeks Senatorship on 'Women First' Platform." *New York Times* (9 September 1920): 1.

"Women Establish a Bank." *New York Times* (5 September 1920): 20.

"Women Open Fight on Beauty Pageant." *New York Times* (18 November 1927): 12.

Woolf, S. J. "The Gibson Girl Is Still With Us." *New York Times Magazine* (20 September 1942): 15–17.

Yolen, Jan. "America's Cinderella." In *Cinderella: A Casebook*. Ed. Alan Dundes. Madison: University of Wisconsin Press, (1982): 294–304.

Young, Iris. *Justice and the Politics of Difference.* Princeton, NJ: Princeton University Press, 1990.

"Y.W.C.A. Opens War on Beauty Contest; Calls Atlantic City Parade Peril to Girls." *New York Times* (18 April 1924): 21.

Contributor Biographies

ISET ANUAKAN is an assistant professor in the department of Africana Studies at California State University, Dominguez Hills. She teaches courses that emphasize the global, gendered development of aesthetics, the emergence of racial stereotypes in folklore, and contrast between African and Western European images in history. She received her Ph.D. from the University of California at Berkeley in 2002. She is the author of the forthcoming, *We Real Cool: African American Beauty, Image and Style.* She is the recipient of numerous grants and her scholarship has been recognized by the American Biographical Institute, The International Poetry Society, The American Business Women's Association and the National Association for the Advancement of Colored People.

GERALD EARLY is Merle Kling Professor of Modern Letters, Professor of English and African And Afro American Studies, Director of The Center For The Humanities at Washington University in St. Louis, Missouri. He is the author of numerous books and articles on the Black experience. His book, *The Culture of Bruising: Essays on Prizefighting, Literature and Modern American Culture* won the 1994 National Book Critics Award for Criticism. He is a member of the American Academy of Arts & Sciences and is currently completing a book about Fisk University.

MARK A. EATON is Associate Professor of English at Azusa Pacific University, where he teaches American literature and film studies. His work has appeared in *The Boston Book Review, Christianity and Literature, Modern Fiction Studies, Pedagogy, Studies in American Fiction,* and *The Edith Wharton Review.* An essay on recent adaptations of Henry James's novels appeared in *Henry James on Stage and Screen* (Palgrave, 2000), and another piece titled "Moving Pictures and Spectacular Criminality in *An American Tragedy* and *Native Son*" appeared in *Prospects: An Annual of American Cultural Studies* (Cambridge UP, 2002). He has contributed chapters to three different volumes in the MLA *Approaches to Teaching* series, and is currently completing a book manuscript titled *Critical Mass: The Literary Uses of Mass Culture in Modern America.* His web-based essay project *Roads to Nowhere: Twentieth-Century Traveling Cultures in the Americas* is available online at www.roads-to-nowhere.com. And another collection of essays that he has co-edited with Emily Griesinger, *The Gift of Story: Narrating Hope in Film and Literature,* is now currently circulating among several major presses.

KIMBERLY HAMLIN is a doctoral student in American Studies at the University of Texas at Austin.

VALERIE KINLOCH is an assistant professor of English Education at Teachers College, Columbia University. Her most recent work investigates democratic learning, literacy practices, and spatial affiliation in the education of diverse student populations. Her book, *Still Seeking an Attitude: Critical Reflections on the Work of June Jordan* (with M. Grebowicz; forthcoming from Lexington Books, Rowman & Littlefield) will be published in the fall, 2004. She is currently working on a literary project on June Jordan. Her work has appeared in a variety of academic journals.

DARCY MARTIN is an adjunct faculty in the department of Women's Studies at East Tennessee State University. Her co-authored article on the Miss America Pageant entitled *The Miss America Pageant: Pluralism, Femininity and Cinderella All In One,* received the Russell B. Nye award for the best article published in the 2000–2001 academic year in *The Journal of Popular Culture.* Her current research focuses on romantic fiction, women and literature during the Civil War, and Oprah Winfrey.

JERRILYN MCGREGORY is an associate professor in the department of English at Florida State University in Tallahassee. She previously served as director of undergraduate studies in the department. She is a member of the Florida Folklife Council. Her specialties include folklore, rural literature, wiregrass culture and African American literature.

DONELLE RUWE is an assistant professor of English at Northern Arizona State University in Flagstaff. She is the author of the forthcoming *Culturing the Child, 1690–1915: Essays in Memory of Mitzi Myers.* She has written on British Romanticism, children's literature, and poetry in various journals and essay collections. She has been a recipient of several awards among them an Amhason Research Fellowship from UCLA's Charles E. Young Rare Books Library and NEH Summer Institute Fellowship. She is also a member of the 18th and 19th–Century British Women Writers Association.

MARY ANNE SCHOFIELD is an associate professor in the department of Humanities at Villanova University. Her scholarship focuses primarily on the study of war, particularly World War II. She is the author of *Fettered of Free: British Women Novelists* published in 1986 and the co-author of *Visions of War: Literature and The Popular Culture,* published in 1992. Her current research examines British and American veterans of the Second World War.

ELWOOD WATSON is an associate professor in the department of History at East Tennessee State University. He is the author of several articles. His work has appeared in *The Journal Of Black Studies, The Journal of African American History, Endarch, Maine History, The Journal of Religious Thought, USA Magazine* and other publications. His co-authored article *The Miss America Pageant: Pluralism, Femininity and Cinderella all in One* received the Russell B. Nye award for the best article published in the 2000–2001 academic year in *The Journal of Popular Culture.* He is currently working on projects that examine the former television program Ally McBeal, Black women in the legal academy, Black Conservatism and Oprah Winfrey.

SARAH BANET-WEISER is an assistant professor in the Annenberg School of Communication at the University of Southern California. She is the author of *The Most Beautiful Girl in The World: Beauty Pageants and National Identity,* published in 1999, and has published articles on sports and gender, children and technology, and children, media and national identity. She is currently working on a book on the children's cable channel Nickelodeon, that examines children citizenship and the media which will be published by Duke University Press.